Born in Greenwich, London, Chris Difford has written lyrics for over forty years, most notably in partnership with Glenn Tilbrook for Squeeze. After the break-up of Squeeze in 1983, Difford continued writing songs with Glenn Tilbrook for artists such as Helen Shapiro, Billy Bremner and Elvis Costello. He has also written lyrics for music by many artists including Jools Holland, Elton John and Wet Wet Wet, has been the manager of Bryan Ferry and The Strypes, and released four solo albums. Difford also curated *Songs in the Key of London*, an evening of music dedicated to the capital at the Barbican Centre, London, in 2011 and 2014.

'A witty, charming, acutely observed and astonishingly honest account of what it's like to be a successful musician. I was gripped and fascinated' Mark Ellen

'With hilarious honesty, Squeeze's frontman reveals how his pop career went well and truly Up The Junction!' *Mail on Sunday*

'Squeeze's music has been a part of my soundtrack since first hearing and seeing them back in the late Seventies and Chris's book is just as lively and captivating. It's honest, poignant, laugh-out-loud funny and is a fascinating peep (warts and all) into the life of one of our most talented wordsmiths. Quite simply, I couldn't put it down' Gary Crowley

'As anyone who has listened to "Cool for Cats" or "Up the Junction" will know, Difford's lyrics are superb at noticing the unconscious poetry of everyday life, and the early chapters of this book are tightly packed with the sights, the sounds and especially the smells of his childhood' Robert Douglas-Fairhurst, *Guardian*

'Loving the Chris Difford autobiography. "Dad said if I joined a rock band I'd be an alcoholic, drug addict & skint. Turns out he was right."' David Hepworth

'This conversational memoir from Chris Difford . . . is distinguished by its admirable candour: Unlike many artists, Difford is reflective about the obstacles he's had to overcome (flying anxiety, substance abuse, relationship breakdowns), and he is direct and forthcoming about how these things inform his life and music, even in the present. However, Difford's dry sense of humour also shines through . . . Lovely and enriching, *Some Fantastic Place* is very much worth a read' *Salon*

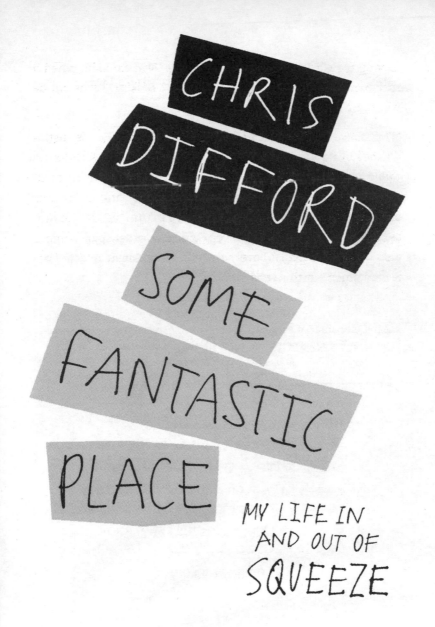

CHRIS DIFFORD

SOME FANTASTIC PLACE

MY LIFE IN AND OUT OF SQUEEZE

WEIDENFELD & NICOLSON

First published in Great Britain in 2017
This paperback edition first published in 2018
by Weidenfeld & Nicolson
an imprint of The Orion Publishing Group Ltd
Carmelite House, 50 Victoria Embankment
London EC4Y 0DZ

An Hachette UK Company

1 3 5 7 9 10 8 6 4 2

A CIP catalogue record for this book is available from the British Library.

ISBN (paperback) 978 1 4746 0568 7
ISBN (ebook) 978 1 4746 0569 4

Typeset by Input Data Services Ltd, Somerset

Printed and bound by CPI Group (UK) Ltd, Croydon, CR0 4YY

MIX
Paper from
responsible sources
FSC® C104740

www.orionbooks.co.uk

For Louise, my beautiful children,
and in loving memory of Maxine, Les and my parents.
Dedicated to my brother Lew.

KING GEORGE STREET

My first home was 98 King George Street in Greenwich, south London. Six prefabs, three pubs, a school, a church and a yard where the electricity board kept cables. Two long rows of terraced houses faced each other at one end of the street; at the other, big houses with big doors and even bigger windows. There was a phone box next to one of the pubs and when it rang everyone came out to see who it was for. It was a tiny road – at one end of which was Greenwich Park. It was heaven being there. Its beauty shone on me from the trees at sunset and from the bushes in the rain. I was there in all weathers. It was 1964, I was ten years old and this is when my memory really begins.

In the early 1960s, our family was working class. We had a green bath and matching basin, a tin bath for outside and a shed. We had a cardinal-red doorstep and a budgie called Joey. Dad had a bicycle but never a driving licence. Sunday roasts were traditional and wonderful; there was lots of it and crumble for afters. The radio played in the corner as we sat and ate our greens. A black-and-white telly occasionally spluttered into life; lines would move up and down the screen until the valves warmed up, and then they stopped. Life was good and I was happy killing ants with hot water and playing games in the garden with my mates, all two of them. Coconut – whose real name was Jimmy Thatcher – lived just down the street. We went to the same school and shared many adventures. He was called Coconut because he had three crowns on the top of his head. My other mate Gary Meades lived what seemed like miles away, by the river. He was tubby and had a ruddy face like me; we shared a love of collecting stamps and model aeroplanes. Each weekend we'd make things and paint them, mostly badly, while listening to the radio. Even today when I hear 'You Really Got Me' by The Kinks, I'm transported back to small tins of paint and a tube of glue.

Our prefab was the perfect home to grow up in: no stairs to climb and a huge garden to hang out in which went up a slight embankment at the back. My mum, who loved me and took me everywhere, was bright-faced and slightly round, like me today. A staunch Protestant from Coleraine in Northern Ireland, she enjoyed dancing and shouting at my dad when he occasionally came home from work drunk. She was a great cake-maker and I used to sit beneath the table and watch her and her friends bake. Icing sugar would fall like snow, currants would occasionally drop on the floor and I would pick them up, chewing the life out of them. It was a bit like being in a Tom and Jerry cartoon – all I could see were their legs and their knees. I was told not to speak unless spoken to. I was given jelly, cake, white bread with lemon curd spread thickly on top. It was all about food and legs, handbags and toys.

Mum and Dad had met in World War II during his time in Belfast. He was waiting for a ship to take him to Africa, Mum was serving up food in the mess, and I guess they saw each other over the steaming Irish stew and fell in love. I can imagine them walking along the docks holding hands, watching the stars and trying to stop each other from crying at how wonderful life was. Her ship did come in but it took my dad away from her, off to war, to fight the Germans. They had just enough time to fall deeply in love – and other stuff. Nine months later, while he was away, a telegram arrived to inform Dad of my brother Lew's birth. It was 1943. Three years later, he came home to see his young boy. There on the dockside was Mum with Lew, waving flags and crying, and down the gangplank walked Sidney Lewis Difford, beaten by the years of war but overcome to be on dry land. His son ran right past him – they were meeting for the first time. The drums must have been banging, the pipes piping and the ship's horn blowing. Belfast in 1946; he wasn't home yet, but peace had broken out and the war was a shadow that would follow my father around for the rest of his life, although he said nothing, ever.

Coming home from war would mean moving mother and child over to England from Coleraine. They went to Charlton, south London, where my dad's parents lived. Reluctantly, Mum moved into the spare room and brokered a deal – she would get to go home every year for a few weeks in the summer. She'd been uprooted and forced to move in with my grandparents, who I knew very little about. I only met my grandmother once or twice; she had a beard and lived in one room in a big house close to the Charlton Athletic football ground. Beside her sat a bell, which she would ring if she needed tea or a newspaper. She lived to the ripe old age of ninety-two and had a colostomy bag for the last thirty years of her life. My uncle Bert lived with her and tended to her every need. My other three grandparents all died of cancer before I was born.

As soon as my mum moved into the house in Charlton, she contacted the council about getting a place of her own. A prefab came up a few miles away in Greenwich and they moved in. It must have been a palace to them, a reward for being together and surviving the war. Les was born in Woking four years after Lew; and I came along in 1954 – an afterthought. They were so much older than I was and they left home before I moved into adolescence.

Dad was tall and handsome; I could imagine him at Monte Cassino, in Italy, charging around with a gun, though this was probably far from the truth. But what was the truth? As much as I asked him about the war, he would never tell me what it was like. He did say that seeing your friends get blown to pieces wasn't a story that needed telling. He was the breadwinner, working as a wages clerk down at the gasworks. Mum managed his income well and we seldom went without – there was always food on the table and socks in your shoes. Dad worked the same job all his life and never missed a day; he was dedicated to the coin. He knew where every penny went, and unlike me, he was extremely careful with money.

Being with Dad was a very different experience to being with Mum. We would cycle to the allotment on a Saturday down by the Blackwall Tunnel, me strapped to the wooden crossbar on his bike. We would take trips up the Thames on the riverboats. We went to his office. The gasworks was a huge place built on marshland called Tunnel Point. It's now better known as the O2. Dad sorted out the wages and all the men on the site had genuine respect for him. In his office I would play with rubber bands and paper clips; there were also yellow Bic pens with 'Gas Board' written on them – well worth nicking at the time. As a young lad I loved being there, surrounded by men, stationery and large dumper trucks. Next to the office was a huge furnace where the coke would be smelted to make gas. It was roasting hot, and massive trains would carry the coal away to a siding by the dock for shipment. I was in awe.

The office was robbed a few times at gunpoint and Dad was caught in the crossfire. I'm not sure about the whole story, but I imagined cars pulling up, men with sawn-off shotguns and hands in the air from inside the office windows. The only security they seemed to have was a floppy plastic disc on a small record player in a cupboard which was hooked up to a phone line and, with the tap of a button, the arm would drop and it would play to someone at the other end over at the Greenwich Police Station. A delicate female voice would calmly say, 'There has been a break-in at the Gas Works, emergency, emergency.' How do I know this? The disc ended up on my record player at home.

The Gas Board held Christmas parties and we would all go for dinner on folding tables and receive little presents from the managers on the stage. It was all very jolly and great for the morale of the workers; bringing everyone together to say thanks was a wonderful idea.

Harry Lynham was a close friend of my dad's. He fell in the furnace one afternoon and burnt his face and hands as he scrambled to climb out of the scorching coal. His leather gloves and his patched eye always scared me, but I could see that he and Dad had a very close bond. They would even hang out at weekends together; a few beers in the Tolly House on Royal Hill. A friend of

Harry's would deliver a wooden crate of beer to our house each Saturday morning; he was tubby with Charles Hawtrey glasses and he always wore a brown cardigan, and his van was full of similar wooden crates.

The allotment was next to Dad's office: he was the manager of this vast marsh on which men would come and turn the soil and grow vegetables. He would weed and sow while I would run around in the dirt with my toys. There was a disused van at the allotment and I would sit in it and pretend to drive – I'd travel as far as I liked, sitting on the leather seats with springs and mud everywhere. People would drop by and buy things from my dad: lime, string, seeds and cane. Across the allotment on a green field, men in whites played cricket at the Gas Board cricket ground.

When Dad wasn't working, at the allotment or in the garden digging up weeds and sorting out the shed, he was a home bod. Feet up by the telly, reading a newspaper, pouring out a beer; this was the man I saw from way down on the rug where I'd be playing with my Dinky toys. And it was from these toys that the roots of inspiration were formed. I created my own world where I could speak as much as I liked, but in happy silence. I had a few buses and cars, a lorry and a tractor; inside my head I had a world of things going on, a whole planet of people and places that only I had the bearings of.

King George Street was a great place to grow up. Milk was delivered by a horse and cart at first, then later by a three-wheeled electric death trap that would slide all over the place in the snow. Bread came from the bread van, rag-and-bone men took your disused bits away, and the fish lady pushed her barrow once a week up to the corner, where she would sing and sell her fresh cod.

Cars were few on the street, but they were mostly black and very impressive.

I would play with my toy cars and buses all day long, and often drove them from one end of the street to the other along the kerb, lying in the gutter with my chin on the pavement.

Life was all bees in jars and Fairy Liquid bottles filled with water on hot days. Rhubarb crumble and yellow custard, green gooseberries and upside-down cake with tinned pineapple. Harry Secombe and Doris Day, Harry Worth and Tony Hancock. Voices in the living room other than our own. *This is Your Life* and *Sunday Night at the Palladium* on the telly; *Watch with Mother*, *Blue Peter* and *The Woodentops*. Mum singing along with Jim Reeves and The Bachelors. There was always music playing – not all of it brilliant. My older brothers Lew and Les were generally out or in their bedrooms; Mum was always in the kitchen. Lew suffered from asthma. His wheezing did not go down well with Les, who shared a room with him. Les was born with a hole in his heart and this made him treasure each day as it came, in a more rebellious way than Lew. The two of them never really saw to eye to eye. I was always on the floor: the pattern of the rug made for a network of roads all leading to the same place, a traffic jam of Christmas and birthday toys all in a row.

Home was warm and black and white while we lived in King George Street. My elder brothers were at school, Dad was at work; it was just Mum and me. I loved being with her. She was gentle and tender, her whispering Irish accent gliding like harp music up and down my spine. As most mothers do, she kept each family member's plates spinning with selfless love. I had my brothers and my dad in the evenings, but during the day it was women who surrounded me. Mum and her church ladies would sit in the front room and talk all day long, or bake cakes in the kitchen. There was always cooking, and Mum's meals were a treat – worth waiting for. To me, cooking seemed like a play with three acts. Preparing – me peeling the spuds and podding the peas. Cooking – me stirring the gravy and watching the meat. Eating – all of us sitting quietly around our tiny kitchen table, which I must have laid in order to gain brownie points. The encore was the washing-up, which Dad always did. Our house was a home full of memorable smells and food fresh from the allotment or the local shops on Royal Hill.

I don't remember too much tension. My many therapists over the years have tried to locate deep-buried memories of conflict and familial unhappiness, but to no avail. Life was normal; we lived simply. Sometime before I was ten, I was joined by my imaginary friends. Only an addict would have more than one. Together we were soldiers, pilots, seamen and spies; in the garden, in the bath and under the table during cake-making manoeuvres. We went everywhere together and were inseparable. My mum cottoned on to how close we'd become and laughed about it with her friends. She even had my imaginary mates babysit me; she'd encourage me to hang out with them in my bedroom when she wanted some time to herself.

I have no idea where they came from. They joined me one day while I was playing in the garden and came back the next day for more; they stayed with me until I was about sixteen years old. We formed a band – but not Squeeze. We were good mates. I never took them to school, but we walked together as far as the gates outside the playground and they waited for me there. We were the Men from UNCLE, invisible and invincible. I can't describe them, but they would have been good-looking and a little burly one moment, and slim and slender the next. They could have been sulky like me. I remember the one called Paul; he wore the same jumpers as I did and the same grey flannel short trousers. Sandals in the summer with socks, Wayfinder shoes in the winter. Together we grew up in summer gardens and in the park. We would talk to each other and romp around. On the way to school, the three of us would pretend to be on a train. We would chug along the park wall, down to the school gates and there the train would stop for me to get off and go to school. They'd be there at the end of the day to pick me up, though I would wait for the bigger boys to fade away before I launched into the full train-like sound. Sometimes steam, sometimes electric – both were as sexy as each other.

August provided holiday time for us all. Heavy-looking cases, two of them black-and-white check, were packed and left in the hall; we were off to Coleraine. We would lock the front door and walk down the side of Greenwich Park to the 177 stop, where we would catch the bus to Euston. Dad would be in a suit. Upstairs was the only place to sit on a bus, my brothers and I pressed up against the front windows looking out over the south-east London landscape of working-class lives. Across Tower Bridge and into the unknown of north London. Euston was a huge cathedral of steam and noise, the smell to be consumed like a stew. My dad would grumble as he hauled the cases onto the train, and then there we all were at the table, heading north. Porridge for breakfast, black faces from looking out of the window at the steam engine up ahead pulling us nervously along the tracks. My imaginary mates would occupy the bench seat with me, and if people came into our compartment my mum would simply say the seats were taken. The wonderful journey would go on for days in my head. For a little boy, it was magical. Steam trains and ships; what was not to like?

When we arrived at Heysham, the train would wobble onto the ferry and we would spend the night crossing the rough sea to Belfast. Our cabin was small and musty, and in it I half-slept and half-imagined being in the navy. With all of us in one cabin, it was our prefab at sea. Bleary-eyed, the five of us would be led back to the train for the last part of the journey up the country to my mother's home town. Aunt Sarah and Uncle Robert were always there to meet us at Coleraine station. She was every bit my mother's sister and he was quiet and gentle. A pipe-smoker. He talked with a whistle, very softly and with a huge grin always at the ready. He was a skilled carpenter and drove a Mini; it was immaculate and I loved to sit on his knee and hold the steering wheel as we went up the back road to the garage behind the house. We would decant ourselves into their small terraced house on James Street. How we did that I'll never know. It was smaller than the prefab; we must have all been in one room. I loved the journey and the holidays we had there – fourteen in total. My Aunt Ginny had a shop just up the street: she sold potatoes, sweets and just about everything in between. This was my Willy Wonka's, and my fingers were often caught in the many jars behind the counter. Out the back in her living room there was the sweetest smell of peat burning on the fire and her pet pig lay snoring and farting in front of it.

Trips on old local buses to the south for cheap fags and gifts, walks along the Antrim coastline to the Giant's Causeway, powerful cliffs, castles and streams. Portrush for Morelli's ice cream, toy shops and naval vessels, all moored up with nowhere to go. Tea shops, fish and chips, playgrounds and funfairs. That was all we needed each day – and the local club at night for a knees-up while the kids sat outside trying to be good. Crisps and orange Fanta. I'm sure there were rows and we used to fight; like any other family we must have had our moments. The great thing is that I don't remember it being anything other than wonderful.

This was mid-Sixties Northern Ireland, though, and beyond our idyllic little world, there was tension in the air. Not that I knew much about it, of course. I was dimly aware of there being a gulf between the Protestant community in Coleraine, of which my family were a part, and the Catholic area. The streets I knew over there were warm and friendly places, where people left their front doors open for each other, while the Catholic parts of town seemed dark and unwelcoming, places to keep well away from.

My mum never made a big thing of the religious divide, even when the Troubles really kicked off in the late Sixties. But she did tell me I must never marry a Catholic – or a black girl. Yes, we used to go and watch the Orangemen march through Londonderry on the Glorious Twelfth, and my mum would sing 'The Sash My Father Wore' as loudly as any of them, and I remember going to Belfast with her and seeing barbed-wire fences and British army vehicles on the streets, but I never identified with the Loyalist cause.

Once at my cousin Trevor's house in Belfast I was shaken in my bed by a large explosion a few streets away. It was very frightening for a young lad like me, but somehow I felt safe in the arms of my family back in the calm of James Street in Coleraine. When we sat together on the rocks at the Giant's Causeway, my mum would stick her nose out to the sea and the sun, and she would pray. She felt her prayers would wrap us all in safety. She sat there for hours on end while I jumped from stone to stone, fishing for reflections in rock pools. I never interrupted her prayers. I was told to speak when spoken to. It has served me well over the years. She, however, was in constant conversation with the Lord and his shepherds.

Ireland was our second home. The Antrim coast was our far-away nest: the cold rocks and the salty breeze, the rain and the long, hard walks up and down the cliffs around the Giant's Causeway. Shopping for handkerchiefs and tablecloths, tea towels and postcards. Pac-a-macs protected us from the constant summer rain and the wind and the spray from the sea.

Once my mum took me to the Lammas Fair, a gypsy gathering in the County Antrim hills. She led me into a caravan to see an old lady who looked at my hand, held my fingers back and in a deep Irish accent told me, apparently, that I would marry several times and have many children, have a long life, play an instrument and find happiness in music.

I was sidetracked by her hairy face and was far too young to know what was being said. Mum told me about it one night at home before she died; we discussed the reading of hands as though we'd just opened a bag of crisps. If it were true, the old gypsy woman was right.

Music was a big part of my mum's life. At home, she'd play love songs – Jim Reeves and Frank Ifield – and she loved to sing and dance to Irish music. On holiday in Ireland, we would go to a pub called The Salmon Leap and listen to folk music; I'd sit there with

my crisps and lemonade and watch as she swayed and sang along
with her friends and family. Her Irish roots were planted firmly in
a fertile soil of religion and music. It's a good foundation for life.

Dad told me that Mum breastfed me for two years after I was
born, and during that time she was drinking Guinness. He said I
slept for days – so much so that they took me to see a doctor. He
saw nothing wrong with me, but thought my doziness might be
linked to the velveteen black stuff. I slept on and the doziness
continues; I was in at the deep end at a very early age.

My mum's connection with the local church meant she did
lots of good things, like taking in a young girl whose mother had
cancer. She moved into the prefab for a few months. My imaginary friends were not impressed. My mother doted on her and for
those few months my nose fell out of joint. Dad meanwhile was
treasurer of the church and also did good things. They were do-
gooders, you could say, but in a nice way.

My mum and dad were on the waiting list for a new house for
many years. We were getting very crowded and there was damp
everywhere – which didn't help my brother Lew's chronic asthma.
In 1965, we moved from 98 King George Street to 98 Combe
Avenue, a house on a council estate at the edge of Blackheath,
built from grey breeze blocks and glass. The fronts of the houses
had no windows; it was the new way, a Swedish design, they said.

Inside it was open-plan: a chimney breast coiling up to the
roof from the large bricked fireplace, the tiny kitchen covered
off with a sliding glass hatch, three bedrooms and a bathroom,
and a green bathroom suite, again. Once more, a house with a
flat roof. Change was unnerving at first, but soon I got into the
swing of living in a modern house on Blackheath. Outside, there

were garages with floors that sloped down under the ground and washing areas to hang clothes out to dry; there were open spaces paved over to play on and across the road the very green heath. On the corner of the estate there was a tower block so ugly that nobody wanted to live there.

My brothers had left school and gone on to work by the time we moved in – Lew was an articled clerk on his way to being an accountant and Les worked in a tailor's shop in Lewisham where he nicked suits at the weekend for parties and returned them on Monday morning. Smart lad. They were both in relationships and girls often came round to the house. Scooters were polished every weekend, music was played on the newly bought record player. A stereogram hogged the whole of the front room; it was fun to listen to and I would lie beneath it with my head on the floor, absolutely entranced. One minute I was bathed in the gentle sounds of The Searchers, and the next the more down-to-earth rhythms of The Rolling Stones or Bo Diddley. Music cradled my little imagination and transported me into a safe place, one that would become my home for life, it seems. Even my mother's records grabbed my attention; Ray Conniff and The Bachelors rolled me up in a passive state of comfort.

I was in some ways an only child, with a mother who let me get away with most things, including staying up late listening to music with her by my side. The smell of Persil wafting from the kitchen and a blast of Jim Reeves: what was not to love? Les came back to live at home every now and again; Lew drifted in and out. He provided the balance in our house when I was young. He was the yin to Les's yang. He always loved me with real and genuine warmth, and introduced me to The Beatles and The Searchers

– music Les would have thought too soft. Lew's asthma meant he would cough all night, keeping us all awake. It was so unfair; Les would just hit him and tell him to shut up. Mum was so worried about his health, she got him to start swimming – an activity that opened him up and helped him breathe without pain. Even though he's now got a replacement hip, he still swims seventy lengths once a week at the golden age of seventy-three. He puts me to shame health-wise. I feel more at home in the shallow end and have never been sporty at all.

The house was a more grown-up version of the prefab. Mum was so proud of it and dusted every day. New curtains and new carpets, a smaller cardinal-red door and a coal bunker. We were living the council-estate dream. Still I hung out mainly with my imaginary friends. They gave me the chance to be sociable in another world, one in which I felt safe, loved and happy. Today I still long for this place. Yes, I have friends, but they sometimes pass like the breeze. Maybe that's my fault though. There's been so much water under the imaginary bridge, so many changes – family, recovery, touring the world . . . It's very different from those short-trousered days when I could storm houses and fly low across open battlefields, and I'm sad to say I think I preferred it the way it was. Back then, my imagination was endless, my hope eternal, and I thank my imaginary friends for being there for me. It's been a gradual uphill climb ever since, but then life seems to be like that. King George Street was the cradle of my youth.

COMBE AVENUE

Walking to school through Greenwich Park was a daily treat. I loved its changing look through the year: the snow of winter, the colours of spring, the heat of summer and the orange-greys of autumn. On its avenues of tarmac I began to stretch my imagination, surrounded by nature and big open skies. Mum walked me in most days, as by now she'd found a job and was working in the canteen at the local police station. This was where, most nights after school, I had my tea. Sitting with the Old Bill on benches looking out over the rooftops of Greenwich right next door to the town hall. The men flirted with Mum and she with them. It was good-natured and all I cared about was the pie and chips, a sneaky teacake and a possible ride home in a police car.

South London was safe in those days for a young lad and I remember that I could ride my bike for miles along the towpath by the river or across the heath and even down to Lewisham. The towpath was my route into the future and my imagination came with me everywhere. I'd pedal past moored barges, bored-looking cranes and tired and silent lorries. This was my manor and I was lord of all I encountered on my green Chopper. I was following in my father's footsteps – feet that had walked across Europe during the war, had walked the steps to the church where he married my mother. They were big shoes to fill.

Mum changed with the new move and the new job; poor old Dad could never stand up to her and would run around like a slave for her. 'Do this, Sid ... bring me that, Sid' – her constant commands would wear him down. And me too. He would dust, hoover and cook while she sat by the fireplace with her whiskey; he would finish work and come home with the shopping while she sat in the garden in the sun. She had changed from the quiet one to the mother with a bee in her bonnet.

Mum was a jealous person and next door to us lived Mrs Jones, who Dad always got on well with over the garden fence. She was attractive and looked a little like Joan Sims. Her husband was a fireman – Mum liked him – and his whistle would sing across the lawn over the picket fence and into my mum's lap. Nothing ever happened, but it was flirtatious. My mother's jealousy sadly made her burn many of the love letters my dad sent her in the war; she struck the match one day when she thought my dad was seeing someone at his Gas Works club. He wasn't seeing anyone as far as I know.

Dad did everything for Mum to keep the peace; even – I believe – turning a blind eye when she became a bit too friendly with a policeman she worked with. There were so many unsaids in our house at that time. I remember silence being a big part of our family life from an early age: on the train going on holiday, on the beach with our jam sandwiches. One summer, en route to Ireland, Dad got off the train at Crewe to get some tea and KitKats, and never got back on. I still don't know why. Mum said nothing; she just sat there looking at her reflection in the glass as the train pulled out of the station. I cried and looked out of the window too. No KitKats! Just the reflection of my mother's eyes straining not to cry in front of me. Two weeks later, we were home again and nothing was said. Dad had come back.

Therapy has explained none of this. Dad loved Mum, of this I'm sure, and in all the pictures I have of our family, I only see the two of them smiling and laughing together. This makes me happy; glad to know that love was there even during what must have been long periods of domestic emptiness. Even now it makes me smile when I remember one night on holiday in Coleraine, Dad staggering home with Mum and stumbling up the stairs. I could hear him singing and laughing, and though he was obviously trying to have his way with her, she was having none of it. 'Go in the bathroom and sort yourself out, Sid,' I heard her say.

By the time I was due to sit my 11-plus in 1966, it was panic stations. Short trousers were becoming a thing of the past and being a mummy's boy was not a cool look around our estate. Gary Meades, who was always allowed to wear long trousers, was my new best mate. Together we had fun being silly on school trips and in the upper forms of primary education. He was chubby like me and we shared a boring hobby: plane-spotting. We also spotted ships and sometimes lorries on the A2 from the roundabout on Blackheath. We were nerds in floppy hats. Once on a school journey to the Channel Islands me and some friends took a boy's pants down and polished his nuts with black shoe polish. I quite literally fell through the bedroom window in tears laughing. The teachers didn't think it was so funny. We'd been to Guernsey to talk about how they grew tomatoes and why the Germans had invaded this small, boring island. A day trip took us all on a ferry to Herm, an island close by, and someone said that Eric Clapton had sailed his yacht up to the beach one afternoon. 'Get Back' by The Beatles was number 1 and two hundred 555s were bought and stowed away in my hand luggage. I smoked myself sick, but it looked good.

Dad had always hoped I'd be a grammar school boy, like he had been, but because he worked so much he could never keep his eye on the ball when it came to me and homework, and I managed always to skip it or disguise the fact that I had any. I failed my 11-plus at James Wolf Primary School and I didn't end up going where my dad wanted me to go. We stood in Greenwich Park by the bandstand and he read me the riot act as he thumbed through my exam results. Mum in his shadow weighed in with her wistful Irish wisdom and we all marched back to the house with me twenty yards behind, head hanging low as if I was on my way to the gallows. I was a let-down. Mum always wanted me to remain four years old, cute and a little bit in love with her. The schooling wasn't a huge issue for her, but she had to take Dad's side and stand close by when he shouted at me.

I spent the six weeks of the long summer holidays nervously building up to the new place – Greenwich Secondary School for Boys. But for the first time ever we went on holiday to somewhere other than Coleraine; we went to the Isle of Wight. Dad, who was sick of going to Northern Ireland, had got his way, so we sat on the beach drinking tea and eating gritty hand-made sandwiches, walked the cliffs and came down in the morning at the B&B to a sunlit room filled with people like us. It was so great to be somewhere new and I think even Mum enjoyed the change, a new home and a new holiday destination all in the space of a few years. We went back a few more times to the Isle of Wight, and I remember seeing the *Queen Elizabeth* sail by each time we were there. It looked so graceful and so much of another world: way above our station.

Lew was now too old for family holidays and Les was trusted to stay at home and house-sit. We came home after one break and opened the door to find the furniture all out of place and the fish in the tank gasping for food. Behind the sofa was a pair of girl's knickers; in the kitchen empty bottles of beer and wine. Mum hit the roof and Dad was hunched over, resigned to something he knew all along – that the boy couldn't be trusted.

The new school beckoned. A 53 bus from the edge of the heath took about six minutes to get down the hill into the dark and dangerous world of Deptford. I had to walk past Carrington House on the corner of Deptford Broadway, a doss house outside which I'd trip over women with walking canes and men with matted grey hair and long, flowing Dickensian coats. The smell was urinal and high in octane – one dropped dog end and the whole lot would have gone up. At first I was petrified. The rest of the walk was along Friendly Street to the black gates of the lower school, passing the corner shop that sold single fags to school kids. I'd heard about the tradition of tie-label cutting and bog-dipping, and I was nervous my head would be stuck in some shitty white toilet bowl.

I said goodbye to my mum at the black gates. I wanted to hug her and cry, just like I had on my first day at junior school, but the new young man inside me dragged me off into the playground – into the lions' den. When I had a chance, I took my own tie label out and threw it away; it did the trick and in some ways made me feel part of the flock. The early years in the lower school were spent dodging games and looking out of the window at the trains heading up the track to London. I had some friendships to build; I also had some old mates, like Coconut, who was big enough to offer me some security. It was time to toughen up a little, too, as without it I'd get eaten alive by the bigger boys. But there was too much Mum in me and not enough Dad.

My classmates and I grabbed each other's balls on the stairs going to and from class, we rubbed bogeys on the banisters so teachers would put their hands in them and we tripped weaker boys up in the main hall at assembly. Hardly tough nuts. I had the nickname Mo; it was seen as an insult, but I had no idea why. I was hopeless at games, so in the eyes of my peers, my masculinity was immediately in question. At best, I played in goal; in cricket I batted like a little girl and in running I walked. In the brutally cold showers our teachers would force us into after every game of football, I found looking at other boys uncomfortable; they never looked at me.

The balance had shifted at home, and Mum working at the police station wasn't going down well with Dad. This was the end of the 1960s and working mothers were still a rarity – especially around our way. Dad was miffed about it, though he was the first to admit we could do with the extra money coming into the house. His problem, I think, wasn't this first flowering of women's liberation, but the fact that she spent her days surrounded by burly, cocky policemen. She seemed happy, though, and was always being chauffeured to and from the station in police cars, which I thought was impressive.

Dad sat at one end of the sofa and Mum the other, then she moved to the chair next to the fire. They pointed themselves towards the TV and watched the heaps of inspiring programmes that came into our front room back in those days. Wednesday plays, *Morecambe and Wise, Tomorrow's World*. The cigarettes seemed more and more important and the new spinning silver ashtray on a pole in the centre of the room was always full. Drinks were poured but each night felt increasingly empty of conversation. Dad worked as hard as he ever did and treated himself to a moped. It was scary to see him ride it, as he'd never driven anything more dangerous than a bicycle. The tubby man with the brown cardigan and Charles Hawtrey glasses seemed to follow our move, and again every Saturday he would pull up in his small van and Dad would smile and pass him some cash.

Dad was frustrated with my schoolwork and the fact that I was academically useless, unlike my older brother Lew, who was as bright as a button and had got a good job and a new home in Overton, Hampshire, with the love of his life, Christine. Lew was the generous older brother who would bring me toys and look after me with a warm arm around my young shoulders. He always called me Henry, my middle name, the only person who does so, and his affection for me made him seem like a third parent. By council house standards he was doing pretty well for himself. Unlike me, who struggled with maths, English and all the things Dad wanted me to excel in. They said I was backward at school – whatever that meant. Dyslexia by another name. Homework was boring and I sat there long-faced as Dad stood at my shoulder waiting for me to turn into some kind of Billy Whizz, which I never did. I turned into Billy Liar instead.

My stammer and my lack of self-confidence slowed me down. I sat at the back of the class next to kids who chewed crayons and threw paper and rolled nose-pickings into a matchbox. I went to elocution lessons in Deptford to try and correct my speech impediment.

I was often gasping for words with my friends at school and this always made me feel one step behind the rest. I felt frightened. I'd never conform to Dad's way of thinking and in the end I think he saw that my way was the only way I'd make myself happy. I was nice but dim, and I was never going to be an accountant like my big brother.

School dragged on. I can't remember too much about the lower school, but once I transferred to the upper school, things changed. The 53 bus took me from the same stop on the heath down to the bottom of the hill again, but not as far as the doss house on the Broadway. The upper school was a tall imposing building and it felt dangerous, bigger boys and bigger balls to grab. In the play-ground there were two long buildings, one for metalwork and one for woodwork. The top floor was where the art room sat – the first class that made me feel engaged in this education I'd previously assumed I simply had to get through. It takes a good teacher to show you that learning can be fun, and we had a few. Good friends can always help, too. Eric Stuckey was my new best mate; he was so funny and so focused on his work. A magnificent goalkeeper, he would scoop the ball in his arms, choose a player on the pitch and lob the ball right to their feet. I played left back so I could be close to him for some chilly laughs on bleak open fields deep in the south London suburbs.

Eric lived right next to the Millwall football ground, and we spent our evenings either in his bedroom or in mine on Combe Avenue. Going anywhere near Millwall filled me with fear. It was such a dark, grey environment, and I always felt scared walking the streets around there. I quickly learnt to keep my head down and not invite trouble. You had to look confident, like you knew exactly what was around you, and to walk purposefully. Danny Baker was a huge Millwall fan; he was in a lower year than me, so full of life and charisma, a good football player and all-round happy chap. And like me, he had a keen interest in music. Danny never seemed to be one of those football fans that would round you up with a few punches and a boot to the ribs.

We shared many of the same experiences in that school; you can read them in his book after you have read mine. The smell of school still lives with me today: the sweetness of timber being shaved in the woodwork room; the harshness of metal being drilled on a lathe. The smell of custard creams being cooked at Peek Frean's factory a few miles away in Bermondsey and, in contrast on another wind, the sickening smell of dog biscuits being made down on Blackwall Lane. Stewed greens at lunchtime, tar soap in the changing rooms, the dry crusty odour of socks in football boots. The smell of boys in grey flannel trousers, and pencils – ah! The sweetness of pencils.

The leap from childhood into teenage utopia seemed to happen overnight. Suddenly I was in a place where girls seemed oddly interesting, where Airfix kits were to be left in boxes and what you had in your trousers was worth occasionally investigating, especially when wiry hair started to take root. I started to notice the shape of things to come – particularly in the form of Greenwich Girls' School, across the road. At the bus stop I became friends with a girl who caught my bus each day; she was taller than me and very serious-looking. A few times I walked her home even though it was nowhere near where I needed to be.

Finally I plucked up the courage to ask her to hop off school with me. To my delight she accepted. My daily routine was this: I'd arrive at the school gates and tumble into class for the register; then, in the first break, I'd sneak back out of the gate and onto the bus. I had a key to the house and was trusted by my parents. She agreed to join me and we met on the bus going back up the hill to my estate. I turned the key and in we went to the cold, empty house. Suddenly I lost my nerve, and after a cup of tea and some awkward chat, we headed up to listen to records in my bedroom. Her hairy legs and her serious face made me feel like crying, and just at that moment I heard the pop-pop-pop of my dad's moped coming down the road. White-faced, I told her to get under the bed, where the floor was littered with electric toy trains and top-shelf magazines nicked from the corner shop. Dad came in and hunted around downstairs; he'd left something behind. He must have known I was home, as the teacups and the sugar bowl were out on the serving hatch. The door slammed and pop-pop-pop, off he went back to work. By this time, any passion I had was gone.

My attention span was minimal. When being taught history, I drifted; when being shown how to make a wooden stool for my parents' kitchen, I lost interest and the stool was forever lopsided. Maths was for the bright kids in the front row of the class, not for me. Geography, though, was something I enjoyed. Mr Cosgrove, our teacher, was seven feet tall and his hushed Irish accent and total love of rivers and valleys won me over. I was gripped by his voice and embraced his descriptions of limestone and clay. We once went on a field trip to Box Hill in Surrey, where he stood in a river in his corduroys to show us how the river was deeper on one side than the other. His enthusiasm drew me in.

I also enjoyed English, especially when, from time to time, it was taught by a stand-in teacher. He was young and tuned in to my dreamy, curvy handwriting, which would dribble words in rhyme onto the backs and fronts of my school books. I knew about daydreaming and I knew about poetry, and to pass the time at school I married the two together. I was fascinated by the rhyming images of Spike Milligan, his humour and the rhythm of the words. Poetry was something I had read, but not understood, at my brother's house in Hampshire when he first got married. I flicked through a book of verse by Tennyson. The pattern of the words and the meanings hung like fluffy clouds above the empty pallet of my receptive young mind. Nobody in my house seemed the least bit interested in words; there were no books except the Bible and a few unread encyclopaedias. We were not a well-read family. I'd been unsure about writing but this teacher inspired me.

In an early long poem, I wrote about a land that could only be discovered from within the lamp post outside my prefab. The cold metal door would open to reveal a mystical place full of friendly children my age who would talk in rhythm and offer you sweets. Day was night and night was day. I went there in my imagination and inbetween the words I had created. Xiom was a far-off land of peace and sunshine, full of little people who lived in cream-cake houses and drove around in sherbet-dab cars and buses. Rivers were lemonade and the clouds were candyfloss; almost everything in the lamp post was edible. I could lose myself in the poems I wrote; along with my imaginary mates I was in a safe place far away from the rigid structure of school.

One afternoon my teacher carted a record player into the classroom and out of his bag he pulled a Bob Dylan album. We studied the lyrics and talked about them. This was new. He unveiled the link between words and music. I must have subconsciously swallowed this idea and the seed was planted gently in the fertile ground of my youth. Most of the other teachers were too old to teach and way out of touch with the music of the day, and sneered at his forward thinking.

One day the careers teacher sat me down in his office surrounded by Join the Army pamphlets and guides to local colleges. He asked me what I might like to do when I left school – something I really hadn't given any thought to. He was a bit of a know-it-all, and whenever I suggested something, he knew better. When I said I wanted to be a pilot in the air force, he laughed and said I'd have to work jolly hard for that to happen. He said I needed to go away and give it some more thought. That same week, I read an exciting interview with Pete Townshend of The Who in *Melody Maker*. He had all the drugs in the world, fast cars, drink and private planes, money and a busy touring schedule. It sounded great. The next time I saw the careers master, I sat down in his room with a large grin and told him I wanted to be in The Who. Again he laughed. Prodding me, he asked me what I'd really like to do. I sat and thought. A pig farmer?

Art wasn't my finest hour. I could paint, but not with anything other than an abstract brush. I was good at matchstick sheep. Our art teacher was good-looking and a bit of an enigma. She had long hair and all the boys and male teachers followed her with their eyes. She drove an open-top car and swaggered up and down the stairs to the art room. She took me to another place. She was young and used music to inspire us in class, which meant we could bring in LPs. My collection at this time was thin, but Eric and I were starting to take an interest in NME and *Melody Maker*. We were watching and reading everything to do with music; it was our hobby. The 53 bus took us up west to HMV to see and hear the albums there. I would listen to Frank Zappa and The Allman Brothers Band, King Crimson and The Who. Those trips were the foundations of my musical journey; the anticipation of hearing new music was so special. Albums were listened to and collected with pride and devotion. It was a boy thing, except she wasn't a boy – she was our teacher, and being asked back to her place was a bit weird. At her flat we listened to albums and sat on the floor a lot. It was all Chicken Shack and wholemeal bread, candles and sideways looks that seemed full of meaning. When she came close to me, I was aware of something stirring in my underpants. But I knew that was a line that could not be crossed, and anyway I was terrified.

Albums were key to all forms of communication; they were the talking points that could turn a friend into a closer friend. Eric had a cool collection including records by Canned Heat and Jethro Tull. He did a fine impression of a man playing a flute, in his socks with a ruler in his hands. I wasn't a big fan of that, but he turned me on to Chicago and a band called Heaven, who reportedly had the most complicated album sleeve in circulation. It opened up into a large cross the size of my bedroom. The music wasn't great. Sleeves were the thing, and with King Crimson we had album sleeves that were so artistic it was hard to believe there could be anything better. The music inside seemed great, too. With a Pink Floyd album under your arm, you could walk through school and say all you needed to say about how you felt about life and who you were.

Eric and I started going to see bands play live – Genesis, Canned Heat, Crimson, and lesser-knowns such as Camus and Gong. The norm was to sit on the floor and nod to the music, coming away with what we felt was an innate understanding of time changes and non-emotional lyrics about mythical creatures and dreams. Lunchtime concerts at the Lyceum were good tickets, but we had to hop off from school to see them. No big deal as our art teacher would cover for us. Van der Graaf Generator, Patto, Atomic Rooster; all great sets, over which the smell of patchouli and fags would hang sweetly in the afternoon air.

We were distracted from our musical adventures briefly when we bumped into two girls in the park. Eric was confident and soon moved into a short relationship with his; me, I stumbled forward like Frank Spencer. Diane Twigg was tall and very lovely; we were both fourteen going on fifteen. She lived in Lee Green, where I made a few visits, soaping up her parents with my good behaviour. I think I even washed her dad's car. Once I was in the family I was allowed upstairs to her room to listen to her records. She put a Leonard Cohen album on the turntable. She gazed into the light of the window; I gazed at my monkey boots. I was not vibing with her on this one. Her dad took us to see Cat Stephens at the Coliseum in September 1971. Cat was magical and gentle, like Diane. The concert was an eye-opener: I had never seen such a soft concert before but I think I loved it. A few weeks later, Diane dumped me. I went and bought the Leonard Cohen album she had played me; suddenly I understood the darkness she was looking at, and now it belonged to me.

I may have been a sort of hippy at school, but such dreamy affectations would never have cut it back on the estate. A skinhead gang was forming as the houses were being put up around us, and the Combe Avenue Killers – a name I once painted onto one of the shed walls nearby – were starting to come together around Les Grimsley and Trevor Chambers, kids a couple of years older than me. Les walked with a limp and his lips were never very far from a cigarette. He could explode at any minute, he seemed to have such a short fuse. Trevor was more cunning in looks and by nature. There were two sides to the gang – those who leant towards creative mischief such as removing people's gates and reattaching them to their neighbours' gateposts, and the out-and-out thugs who were into nicking cars and breaking into houses. At first, they petrified me (I'd always veered towards the nerds in floppy hats), but ours was a small estate and social options were limited, so I was soon hanging around with them once school was over. It was boredom relief. We would often gather on the heath on a piece of rough ground we called Cowboy Land. Snogging in the bushes and lazing about being hard was the nature of the beast.

One night a man arrived on our estate delivering the football pools; he had a small black car and was very friendly. He asked me and a mate if we wanted to help, and told us we could earn a few bob too. I went around posting the forms through the doors of our estate and others close by. One night he took me to an estate on the other side of the water, in east London; it was scary and exciting. He asked me if I liked model aeroplanes, which I did, and the next time he picked me up he had a box with a model Lancaster bomber in it. My face lit up as he rolled another cigarette.

He then drove the car into a dark spot off the heath and touched my leg, smiling and in search of reward. I slammed the door and scarpered. The following day I gathered my mates together and we went to his house. We broke into his car and rolled it down the side of the incline that would become the new A2 bypass down to the Blackwall Tunnel. To top it off, we smashed his front window. Nothing was said. I'd dodged a very hairy bullet.

I did have some softer friends on the estate. John Barnes lived just behind us, and his parents often took me with them for Sunday lunch in a folk club down in Kent. We sat outside submerged in the tenderness of folk tales played on fiddles and banjos. I do recall a woman singing songs one afternoon and being smitten by the storytelling value of her words. John and I got on well and I found his home a place to retreat to when things got hot under the collar around the washing lines. Other softies included Andy Driscoll, who played the drums in his bedroom, much to the annoyance of his neighbours and his parents alike. He lived opposite two boys who were into The Who and The Small Faces. We would bounce off their parents' sofas with tennis rackets singing along loudly to 'Lazy Sunday Afternoon' and 'Happy Jack'. The estate was a mixture of emotions: one minute I felt safe in a woolly jumper, the next on edge in a pair of turned-up jeans and a Fred Perry shirt.

The skinhead scene may have become synonymous with racism, but in our corner of south London that couldn't have been further from the truth. A lot of people in the area were uncomfortable with seeing more black and brown faces on the streets in the late Sixties – I remember my dad once telling me he'd got off the bus and walked all the way back home from Lewisham because three 'darkies' had got on and sat behind him – but ours was a very white estate so it just wasn't that much of an issue for us. Plus our gang had huge respect for Jamaican music, so the black kids we'd go clubbing with were good friends. There was a definite sense of segregation at school. The Jamaican and Ghanaian boys gravitated towards each other in the playground, and the white kids hung around in separate groups. But there was never very much tension. I was once in a fight with a boy called Dingle Fullerton, who stabbed me with a fountain pen on the ground outside the woodwork room; there was a stand-off around us, but it was soon broken up by the seven-foot geography teacher.

I loved the music I heard at the Tamla Motown parties I went to with my skinhead mates every Saturday night, followed by the Savoy Club in Catford on a Sunday. My record collection was full of reggae and ska; my wardrobe consisted of tonic suits and polished shoes, white shirts and white socks. Brut and spray-on deodorant was a mixture I won't ever forget the smell of. My skinhead days intertwined with my early days in the upper school and my dual life split me into two camps. Combe Avenue, and the estate I lived on, provided the lads and the little masculinity I managed to harvest; school nurtured the more feminine musical-poet teenager who was focused on doing as little as possible but enjoying the ride. Being a skinhead made me walk tall and connected me to dancing and girls.

My skinhead girlfriend was Sharon, she was as skinny as a rake; we dressed the same and danced the same, but somehow I always knew she was looking over my shoulder at better-looking boys. I say girlfriend, but nothing ever happened; it was a long walk home for a kiss. Nothing else. One night we won a dancing competition judged by a slick black DJ in a reggae club. I was buzzing. Outside I was talking to a very pretty girl in a Prince of Wales check suit. From behind me leapt Sharon, who stabbed me in the hand with her silver comb. We fell to the ground and had to be pulled apart. It was over, and she moved on to a taller skinhead with a chiselled face, sculpted no doubt by large amounts of uppers.

Speed was the first drug I ever took; it pinned my face to the back of my head and made my teeth grind like millstones. We danced all night and we danced all the next night too; me and Trevor at his mum's flat on the estate. He was a thug and started aggro without any fear. Together we often picked fights with hippies on the street – easy targets. But then he beat up a boy on the heath whose dad was head of CID at the local police station. Not so bright. He was arrested. A big black girl and her sister joined the clan; she was a nutcase from Lewisham and punched people for no real reason at all. She terrified me. One night she tried to force me to take my pants down on the heath. I ran away and hid under the washing lines. Another girl, Chrissy Mayers, was connected with friends in local record shops in Deptford so we always had the newest releases from Jamaica on the decks. My life was livening up.

I was once caught in a house with Trevor and some other boys when the police raided the place for drugs after a tip-off from a neighbour. Handcuffs were exchanged for held-out arms, but not me: I was taken to one side. The policeman I knew from my mother's canteen gave me a stern talking-to in the back seat of the police car just up the road and then let me go. Mum was none the wiser. A few years later, I walked into our front room at Combe Avenue to find the same policeman in my mother's arms. He was sitting on her lap; I could see her stocking tops. I think they were both on the brandy. I ran upstairs to my room to sit with my tropical fish and my record player. I wasn't sure what to think or feel, so I played *Beggars Banquet* by The Rolling Stones. A few days later, I found him waiting for me outside the house in his car. He got out as I walked past, and gave me The Beatles' *White Album* as a gift. I took it from him and went to my room trying hard to pull a long face. I don't think I said thank you. The record still sounds amazing despite its connections to Greenwich CID. He wasn't *The Sweeney*, more *Z-Cars*. A nice man with a soft Irish accent. I left a big scratch on his car with my front-door key. Revenge was not sweet. Playing 'Revolution 9' loudly every time he came round to the house was.

On Saturday, 26 April 1969, Leicester City played my team Manchester City at Wembley Stadium. Colin Bell was my hero. Dad got two tickets and took me to see the game. The journey through London on the bus and the tube swallowed me up. I was fifteen, but I still held tightly to Dad's hand. The experience of being around so many people, mostly men, made me scared and anxious; I was not so much excited as petrified. We stood in the stands as the crowd as one swayed from side to side, men in hats, boys in scarves; it seemed powerful. Dad stood by my side while I tried hard to see the game on tiptoes. The winning goal was scored by Neil Young – the other Neil Young – and the place erupted, except for my dad, who stood silent and motionless. I was beside him trying hard not to explode; I was the firework that fizzled out under my father's giant shadow.

Manchester City won the cup and we returned home on the tube and bus. It was a damp squib of a day, but the journey and the vibrations of so many people in one place stayed with me for a very long time. It was tribal if nothing else; it's just my dad wasn't into crowds and expressions of manhood. Back home in my bedroom I looked at the poster of Colin Bell on my wall, next to the one of The Who's *Maximum R&B*, and beamed with pride as I took it down. It was replaced by a poster of a girl scratching her arse while holding a tennis racket. On my copy of The Small Faces' *Autumn Stone*, I can still see the words 'Man City' written in biro on the front of the sleeve. Mixed-up days indeed. I didn't go to another football match until I was in my thirties.

Our rival skinhead gang lived in Charlton – just above the Valley football ground on the Charlton Road estates. They were into causing trouble at Charlton Athletic games, a new kind of fun for many young working-class boys in the late Sixties and early Seventies; and something my dad, a lifelong Charlton fan, could never understand. We couldn't be bothered with that, but we were always up for a fight with the Charlton mob. Equidistant between us was The Standard pub, which was the crossing line. You had to go mob-handed if you went anywhere near it, as once you passed it, you were in enemy territory. The fight would normally be led by one or two people – the gang leaders – who would start rucking while everyone else stood around and occasionally stuck the boot in. Then, when it got too much, we would all run off in different directions. There was another gang over in Kidbrooke, which included the comedian Jim Davidson and his brother, that we had an easier relationship with. I remember teaming up with them to oust some Hell's Angels from their local pub, The Dover Patrol. But when we got there, the Angels came out of the door and we all legged it.

These sorts of events were seemingly all in fun, if a little nasty in reality. All local gangs would taunt each other but it never seemed to reach me on a deeper level. It was all part of being a lad. Les Grimsley and Trevor were more cut out for villainy than me. They had anger issues and liked to get involved in any kind of scrap. One evening they pulled me into something I knew was going to be uncomfortable. They needed money to buy drugs, mostly speed, or wiz as we called it. It was such a misty night, they suggested we just grab someone on Blackheath and rob them. We hung around the bus stop for a while, waiting for someone to get off, but no one did, so we went down Langton Way, a narrow, dark lane, where we saw an old woman walking a dog.

It all happened quickly. It was a misty night and I was choking with fear. As things started to escalate, I knew I was doing something that wasn't really me. It shook me up and made me think about the peer pressure that I seemed always to be under. I was impressionable and drawn into the danger of teenage stupidity. We were like a pack of wolves as we ran towards the woman from behind. She was knocked to the ground, the dog was kicked into a hedge and the bag was wrenched from her shoulder. And for what? All that was inside was a pack of Polo mints, a couple of quid and some keys.

I felt terrible all the time we were doing it. Really upset. We'd tipped the scale too far and I realised I'd had enough – that my journey onward wasn't going to be with the gang. Les was the sort of person who had no fear and little emotion; he was clearly destined for prison. Many years later, he died outside his home, frozen in the snow, high on drugs. Trevor went to prison and later died from an overdose. The day after the mugging, I had to take the victim's handbag and lob it in the Quaggy River at Deptford Bridge. I was petrified and tearful; I knew I wasn't cut out for the danger and the violence of council-estate life. Deep down, I was still under the table watching my mother bake cakes: a sheep in wolf's clothing.

I loved my estate and all of the people who lived there; we had a good laugh and grew up with equal amounts of danger and fantasy. Our parents worked hard for the rent and with some ducking and diving we all managed to scrape by. People kept themselves to themselves but I always felt that the arm of friendship was always close at hand. I loved it despite being dragged into some sticky situations.

My hair started to grow longer, and heavier music appeared on my turntable. I was moving from the dance floor to the bedroom floor, from Marvin Gaye to The Nice in one short year. Prince Buster made way for Pink Floyd. My parents were confused and the poems I began to write were a constant amusement for Les and Trevor and the rest of the gang. One minute I was coming home high on speed from a Tamla Motown party, tanked up on a Party 7; the next I was slow as a snail glued to the sounds of Black Sabbath or Cream. The role change was very swift, but I think it probably saved my life. We went our separate ways; the gang got more and more dangerous and I grew more reserved and introverted. I was seventeen and all over the place inside, until the day I heard some loud music coming from the end of the block.

THE THREE TUNS

Some boys followed football teams and the muddy world of the leagues. But I wasn't into that; I followed the charts. I tracked record companies and their acts with passion. I read music papers as if my life depended on it. My hair grew down my back and my world focus zoomed in on music and groups. Some boys thought I was a girl. I was sliding down some scary helter-skelter on a rug made of surreal lyrics. The best thing about adventure is not to question it, and I didn't know what to ask it even if I could.

Bob Blatchford lived a few doors down on my block in Combe Avenue; he was heavily into music and making model planes, which we often flew on the heath. His fingernails were mashed to shreds from catching his fingers on the rotating propellers. He had a small moustache and slicked black hair. He smelt of 3-In-One oil, and wouldn't have been out of place taking tickets on the dodgems at the fair. Bob was older than me by a few years and came from a lovely family. His father was a trade union leader on the docks, and looked angry all the time. Bob adopted me and introduced me to an alternative lifestyle. He had some loud records by MC5 and The Stooges. He would pump up the volume and his big black speakers would rattle the windows. I held on for dear life. I borrowed his guitar and took a chord book out of the local library, along with a Donovan album called A *Gift from a Flower to a Garden*, which never went back. I'd started writing songs in my bedroom and, heavily influenced by Bowie and Donovan, was making my first attempts at putting words to music. Bob heard me strumming these and recorded them for me on a tape recorder and some microphones he owned.

I have to thank Bob for inviting me into this world. He listened to me, and took interest in my growing passion. Times were moving on and poetry was my thing, now in full motion. Across the street were the remnants of the Combe Avenue skinhead fraternity; they had whittled down from about twenty to just three or four of them sitting on the wall, gobbing and trying to look hard. But I'd hung up my Doc Marten boots and was now mincing around in plimsolls. We would nod but seldom exchange words; the whole mood of the estate had changed and I was moving on with my life. Two other boys from the estate toyed with music, one with a drum kit and one with a guitar, though it was only a passing fad. But I was not letting my focus shift like the others and spent more and more time with Bob.

Bob took me to Cambridge one afternoon in his father's Austin Metro, and there we hung out with his mates in a student flat where there was a party. I may have rubbed shoulders with my heroes; there were meant to be members of Pink Floyd hanging about but I'd never have known, as I was indulging in the room spin of my first joint. Meeting David Gilmour would have certainly made my year. The odd thing is, maybe I did. The party was slow; we sat on the floor and listened to music, but there was no Smokey Robinson or Prince Buster in sight. Skinhead parties were all about dancing and holding onto the girls, the music steaming up the rooms. Now it was time to sit down and take it all in. There was a lot of dope smoking going on, something I was new to, but joining in seemed the best thing to do, and it didn't take long for me to become very passionate about rolling joints. I rolled them as if my life depended upon it; they were neat, round and tipped to perfection. I had a friend called Keith who lived across the road from the estate. Together we smoked our way through Pakistan and back, his eyes squinting narrowly together. His brother was a dealer; we got all the good stuff, and sometimes the good stuff made me sick. Other times it would make me giggle all night long. It was delightful.

One of the first concerts I went to with Bob was Pink Floyd at Crystal Palace; they were supported by The Faces, Mountain, the brilliant Sutherland Brothers and Quiver. On the top of the 75 bus from Blackheath, sitting right at the front, I found myself surrounded by hippies.

One with a sweet bag offered me a mushroom – it was a magic one and I obliged. By the time we made it to Penge, I was flying. The bus had become a spaceship and I was the pilot. I giggled all the way to the front row, where I sat down just in time to see the show. The Floyd were amazing; they inflated a massive octopus from beneath the lake in front of the stage. This was it, I was in heaven, and it tasted like mushrooms. The whole experience was enhanced by quadrophonic sound and a dark-blue overcast London sky. My early experiences of going to gigs were mostly like this, stoned and happy, studying every aspect of what the musicians were doing, staying up late and being in a haze of quietly spoken friendships. Nice one.

I would walk across Blackheath with my imaginary friends, and we would often form a band and make up songs, some of them long and progressive like ELP or King Crimson. We were forward-thinking with our bass and drum solos. I would sing and play guitar like Jerry Garcia, then switch to being like Frank Zappa. I would make up lyrics and if, when I got home, any of them were worth keeping, I would jot them down in a notepad. I still do this today, but without the bass and drum solos. When people walked by, I would quieten down and hum softly until they had passed, then crank it up again. If the concert wasn't over by the time I got home, I would walk around the block a few times.

Walking and being in the imaginary band helped me to find words and melodies. My days would be full of drum crashes and guitar strums, keyboard swells and crowd noises, and even introductions from the DJ. It was a full-time job being in an imaginary band. We never got on *Top of the Pops* or *The Old Grey Whistle Test* but we had a good go at being famous in my head and in my bedroom, where we imitated every record that hit my turntable. Once I saw Soft Machine, though, my walks with the band changed shape. I suddenly found myself in the world of slow jazz pieces complemented by sporadic vocal lines; often this would go on all afternoon if the weather was right. I realised, though, that any band I played in could never be as intelligent as Robert Wyatt or Mike Ratledge. And I'd never have the sheer musical talent of Keith Emerson of The Nice, who I also saw play around the same time at the Festival Hall – he was another hero of mine. This was a huge realisation for me, and one I'm probably still coming to terms with. I wasn't to know, but a real band would soon follow and my imaginary band mates would take a back seat while I learnt to bluff my way around the local music scene.

Tony Bachelor was a close, quietly spoken friend from school; he rolled the best joints in the class, apart from me, that is. We enjoyed the same kind of music and it was with Tony that I played my first few songs. I had a bass guitar – a Bill Wyman Vox from a second-hand store in Lewisham – and he had a drum kit, and we played in his bedroom in New Cross. His mother was usually downstairs glued to the TV; she was housebound with agora-phobia. She liked knowing where Tony was, so she put up with the noise. We were rough, but it was fun. And the more stoned we got, the better it sounded. We jammed for hours on Velvet Underground songs; it was perfect. Eric Stuckey faded into the background as he needed to study for his exams. I was intent on learning the bass and playing music for the rest of my life – I'd decided exams weren't going to get me anywhere. Tony was like me; we couldn't care less about grades. Cheese on toast round at his and a few hours of 'In-A-Gadda-Da-Vida' was all we needed to get by.

I formed my first band in 1972. It was called Porky's Falling Spikes and was a mixture of jamming, dope-smoking one-chord wonders and good intentions; at one point we had two drummers and I played bass. We played a few shows I managed to sort out in a local pub. The band was made up of some school friends; they weren't as good as my imaginary band, but for a while they helped me live in the real world. As I remember, I wore a boiler suit when we played; I thought it would make me look like Pete Townshend. I had the look – just not the style or the talent. I had learnt how to play bass by pressing it up against the wardrobe to amplify the sound, and slowly plodded along with some Velvet Underground songs on my record player. I took the root notes and made the most of it. We supported Nick Lowe's band Brinsley Schwarz. Nick was a real gent, and kept me in jokes and roll-ups all night long.

Our second gig was headlined by The Flamin' Groovies and Dux Deluxe, a fair old night. The pub was called The Harrow Inn at Abbey Wood, and I made the stupid mistake of wearing silver make-up and getting it all over the neck of my bass guitar. I slid up and down the frets sounding dull and wrong. But I looked good. Tony's mother had put me in touch with a charity who were trying to raise awareness of agoraphobia, so I made a few calls to managers and agents and put the show together. I was boldly going in a direction I had no clue about, but it worked. We raised £250 and even made the *Daily Mirror*.

We did have Nigel, who had joined the band and wrote most of the songs; he was a grumpy sod, and everything had to be his way or he would sulk. It seems that every band has this dynamic from time to time. The syndrome. Nigel wrote some good songs and so did I; we swapped ideas and met in the middle. I was just a pothead with some decent poems on lined paper. He played a Telecaster and was a real musician. I never liked him. Our covers would include 'White Light, White Heat' by the Velvet Underground: it sometimes went on for days. Plonking around on a bass guitar was very satisfying, but I knew that one day I would progress to something a little more musical. Eventually the band broke up. I'm not sure why. I think it was due to apathy, not enough skins, a lack of cheese on toast – or any fans.

Then there was the hippy band. A fiddle and a mandolin, a twelve-string guitar and a cello, some drums and me on piano.

The bluff was total. I had a piano in my bedroom at home and over time it became a place where I would try and practise being like Keith Emerson. I got as far as stabbing knives into the keys, but beyond that I was hopeless. I couldn't play the piano, but I could score drugs, load the truck while on acid and add lyrics to some otherwise average folk songs. Barry Bartlett was our leader, a tall, thin, angelic chap with a love of all things Neil Young and Stephen Stills, and a beautiful girlfriend who came everywhere with us. Barry was a fine player, the first person I'd met who carried a capo. I'd just left school, so we went to a small village in Wales called Boncath to get our heads together; the rest is a blur. I do remember an owl being nailed to the front door of our rented farmhouse. I was tripping and it freaked me out. That evening we sat around a fire and listened to *Dark Star* by The Grateful Dead, then jammed all night and went for a walk. We played some music as we drifted over the hills.

Our driver John Reed was a lovely chap with a long beard that he loved to stroke. He smiled all day long and scored the drugs for most of Blackheath and Greenwich. Acid was his drug of choice and sometimes I'm sure he drove while tripping. It was hairy stuff. I recall being on stage in a local hall in the middle of Wales. We were in the heat of a set, intense then laid-back, with long fiddle solos followed by delicate guitar, followed by silent piano parts. I was bluffing, remember. During one solo, a tin of blue pills fell to the floor and opened up; the pills all rolled out and fell down the gaps in the wooden stage. The music stopped as I got on my hands and knees to save them from the void. After the show I went beneath the stage to find the ones that had got away. The addict had landed. We stayed up all night on the back of the pills

I'd prised from the floor. It was my first summer of madness; it was wonderful.

When we got back from Wales, the band split up – just when I thought I would be on *Top of the Pops*. I wasn't ready. We weren't ready. Life was on hold. When I returned home from my adventure, I walked into my bedroom to see my upright piano had been removed by my parents, back to the church hall where it had come from in the first place. They could see the disappointment in my gaze as I lay on the sofa dreaming of buying a Hammond organ.

I'd left school, and unlike the kids who were sent out into the world just a few years later, there were plenty of jobs available for us. The problem was that they were all crap. At school we were taught how to make things out of metal and wood, and how to kick a ball around. Nothing practical. There was no one attempting to guide us down a suitable career path. None of this mattered to me. My only intention was to play music. But my mum and dad were determined I should have a proper job, so to keep them quiet, I worked at a succession of rubbish places in between signing on for the dole. I did a week in a cardboard factory, flattening boxes. Another job involved editing soft-porn films onto reels of Super 8. It was an eye-opener, hot work and very tedious. It was all very tame, with naked men and women bouncing balls over nets; it was topping and tailing, making tea and watching the clock. Mum and Dad were sleeping in separate rooms at this time, apparently because of his snoring – he had massive problems with his sinuses. In Dad's bedroom, which was the larger of the two, hung his neatly kept work suits. One afternoon I had a feel around his suit pockets, and to my surprise I found he kept small wads of cash in them: each suit had different amounts. I fell into a bad habit of removing a few large notes from time to time, small numbers so he would not notice. I wonder if he did. Sometimes I would find myself at the bar in the pub with £100 of my dad's hard-earned cash making its way to the till. It was not a nice thing to do, but it helped tide me over between jobs.

For a while I worked as an office clerk for a local solicitor's office run by a tall, scary-looking lady called Miss Griffiths and a thin, tired-looking man with glasses called Mr James. They seemed to never speak to one another: I was working for my parents, it seemed. There was a staff of about twenty spread over two offices – one in Tranquil Vale in Blackheath, the other in Charlton. My job was to fetch files from here and there, and take them up to London to the law courts. On the train from Blackheath to Charing Cross, I would write poems that I had started to fall in love with in my notebook and dream of better days ahead. I enjoyed the work as it took me to a wonderful part of town where history loomed down on me everywhere I walked.

They liked me there and my £15 a week was soon raised to £18, plus travel and notebooks by the score. My parents were happy. I looked smart and I had a job; I was on the road to great things as far as they were concerned. One day I might even be a lawyer. After ten months of being a good boy and arriving on time I was given the keys to the office. I was such a nice lad. One of my jobs was to close up at night and tidy the desks. But after a year in a suit and tie, I decided that life was too precious to waste on studying law at night school, and going up and down to London on the train in clean underpants. My social life seemed a better alternative to the working one, so one Thursday night I emptied the safe of the entire wages tray – all neatly collected and counted in brown envelopes. I was loaded and it felt fantastic. It simply didn't occur to me that I wouldn't get away with it. All I had to do was cover my tracks, come up with some story and it would all go away. It didn't bother me at all.

That night I went to the pub, The Three Tuns in Blackheath, and scored some speed. I bought some albums and still had enough left over for the deposit on a rented flat of my own. I was off sick for three weeks, spending my way around London, then my dad got a letter asking where I was. I was busted. No more carrying briefs for barristers in chambers; no more arse-licking Miss Griffiths in the office; no more job. My dad promised to pay them back the money so long as the police weren't called in.

I was a chancer and I was stupid and naive to even try to rob people of their wages, but at the time I was dipping in and out of reality, in and out of drugs and in and out of the pub. I was not thinking logically. Dad was losing the plot with me; Mum was drinking too much and generally losing the plot, but not the same one as Dad. It was time to move out. School was done, skinheads were done, but the bug for music was just getting under my skin. I was in the very small world of experimentation and song. I was writing three lyrics a day, I was in another place. Mum and Dad got the raw end of the deal. I remember standing in the kitchen at Combe Avenue with my dad, and him saying, 'If you join a rock and roll band, son, you'll end up an alcoholic, a drug addict and skint.' And, as it turned out, he was absolutely right. I was tripping, though, and in no mood to listen. I was more amazed by the fact that I was able to put my hand right through his chest and watch it come out the other side.

'What are you doing?' he asked.

'That was amazing,' I said.

'Have you been drinking that cider again?'

They asked me to move out the next day.

I had started spending all my time in The Three Tuns, a pub Bob had introduced me to. It was a bohemian kind of place with jelly babies stuck to the walls, where hippies and builders mixed with local villains and estate agents. The landlord had a moustache and was very shady; it seemed like everyone had a moustache in those days. He smelt of roll-ups and, with his very tight jeans, wouldn't have been out of place in a porno film or alongside Bob on the dodgems. He was strict but smoked dope like we all did and turned a blind eye to most things. It was there that I met Jim Giles, who ran a sheet music shop in Soho. Across the road from Jim's shop was Dean Street Records, where I spent many an hour thumbing through the collection of musical and theatrical cast records. I bought Judy Garland albums and musicals as wide-ranging as *Easter Parade* and *West Side Story*; I was in love with the diversity and the brilliant songwriting. My dream was then, as it is today, to write the lyrics for a musical.

Jim took over where Bob left off. He introduced me to many great things and took me under his wing. We became like brothers, and he was the conduit for my transformation from schoolboy to unwashed dropout. I went to stay with him and his girlfriend Christine on Shooters Hill Road. It was 1972 and life was good considering I had little money and no real focus. Christine seemed to like having me around, and when Jim was at work, we hung out together in Blackheath or in the park. Jim had thrown out a met-aphorical rope and I hung onto it, as I knew it was taking me out of my home life and into a new and magical place, away from the drabness of the estate and the lads. He loved my songs, and one day he took me to see where David Bowie lived. We stood outside in the darkness for an hour; I'm not sure why. Bowie wasn't there, no lights were on. I imagined he was in some smart Soho club mincing around drinking cocktails in a serious mime pose.

Blackheath was becoming the well where I would fish for reflections and replenish myself with love and hope. I was in a place where I could now blossom. I picked up a girl from the pub called Diane. She was blonde and from Sweden, and she was a nanny for a local well-heeled family. I bored her with music and dope. We lay in my room at Jim and Chris's flat with its black walls and tried to keep ourselves from falling off my tiny bed. I played her Todd Rundgren's *Something Anything* album and tried to have my way, but she was cold and left me hanging. The album's total length gave me enough time to gently wrap my arm around her and try to nestle in for the kill, but I was very Woody Allen yet again and slipped from the bed on to the record player. We saw each other a few times but it never really worked out as it was planned in my mind. And then there was Tina, a girl I met on an acid trip at a friend's party. We gelled well, but a month later I came down and so did she. We had fun and explored the possibilities of a long-term relationship while rolling joints and snogging, and I introduced her to my mum, who hated her. She was both Catholic and black. Up in my bedroom I could feel my mother seething in the living room below. Love felt like something far away. I had no idea what it really looked like; all I really loved was music and the idea of playing in a band.

To pay my way, I got another job, this time at the Ready Mix concrete plant in Catford. This had a Wednesday-afternoon film

club, and it was my job to shut the curtains, bring out the pro-
jector and load it up, then stand at the back as the film clicked
through the shutters and the drivers watched with sandwiches in
hand. I saw some smutty films at that place. Nuns in trouble on a
bridge over a stream; one was drowning. Oh no! Mouth-to-mouth
resuscitation was needed, and the habits were off. Film over, back
outside to sweep the gravel. It was filthy work.

I ended up working down by the docks with my brother Les in
a huge warehouse stacked high with forty-five-gallon drums of
oil. My job was to count the contents of the trucks as they left the
yard. Drivers would give me money and I would turn a blind eye. I
was young and the cash was burning a nice big hole in my pocket.
Mum and Dad weren't happy. I'd gone from wearing a nice suit
and tie to jeans and a T-shirt, smelling of beer and cigarettes. But
to me, Les seemed like a safe pair of hands; elder brother, what
could go wrong? We went to the Rose of Denmark pub on the
Woolwich Road at lunchtime to watch strippers dance to Slade
songs. Sometimes I'd spend whole afternoons at the back of the
pub, sipping lager and just watching naked girls dance in and out
of time to the hits – even 'Clair' by Gilbert O'Sullivan got a past-
ing. It was never Legs & Co; never anything more than a clumsy
ballet in front of sixty men in overalls dripping beer onto the floor
through a fog of cigarette smoke coloured by the cheap flashing
lights on the makeshift stage.

I was a man – well, a boy who was pretending to be a man
by smoking untipped fags and walking home with a stagger on
a Friday night. Naked women, money in the pocket, drink and
drugs, record shops on a Saturday, pubs and nicking things. I loved
the warehouse world and forklifts. I loved the smell of oil drums

and the lorry drivers with their wives waiting at home and their dinner in the oven. I loved the sun coming up over the warehouse in the morning and the moon when it rested on the roof of the pub when it closed. Life was sweet. *Minder* and *Top of the Pops* on the telly; 'Maggie May' on the jukebox. Working with Les made me feel protected. With him and his dodgy mates I started to feel and smell the first signs of adulthood. Long hair was not an issue at the warehouse gates as it had been in the cosy confines of the solicitor's office in Blackheath. But then the company went bust and we all lost our jobs, the warehouse was closed and the strippers went home. I was back in a void.

Jim and I went on a trip to Devon together in his old London taxi. We went down there to drink cider and find ourselves, but in fact we found ourselves calling the AA every day as the taxi wasn't built for long journeys. In Plymouth we made our camp as we waited for the spare parts to arrive from London by train. We went to see Arthur Brown play, dropped acid and turned into versions of ourselves that resembled elves in a Disney cartoon. Jim was a dealer and drugs were never very far away; people called for him at night, they met him on street corners in Soho and we often had the leftovers. Devon was slow; we crawled back and slept in the car park at Stonehenge, having stopped off at a festival along the way, possibly Glastonbury. It was magical, cold and damp. The sun came up and we struggled homewards up the A303. I moved back in with my parents as I'd run out of money and food.

It was only a few years after that that Jim died. It was very sudden and very sad; he caned the old drugs and died from a brain tumour. I once slept in his shop in Soho. He sold sheet music, and I tripped to the faces of all the greats there staring at me; I was on a wild one. Soho was a dark place and Jim was well known around the local pubs. He passed the social baton on to Will Palin, who worked for David Bowie's Mainman company.

I met Will in The Three Tuns one night, when we started talking after he recognised me from the hippy folk band. All the girls fancied him. He was tall and impressive, suave and blond, and so gentle in everything he said and did. Will looked out for me, and when Bowie played a show in Lewisham, I went to watch the Thin White Duke sound-checking. Angie was there making tea backstage and Mick Ronson was amazing to watch. Will and I went to a builders' yard and came back with some wood and paint; we made the lightning strike on the circle that hung above Woody's drum kit. This was Ziggy and he played guitar. It was a very inspiring night. The band were so thin, they were from Mars, though we all knew they were really from Hull. I thought they were taking speed, so that night I went to the pub and scored some for myself. My teeth almost came out as I tried to sleep that night. Grinding my upper jaw with my lower. I'm sure I woke my mum up at one point as I lay there watching the bloody sun come up, again.

Bowie was a big figure for me. I always imagined he must have had many imaginary friends too. Through his lyrics he told me it was OK to be spaced out and in another world. He gave me the right to be feminine and lovely, to wear big hats and walk with a wiggle. His songs lured me into a place of hope. I saw him play once at Eltham College. I loved the way he walked into the crowd with his blue twelve-string guitar and handed it around. We were all sitting down – that's what you did in those days. That or idiot-dancing, when hippies used to leap about in the air as though they'd got electric shocks going through their testicles.

They should bring that back; it was so funny to watch. In my diary at the time I recalled walking home to Blackheath with a bottle of wine and my friend Andy; I was planning to write more songs and wanted nothing else but to be like David Bowie. He must have ignited so many dreams for so many young people at that time, and I was one of them.

After living with Jim and Christine, I moved into a flat with Graham and Suzy, another fine close couple from The Three Tuns. Graham was a chippy and was always working; at home I lay stoned in front of his hi-fi, zoning out on Stevie Wonder and *Tubular Bells*. I was transfixed by the album's cadences and its magical production, but I'm sure being stoned helped. When I hear it today, it sounds shit. We had a three-bar electric fire which we toasted white bread on when we couldn't be bothered to get up and walk to the kitchen. We put our electric train sets together and sent joints around the room on wagons. They lit up as they went through a tunnel made of a cornflakes box. We were too stoned to do most things and just giggled our lives away, it was hilarious. I was falling around on other people's floors, paying little rent and learning how to listen to music from a different angle. Horizontally. The flat was too small for us being stoned all the time, and they needed some head space of their own so it was time to move back in with my parents again for some home cooking, a washing machine and the start of something very special: the rest of my life.

LLOYDS PLACE

Blackheath was where I first met Glenn Tilbrook, back in April 1973. I put an advert in a shop window for a guitarist to join a band. I had no band. It said I had a pending record deal and a tour lined up. I had neither deal nor tour. The advert cost me 50p – I took the money from my mum's purse. That 50p got me to where I am today, which is some journey. I was looking for a friend. I was a lonely young man, fresh from being a skinhead and now, with long hair, slipping into flared jeans and leaning gently toward the hippy. From beating people up in Dr Marten boots to loving people in bare feet. A change of clothes, a change of music and now a change of friends.

Maxine, Glenn's girlfriend, talked him into calling the number on the ad. At home my mum had a phone table by the front door, and when the phone rang she would take her time perching on the velvet chair next to it before lifting the large green plastic receiver. It was like she was pretending to be royal. 'Christopher,' she called. 'It's for you.' I raced downstairs and spoke for the first time to Maxine – Glenn was too shy – the only person to call in two weeks of the ad being in the window. I was thrilled.

We met a few weeks later at The Three Tuns. Through the

frosted window I could see two young hippies standing around outside, one in pink trousers with no shoes, the other in an angel-like white dress and sandals. They both had long hair and looked like brother and sister. I recognised the boy as being that annoying hippy who played mandolin by the zebra crossing in the middle of Blackheath Village. At other times he would sit in the flower beds playing guitar and looking like he floated rather than walked. I also remembered seeing them together at the Osmosis Club in Kidbrooke, idiot-dancing to 'All Right Now' by Free on the dance floor; he looked like a deer caught in the headlights as he leapt around the hall. I didn't know what to do. But as fate would have it I strolled outside and introduced myself.

. When Glenn and I first met that day outside The Three Tuns in 1973, I was wearing a psychedelic coat made of paisley tinsel, which I'd found in the local Oxfam shop. At least that's how Glenn remembers it. I seem to recall I was wearing a donkey jacket of the highest order. Either version will do – they're both sides of the same coin. Glenn and Maxine were dressed in silks and cotton, cheesecloth and beads. Shoeless Glenn looked like Jesus without a beard; Maxine like an angel – beautiful and glowing with life. Glenn I knew from the long hair falling over his pretty face, and Maxine because she was always by his side, looking so calm and beautiful. They were like Mary and Joseph. I may have been the donkey.

I got the sense he was more nervous than I was as we stood there outside the pub. We talked for about ten minutes, then they said I should come to Maxine's house, a short walk away, to hear Glenn play and hang out for the afternoon. I was still very nervous and unsure. One side of Tonto's Expanding Head Band later and

we were joined at the hip. The house was on four floors; it was the
first posh home I had ever been to. It was like a palace to me – I'd
been living on a council estate made of breeze blocks. In Maxine's
bedroom, Glenn played along with Jimi Hendrix, and I sat and
watched as he effortlessly ran up and down the guitar fretboard.
She made jasmine tea, which I'd never heard of. I was in love with
them both from that moment and I went home that night lost in
the idea of being part of this new world. They were the opposite of
anyone I'd ever met before.

Glenn was locally famous for being kicked out of school for
refusing to cut his hair, and had been in the local paper. Oddly,
it was the same school Boy George attended. A rebel at an early
age. He seemed similar to me in some ways. I think we were both
a bit lost – musical, but with deep distant dreams of stardom at
whatever level. Glenn had a small band of friends at the time who
all seemed soft-natured and very gentle. I had not had people
around me like this ever; it was quite a wake-up call. I felt like a
leaf that had fallen from a tree onto a bed of flowers.

Shortly after we first met, I called and invited them both over to
my house in Combe Avenue. We sat on my single bed and I played
some of my songs. They seemed impressed, and before long we
were seeing each other from time to time as we built up our
friendship. Within a few weeks they were inviting friends around
to hear my songs too. I would sit cross-legged on my single bed as I
treated people to 'Welcome to Mars', an earnest song about space
travel that was inspired by the lyrics of Peter Hamill from Van der
Graaf Generator; or 'To Catch a Girl's Eyes', taken from the paws
of Neil Sedaka, a mixture of light and shade, minor and major
keys. My small audience filled my bedroom. I was an indifferent

guitarist but managed to make my way through the chords I had written for what were mostly naive lyrics. Glenn played me some of his songs too; it was as if we were courting each other. My parents, who were sitting downstairs watching *Some Mothers Do 'Ave 'Em*, had no idea a partnership had just been born. Neither did I.

Glenn and I got on well. I'd never been a great communicator and I wasn't really sure what 'well' was, but I think we achieved it. He was often shy like me yet had the ability to suddenly entertain the whole room with songs plucked out of thin air. He was a big fan of 'Summer Holiday' by Cliff Richard; like Cliff he could smile and play at the drop of a hat. Glenn's own lyrics weren't as deep or as floral as mine, though my chords were more basic than his textures and arrangements. He began to teach me some new chords and slowly I found myself more at home on the fretboard, though never as fluent as him. He could tune a guitar, something I couldn't do. His singing style was way more versatile than mine; his high-pitched and mine drone-like. I would sing like Lou Reed while he was more like Paul McCartney. It was a good mixture. Those first few months of our friendship were a lovely time of tea-drinking and strumming. We were sifting around at the bottom of the riverbed, searching for flecks of gold. They weren't far away.

Glenn had a narrow face with a distinctive nose, and long hair that fell to both sides of his cheekbones, and he spoke softly – almost with a lisp. He wore stuff from Oxfam that was perfect for his angelic features. He and Maxine would sometimes swap clothes. I'd not seen this before and thought it sweet. I found him an incredibly soft character and I never felt threatened by him. I'd grown up on an estate full of hard nuts, so Glenn was a revelation. He was from a working-class family who lived close to me in

Blackheath. His parents had split up and he lived with his mother but spent most of his time with Maxine at her house. His mother, Margaret, was lovely and welcoming; his stepfather less so. I once stayed at their flat and borrowed his stick shaver; he hit the roof. I was not welcomed back very often. Glenn's dad Peter lived all over the place; he was a welder and travelled around Europe where the work and money was.

Our first mentor and manager was Ron Reid, an Australian photographer who was a friend of Maxine's family. He lived in Notting Hill with his boyfriend Johnny, had long wavy hair and was considerably older than us. The first time I went to Ron and Johnny's basement flat in Notting Hill Gate with Glenn and Max, I got nicely stoned and sat around playing songs. After a full-on night of dope-smoking, I fell into a very deep sleep. In the morning, Ron, who was a vegetarian like Glenn and Max, prepared a healthy breakfast of muesli, something I wasn't used to; I was a cornflakes boy. Johnny raved about this cauldron of white goo and rolled a joint to accompany the delight. As I took my first mouthful, Ron gleefully told me that he and Johnny had both ejaculated into it. They giggled like Cheech and Chong. I felt the gluey lumps in my throat and didn't know what to say. I swallowed. Soon I was a vegetarian myself; it seemed to make life easier, as by this time we were all living together and Maxine and Glenn were both streets ahead of me in the health stakes. I missed the bacon, if I'm honest.

Ron was a softie: he managed to find us gigs, which was helpful. He would drive us around in a converted transit van with a double bed in the back, which he called his 'fuck truck'; it was in here – while driving along the A4 – that Glenn and I wrote our first song together. I gave Glenn a lyric, he sat on the mattress and strummed, and the next thing I knew we had a song. It was simple and brilliant. I decided to put down the chord sheets and just concentrate on the words from that point. The song was called 'Hotel Woman'. I had no idea what that was, and had no experience of prostitutes, but my imagination had a good go at it. The song was rocking and bluesy; Glenn sang like a bird and so our partnership was formed. My groaning theatrical voice took a back seat, and my Bowie-like cadences slipped slowly into the sunset. Ron got us our first ever gig, at The Butts – a small bar up at the Elephant and Castle – and followed this up with a slot at Trentishoe, a hippy festival on the cliffs in north Devon. He managed to squeeze us onto the bill between the Pink Fairies and Hare Krishna – obvious bedfellows. On stage, Glenn and I were about forty feet apart and totally unable to hear each other. We ploughed on, though, and went down awkwardly. Ron looked out for us and found us some more shows. These were more festival gigs, and we were shitting ourselves in front of bigger crowds as we tiptoed through our acoustic set (we stayed a duo as we couldn't fit a band into the fuck truck). We ate wholefoods, smoked joints, painted our faces, laughed and danced, shat in fields and tripped out to midnight fires and Hawkwind.

Within a few months Glenn and I gathered some other people around us and formed a band. Norman – another long, thin person with a big nose – on bass, and John, who had curly hair, round glasses and a huge smile, on drums. We worked hard, and though the band was fragile in its commitment, it sounded OK.

Windsor Free Festival was very special and was our first real gig. I played without a guitar in bare feet in front of a few hundred unenthusiastic stoned hippies who were surrounded by police officers. It was an illegal festival in Windsor Park which ran for a few years and was always watched closely by 'the pigs'. We played before Ducks Deluxe Camel and Ace, who had Paul Carrack as their frontman. I felt like one of the new generation of layabouts, creatives on dope ready for the revolution that would never happen. We were giving power to the people in our three-minute pop songs.

In the first year of meeting Glenn we had chalked up no less than 137 songs – 'Take Me I'm Yours' was one of them. We were so happy writing and we seemed to impress each other with each new tune. Golden days. We wrote some obscure songs – 'Clipper Ship' was about a sailor on a clipper ship, can you believe? – we wrote songs about distant lands and fanciful tunes about strange places beyond the mind; songs about being sixteen and being in love. We sang together and Glenn would teach me the chords. I found some of them tricky – something that hasn't changed – but I persisted. We sang into the night, candles flickering, joints burning, friends sleeping and record decks revolving. If the sun came up while we were still singing, it was normal. Hundreds of songs were born in that period. We were like sponges absorbing all the music we could, from Sparks to Elvis and back with a bit of Jake Thackray and Pete Atkin in there for good measure.

I was constantly surprised by how different we were as people. He was outgoing and I wasn't. He would jump on the table at parties to lead singalongs on his guitar, while I sat in the shadows at the back pretending to be Leonard Cohen (I'd get girls, but they were the intense, gloomy ones in delicately printed skirts). Our friends loved the fact that we were so different, but even then we often found it hard to communicate directly. Maybe we were just shy of each other.

Maxine and Glenn's friends soon became my friends, and my old mates faded into the background. That's a lot of people. I had to let them go to make the next move of my life, though I didn't really know I was doing it at the time. My skinhead mates were gone, my folk music friends had gone; I was in the world of experimentation and song. It was like being in a fairy tale. Maxine was Glenn's angel and sometimes I felt jealous. I was embraced by her beauty – most people were. I remember once seeing her in a towel. She'd just taken a bath. She was standing with me in her father's study, and as we talked, I felt something I'd never felt before. I had never been around a woman who was so natural and at one with her body; I was used to fat skinhead girls who were welded into tight skirts.

Maxine's mother Anthea was wonderful too – the first person ever to call me 'darling', while holding a gin and tonic and smoking a fag. She was so full of love and life, even when she was pissed, which she was most days, and she seemed constantly to be playing a part in a Richard Burton film; everything was done with such grand, dramatic gestures. She let me stay at the house, and I came and went as I pleased. Often I would sit by her bed and talk her down from a heavy hangover or listen to her jealous ranting over the love of her life, Maxine's father Felix. He was a lush with the women and would call me 'dear boy', which he did with a great sweep of his voice – condescending, but with grace. I loved his study on the top floor of the house; it was full of books and dust and newspapers. This was an inspiration to me. Sometimes I would sit in that study and pretend to be educated, like Maxine's elder brother Kent. I was never sure how he felt about us invading his house while he was at university, but I do remember him being very stern with me when he caught me and others smoking some of his cigars by the fireplace.

My moods were up and down at the time. Glenn and Maxine's relationship was inspiring but at the same time made me think that I could never have anything so warm and tender myself. One night the gin from the sideboard laid me low with loneliness and depression. I locked myself in my room and started to cry. I had the wardrobe against the door and I was ready to take some of Anthea's pills. Everyone else was downstairs watching the TV. When I realised that nobody could hear me, I removed the wardrobe and stood outside the room. Then I sat on the stairs. Eventually I made my way to within earshot of the TV room. Max came to rescue me. I was a sorry case, looking for attention in such a dramatic way. Maybe it was the gin talking; maybe it was a cry for help, or the start of something deeper. I cheered up once I was sitting and watching the telly with everyone else, and Glenn started to play the guitar along to The Monkees. He never put the guitar down and would accompany bread being toasted. It was something different for me.

During our first summer together, Maxine took me to her family's country home in Benenden, Kent. The house had been built around the time of Shakespeare. It had wooden beams that twisted across the ceilings, bedrooms with floors that sloped to one side, huge open fires and acres of garden with a lake. It was my first smell of country life. One night we had a bonfire and sat around with loads of our friends; her parents were asleep but they didn't seem to mind. When the fire ebbed down to a glow, we decided to lob on some old deckchairs we'd found leaning up against the house – fine Victorian ones, as it turned out. The next day we were raked over the coals by Felix. I walked to the local pub to get out of the way. I'm good at that; walking away is a dance I can do standing on my head. Her dad wasn't impressed, though Kent found the situation very amusing.

Maxine gave me the space to write by letting me stay at her house. She gave me the love that no other woman had before, not even my mother. She introduced me to femininity, to beauty, to jasmine tea and sunflowers, pretty music and Marmite. She showered love on all of her friends. She and Glenn were so generous with their love and with their passion for all things rock and roll.

The band's first name was Cum, but it didn't stick so we changed it to Squeeze. Maxine's mother picked the name out of a hat for us, after the terrible album The Velvet Underground released when Lou Reed left the band. Unfortunately, we'd sprayed 'Cum' all around Blackheath with a stencil. Maxine kindly invited me to move in to her brother's room while he was away at Cambridge. I soon got into the swing of writing words and leaving them on the stairs for Glenn. I'd then listen to him plonking on a piano upstairs or strumming on a guitar. He'd spend hours up there with Max by his side, weaving melody around my words in the most beautiful way. It was fun and gloriously uncomplicated. Glenn and Maxine introduced me to Jools Holland, who would come around to the house on his motorbike and play the piano. I had never heard of boogie-woogie music before and was mesmerised by his left hand, his ability to plough through so many notes and make it all sound so great. His tasselled leather jacket always seemed strange in the context of our hippy-trippy world, but he wore it well and his motorbike looked brilliant.

The girls loved Jools and I loved him too. The two of us quickly became close friends. Jools added such great things to our songs. I was attracted to his masculine side – it reminded me of the skinhead in me – and soon I was hanging out with him more than I was with Glenn. Jools felt dangerous to me. He was much more of a lad. Like Glenn, Jools could hold court with his wonderful musicianship and knowledge of rock and roll. I was blessed to be around the two of them.

In the summer of 1974, Bob from the estate asked me to help him down at Charlton Athletic Football Club. I walked down the hill to where The Who were headlining with Little Feat in support. That night, 120,000 people filled The Valley – a record that has never been broken. Backstage, I loaded charged batteries into walkie-talkies for the road crew. I sat and watched Little Feat play, then I watched Keith Moon slide around on flight cases while playing the drums. I was only feet behind him. It was amazing to watch. I sang 'Magic Bus' all the way home with my imaginary band, the percussion part going on for days. I could smell the fame, I wanted it, and I could sense that, if I was stupid enough, it might just happen. I didn't want to load batteries, I wanted to be on stage. I had a feeling that one day Glenn and I could be in a band like The Who, just like I had wanted at school, and with Jools in the team I knew it was going to be something very special and possible. All we had to do was believe in ourselves and fall in with some luck.

Jools was, and still is, blessed with luck. I loved to ride on his motorcycle, and without crash helmets it was even more fun. We raced down to Benenden along the A21 one weekend, the sound of his Velocette throaty and majestic. We were pigs in shit . . . until we got arrested for driving without an MOT or licence, for being underage and for not stopping when asked to by a policewoman on the Sidcup Bypass. As luck would have it, Jools's dad, Derek, came to bail us out of the nick in Eltham. When the police took us home, they saw all the things we'd stolen on our journeys in Jools's garage – road signs, cones, bits of old bikes. Nothing was said. Derek covered for us. He was so supportive of the band and, like Glenn's dad, gave us the space to do what we needed to do. My dad less so.

By now, Jools had officially joined the band on keyboards, with Paul Gunn on drums. Paul was a really nice person but he wasn't a strong drummer; his timekeeping was always up for discussion. Norman was on bass again, but he soon left, to be replaced by Harry Kakoulli, who came equipped with a new bass, leather trousers and a tasty wife called Mary. Harry looked the part and he made us all laugh. He was a lazy bass player, paradoxically full of energy. He looked as though he could have been in The New York Dolls, who I loved and had seen play once at The Rainbow Rooms above Biba in London. His mop of dark hair and Mediterranean good looks attracted the attention of our local female fans. He was quiet but not shy and loved to be funny for the sake of it. He was also a keen dresser, more so than the rest of the band. I really liked Harry: he was simple to hang out with and never went over the top drinking in the pub. Unlike me.

Together we got a set together in a rehearsal room in Greenwich. We played in pubs for beer money and slowly managed to attract a local crowd. Glenn led the band from the start and always knew instinctively how the songs should sound. He draped us in his ideas and moods, and we coiled around his playing, his fantastic voice and ability to lead. He was a born leader – something I've fought against from the start, for no real reason. After all, I could never do it myself. The rehearsal rooms were dark and mysterious, down there under the street; sometimes you would cross paths with Jeff Beck or musicians of a more mature persuasion. David Bowie and Lou Reed had rehearsed there too; it was a cool place to make some noise.

Glenn and Jools were close in a musical way; they could reach each other as they flew through the songs, even if it was just the two of them in a pub. They loved the same kind of music and would jam for hours, playing twelve-bar blues. I tried to dig in, but I was never very good and could only support them by buying drinks. We also rehearsed at Max's house, and sometimes over at Jools's. He had a huge piano his parents had treated him to. Once or twice I slept there beneath its ceiling of notes, wood and strings. His mother, June, would look after us all and make us feel welcome; later in our lives, she became our fan club manager.

Those were the days. Our first studio experience was in Polydor Studios just off Oxford Street, recording one of my songs, 'Black Jack'. I have no idea where those recordings are and I can't remember much at all about the session. In May 1974 we played at the Northover pub in Catford; later in the year we played at Camden Girls' School, supporting the band Deaf School. My diary of the time says we all played well but Paul was not very good with the endings.

As Squeeze, our first real show was at Greenwich Town Hall in April 1975. My friend Will Palin helped us by letting us rehearse at his house in Devon, and by supplying a huge PA from Mainman, Bowie's own PA company. The cavernous hall could not stand the sheer weight of sound, and the few people who were there went home deafened by our excited set of twenty three-minute pop songs. We then played at Catford Girls' School and my new girl-friend Nicky thought I might like to wear make-up like her idol Marc Bolan. I went on stage looking like Lou Reed. It was a great show and I think the girls loved it.

Nicky looked very much like Marc herself, with shoulder-length curly hair. She once took me up to Bond Street to wait outside his offices. We were there for hours, and I got very bored. She was in a gaggle of girls all waiting to see him. Eventually his green Rolls-Royce turned up and out he got. He walked over towards the door, pinned Nicky to the wall and seemed to put his tongue in her mouth in a huge passionate kiss. I was shocked, but it seemed that Nicky was over the moon. I was forever walking home alone in those days, second best, it seemed, to men of a more fabulous nature. I did briefly manage to pull myself from under Nicky's spell by going out with her posh best friend from Golders Green. One night I sneaked into her house for a sleepover. In the middle of the night she screamed out so everyone could hear – every-one being her parents – 'There is semen all over my leg!' She was being overdramatic, but the next morning her father sat me down in the front room and asked me what plans I had in life. I said I was in a band. I never heard from her again. I did write a song for her, with the lame lyrics, 'Nicky D, Nicky D you're the one for me'. It was early days.

Ron felt we needed a more dedicated manager, so he introduced us to Mark Cooper, a suave, impressive, suited man with ideas and money, and a smart office in Pimlico. He'd formed a company with John Leyton, who was famous for singing 'Johnny Remember Me' in the early Sixties and being in films with Frank Sinatra, but who was running a food stall at Waterloo station by the time we met him. We had a promising early meeting with Mark and John, in which we discussed some lyrics of mine going into a book to accompany Ron's photos of the festival scene, but the whole thing was doomed to failure. John dropped us off at Waterloo after the meeting, and as I stepped out from his brand-new Ford, a bus shot past and took off the door – and very nearly my leg. The one thing Mark and John did for us was to buy Glenn and me some leather trousers. That tells you everything about how wrong their vision for us was. They quickly faded into the background. The book, *Tomorrow's People*, did get released; today it's hard to find and very rare but worth the search just to see Glenn and me with painted faces at a festival somewhere, not to mention my lyrics, so juvenile and harmless, printed on the page.

Our first serious manager, Lawrence Impey, was introduced to us by Peter Perrett from fellow south London band The Only Ones. Glenn had played guitar with them at one point and our bassist Harry was Peter's brother-in-law. I felt threatened by Peter and always thought that Glenn would jump ship and end up in The Only Ones; that gave me a few sleepless nights to deal with along the way. By that point we had only really played a handful of local gigs in pubs and we didn't have two shillings to rub together. There was nothing any of us wanted to do more than be in a band.

Lawrence was a young, skinny, curly-haired, well-spoken, well-educated chap, who couldn't have been more different from us. He drove a flash new car and had wealthy parents who lived in a big house in Bournemouth. He introduced me to some Bob Dylan songs I had never heard, and they inspired me to push harder with my stories. He also turned me on to Carmen McRae; her voice charmed the long nights at his house. His father was a very successful lawyer in Nigeria and in the garden of the house they had a servant who lived alone. Thompson was always on hand to supply sandwiches and drinks. One night Lawrence hired a small truck and I went with him to collect two dozen three-wheel dis-ability bikes, which he then shipped to Nigeria – I had no idea why. We got home in the early hours and Thompson rustled up some breakfast for us. We got on well. Soon Lawrence was carting us to and from local gigs in hired vans, and running up a big tab. He was out of his depth, though, and we all knew he needed help. Then one day he revealed he'd been to school with Stewart Copeland, who was the drummer in Curved Air. Copeland's brother Miles was a proper manager. It was all falling into place.

Miles Copeland became our manager in 1975. He bore a strik-ing resemblance to John Denver, wore a tweed jacket and grey trousers, and had a convincing optimistic chant about life that at the time I found appealing. He walked into our rehearsal room beneath the A2 on Blackheath Hill with his brother Ian (who would later become our touring agent in the US), we played him a few songs and his eyes lit up. It was our moment. The Copeland family were a dynasty of some note. Dad was head of the CIA in the Middle East. What could go wrong? Within a few months a contract had arrived from Miles, a thick wad of paper.

None of us could understand it, so we showed it to our parents, who also had no idea what it all meant. We signed it anyway, and wrestled £15 a week out of Miles, as agreed. Miles was convinced we would be as big as The Beatles, which made us all feel really good about ourselves, and he quickly found us some gigs so we could sharpen up our act. We supported bands he had floating around on his prog rock and blues label BTM. It wasn't really our cup of tea, but it was work. We were soon playing up and down the country with Curved Air and The Climax Blues Band, Renaissance and Caravan. It kept us off the streets and firmly in the back of a noisy Transit van. Miles would always put us on right at the beginning of these shows, in front of audiences that couldn't have given a toss. They didn't want to see us. Plus the headlining bands wouldn't move any of their equipment to fit us in. Caravan would set up with Hammond organs and mellotrons, leaving us two feet at the front of the stage to play on. I loved the album *In the Land of Grey and Pink* so I stood and nodded along secretly with the crowd. At least they let us sound-check.

I thought Darryl Way, the violinist in Curved Air, was a complete dick; on the shows we did with them, he told us he needed all the time before the gig to get his sound right, and we'd just have to make do setting up as the doors opened. I remember watching him perform these endless, boring violin solos, with his long hair flowing behind him like an Afghan hound in a gale, and thinking, 'What a tosser.' He was everything you didn't want to be.

The touring began in earnest at the Marquee Club in London. At the opposite end of the scale we played at RAF Brawdy in Wales. It was exciting to jump in the van and head off all over the country, playing to people who mostly didn't want to see us.

Throughout 1976 the band also built up a sizeable south London following, securing a residency at the Bricklayer's Arms in Greenwich, run by Harry Rodgers, who paid us in lager. Here we cut our teeth covering songs and slipping in many of our own along the way.

Travelling in vans all the time was boring. We played cards to see who would go in the front, and the losers would sit glumly in the back as we weaved our way out of London towards various motorways. One afternoon on the A40, I was in the back of the van with Jools and our friend Mark Smith. Bored, we wrote messages on pieces of paper and stuck them up at the window. One of them said: *I can see your tits, now show us your cunt.* Behind us in the traffic, though we couldn't see her or her motorcycle outrider, was the lady mayor of Acton. The van was pulled over – much to the confusion of those in the front – and the next day we had to appear in court, where we were fined. We missed the gig and Miles made us send flowers to Annie Haslam from Renaissance, the band we were meant to be supporting.

We wrote new songs and recorded them at Pathway Studios in Islington; sixteen songs over two weekends in a tiny space. The recording was funded by Miles and it was an incredible experience; the first time we had heard our songs up close. The studio was a place that Glenn seemed at home in; he always paid more attention to the detail than Jools or I did. The engineer was called Barry, and he did a fine job of easing us into this new world of recording as a band. The light would go on and we would play the songs we had rehearsed back in south London. Overdubs were few, but Glenn seemed to know better than the rest of us just what the songs needed. I really liked recording but always thought it took too long to get the right takes, though maybe that was the band and its inability to glow in the dark of a small room covered in orange and brown pegboard.

Shortly afterwards, we recorded with legendary producer Muff Winwood – famous for producing The Bay City Rollers – at Basing Street Studios. Although Muff seemed to be on the phone most of the time, he did come out of the control room to express his doubts about our drummer; it was becoming increasingly apparent that Paul's days with the band were numbered. Being in the studio was a new experience for us, and it felt as though we'd suddenly stepped into the real world of being in a recording band.

When Glenn broke up with Maxine, I was devastated for both of them. Their long and beautiful love affair had come to an end. Glenn and I moved out of Lindsey House, Lloyds Place to share a flat in Bennett Park just down the hill in Blackheath Village. It was our first step into the real world, and we confronted it head-on by writing songs and recording demos all day long. Glenn was providing more and more amazing music to my lyrics; his arrangements were melodic and beautiful. Together we had carved out a new way of writing and it had begun to hit a new peak. We ploughed on, hoping we would get a record deal full of cash to hold us up while we wrote some more. After Maxine, Glenn started seeing Nicky. He went out with her for a few years; she then started seeing Jools (or was it vice versa?). Our band was a right old chicken run in those days; we stood in each other's shadows but nobody seemed to mind very much, which was just as well.

The flat was in the basement and our landlord was insane. He told us that he worked for the secret service and that he knew all the nuclear codes for a war. We kept him away by building a wall of cardboard on the stairs. I would work in the room beneath the stairs and Glenn in the living room. It was tidy most of the time. Ron came to shoot our photos there once and invited all the girls from the girls' school across the road. They were younger than us and it looked and felt wrong. We sipped whisky and giggled a lot. One night the cardboard wall came crashing down and in fell the landlord, swearing and sweating. He accused us of being Russian spies and tipped us into the street. Next thing we knew, fire engines were racing towards our flat; he thought it was on fire. Joss sticks were calmly burning in a jam jar. We moved on. He was sectioned and never seen again.

We went to Island Records and Richard Williams, the label's A&R man, turned us down, again pointing towards our drummer. Glenn and I were no longer writing about clipper ships. We'd set sail on a new course – writing about love, and imaginary people and places. We even wrote a short musical called *Trixie*, influenced by reading Damon Runyon and indulging in Sparks, a band we both loved. The song cycle was ambitious and ahead of its time for a young band like us. My lyrics were dreamy and colourful, and I'm proud of them to this day. But in the Island audition, nerves got the better of us and we stuttered through the arrangements. Paul was all over the place and possibly more nervous than the rest of us. Richard looked on from his chair in the corner of the studio, and Glenn and I were convinced this was it. Luckily it wasn't. I have always been so pleased that Richard passed on us; the cake was still in the oven and nowhere near rising at the time. Richard crossed the hall into the next studio to carry on working with Bob Marley.

We put an ad in *Melody Maker* and auditioned drummers in a rehearsal room beneath the main pool at Greenwich baths. Paul had his P45 and had left the building. It was loud in there but upstairs you could get a bag of chips and a white slice for 50p. The space was handy for when we played the Bricklayer's Arms next door. Gilson Lavis, a former session drummer, turned up in his mother's Mini with all his drums stacked inside. As I helped him unload, I could hear the clink and rattle of empty whisky bottles as they rolled around the floor. Gilson's drums took up most of the space in our rehearsal room. He played with six toms on racks; it was ridiculous but it sounded amazing. He got the job. All the others we'd heard that week were so tippy-tappy compared to this powerhouse. Our songs sounded brilliant with him playing on them. We were complete. We were Squeeze. Gilson was a big fella with a lovely chunky cardigan with a zip; it opened up to reveal a hairy chest and a cigarette lighter on a cord. He was vocal about arrangements and came from the world of session playing – he'd just been on tour with Chuck Berry and Johnny Cash, no less. He had also auditioned for Wings. We naturally were impressed by his CV.

Gilson lived in Bedford so it was a trek for him to get to us in south London, but he always turned up when needed. He liked a drink, it's fair to say, and with him in the band I felt we had grown up both musically and at the bar.

Since we'd met in 1973, we had grown into young men. I was twenty-two years old. It was now 1976 – pre-punk, the tail-end of hippy and all things self-indulgent. Glenn played the guitar like no one I'd ever seen before – he was amazing around the frets, and with him and Jools in the band, we had a fantastic line-up. Gilson brought up the rear with his inventiveness and flair, and Harry plodded along behind with me. We had tons of songs and we rehearsed all the time before trying out numbers in the Brick. We were on fire most nights and we packed the place out. We played for the booze and for the fun of it all. Covers went down well, as well as our own songs. We played 'Junior's Farm' and 'Get Back', and some obscure Merrill Moore songs that Jools brought to the table. Jools sang some and I sang some, but Glenn sang the most. He had the best voice by a mile. When he sang 'Riot in Cell Block Number Nine' everyone's jaw would drop open. Gilson was so loud; his drums took up all the room and he was not a light player, but he could be tender when he wanted to be. I was out-of-tune, pissed and having a great time of it all.

Miles got us a meeting with RCA. They sent us to Rockfield Studios in Wales, where we recorded with the BBC Welsh Symphony Orchestra, no less. The songs were sweet but not sweet enough for the label bosses. Here we recorded 'Take Me I'm Yours' for the first time. We also nailed 'Cat on the Wall' and 'Night Ride'. This was the first time we had been away from south London as a band together to record, and it was the first time we witnessed how much experienced drummers could drink. I was impressed and found it hard to keep up.

That summer Glenn's dad Peter booked us some shows in Holland. Some nights we played three sets, mainly for beer. After two sets one night, I was so drunk I had to sit the third out on a beer crate. It was good fun and being in Amsterdam meant real bonding sessions for the band. A museum with Jools by day, a seedy bar by night. We drove around in a Luton van, playing cards as usual for the front seats; if you sat in the back, your view of Holland was through a small hole only fit for one eye at a time. Fame trickled in slowly in those days. When we went on stage one night in a place called De Brak, a huge potted tree was put in the middle of the dance floor. It turned out to be a marijuana tree. A handful of giddy people arrived to hear us play our rapid and excitable set. By the end of the evening we were all doing the hokey cokey around the tree, giggling and falling over each other, having a really good time. Thanks to Peter, we learnt how to have fun and play music with people with broken English.

Those dates in Holland further illustrated Gilson's thirst for a good time. He was often angry but I was never sure why. He tried to get off with our roadie's girlfriend; he tried to pick a fight with a hotel manager in Amsterdam; he threw a bike into the canal. But then, who didn't? We all liked a drink in those days, but Gilson had a completely different threshold to the rest of us.

One night at the Milky Way club we all succumbed to some space cake, and after about an hour we were off with the fairies. When the police came in to ask us to move our van, three of us took the back of it and the other three the front, trying hard to push it. It had broken down and we were in no fit state to move it, or play a set. We did make it on stage, though, and I remember well the feeling of not knowing what a guitar was for, or why it was around my neck. Jools's keyboard sounded like shards of ice dropping from the sky, Gilson had rubber sticks, Glenn was Hendrix, in my head. Harry was cool and posing as usual at the front. My jaw remained sealed for days after so much laughing and giggling like a child.

Our roadie on that tour was Les Grimsley, skinhead from Combe Avenue. I thought it would do him good to get him out of harm's way. He drove the van, and in one small town took the awning off an ice cream shop.

He got stopped by the customs officers at Dover and was asked to unscrew all of the speaker cabinets, at which point he handed the screwdriver back to the officer and said, 'If you want to see what's inside, go ahead.' They were having none of his lip. Les took the speakers apart and two hours later we moved on. He was a handful, as he had been on the estate. There was no getting him out of harm's way.

Our only other ventures into Europe included a brief trip to Denmark where we visited the Heineken factory in Copenhagen and came out much the worse for wear, having sampled a few gallons of Elephant Beer. The other time was a trip to Sweden where we were invited to a party by one of the girls from Abba. Phil Collins was there as he had produced her album. I got very silly, I was also hallucinating on some heavy dope I had been smoking, which made me feel slightly paranoid. I was in a hotel room with a man dressed as a woman. I made a hasty exit when I figured it out. Back down in the bar Phil kept us all entertained with his Genesis stories. I felt like the lamb that almost laid down in Gothenburg that night. Europe was never a big marketplace for Squeeze. I think my lyrics were lost in translation along the way, which is not surprising.

Suddenly, in 1977, punk happened. Fashions changed and we watched, slightly bemused, from south London. Touring was our staple diet; we seemed to always be on the road trying to impress people with our outrageous energy and short songs. Miles had several punk bands on his books, so we mixed with them a lot in those early years, but I never really liked the music. I was always looking for the lyric and I felt there was no depth to it; it was just kids trying to get a record deal. The music sounded like it was falling down stairs. I moved to a flat on the Crossfields estate in Deptford, and it wasn't until Dot, my flatmate, played me the first

Clash album that I heard a punk record I loved. It had a depth and energy to it that was totally lacking from stuff like The Sex Pistols. They annoyed me in the same way that Les Grimsley had done when I was a skinhead. The aggression was too much for me to handle. I was leaning more toward the pub rock troubadours and their gentle venom which I knew was only skin deep. Downstairs lived a band called Dire Straits – how they survived the headwind of punk aggression I will never know; maybe it was the constant rehearsing in the flat. To me it sounded like they were knitting; it was polite and drifting. But then what did I know? They seemed like nice lads. Glenn and I were never natural punks, but we tried our best. Jools, though, couldn't be persuaded at all. Miles wanted us to ride the bandwagon, so we untucked our shirts and I bought a few safety pins that I wore like brooches on my shirt. I didn't mind dyeing my hair either. It was blond for a while, then orange, then blue.

Punk meant that record companies would now make the effort to come and see us play, and so Miles had an idea. We'd record an EP, which would send a signal out to record labels that we were serious. He and his brother Ian were promoting a tour with John Cale, who happened to be in London biting the heads off chickens, and was invited down to hear our songs in a rehearsal room in Chelsea. I was beside myself. My hero from the Velvets was coming to hear us play! I sharpened up my act; I found some cool dark glasses and a leather jacket and tried hard to look out of it all the time. Cale walked in and sat down, and asked us to play for him. We raced through twelve new songs; he fell asleep. We prodded him but he wouldn't wake up, so we moved the PA closer to his head and ploughed on. Still no life. Then Jools grabbed a marker pen and wrote 'I am a cunt' on his forehead. We woke him up and sent him in a cab back to his hotel. The next day, he came back to the room. The writing was still clearly visible on his head, though it was a little faded, but nothing was said. He then got us to play again before stopping us mid-song and telling us our songs were all crap and we should rewrite everything.

We chose three of our current crop for the EP and quickly recorded them with John Cale at Surrey Sound, an out-of-the way studio in Leatherhead, Surrey. 'Cat on the Wall' was a fun song to play; it had shades of The Who about it, and was noisy with grains of attitude. 'Night Ride' was in the same boat. 'Backtrack' was also lively and mildly aggressive. All three songs promoted the use of Gilson's drums. Toms were the order of the day – he played an Octaplus drum kit at the time – served up on a bed of brittle guitar in a gravy of lumpy bass sprinkled with some flakes of fine keyboards from Jools. Glenn and I were the salt and pepper.

John Peel played the resulting *Packet of Three* EP on Radio 1. It was pretty amazing to hear our record for the first time in full mono on a small transistor radio in the kitchen while the cheese was melting on the toast. We were on the radio, everything was new and exciting, every day was a huge adventure on a journey I instinctively knew I had to make. *Packet of Three* sold 25,000 copies on our own Deptford Fun City label. We were courted by other record companies and most of our London shows were all about impressing A&R men: Sony, Arista, Warner. We eventually ended up at A&M Records on the King's Road. Miles walked us in and dropped us off as though it was our first day at school, and I loved being there. The staff were welcoming; the whole building was alive with music and people who loved music. It was a breath of fresh air. A&M were really great at developing their acts; they gave us time, there was no rush to get things right, which was just as well. We were stablemates with some odd people, but it was 1977 and that was all about to change. Supertramp were giving way to The Sex Pistols. Punk and new wave were marching towards us up the King's Road.

WILLESDEN HIGH ROAD

Recording our first album was like a daily trip to the moon. John Cale had booked us into a studio in north London that took us an hour or more to get to, and when we did get there, there was nothing to do. Willesden was an oasis of kebab shops. We spent our days setting up and trying things out. John hated everything we'd written up to that point; he just wanted us to be vulgar and rough, so all our lovely pop songs were put away for another day and we charged into the unknown, with guitars being dragged across chord changes that were out there (though, somehow, Glenn managed to shine through it all). Jools's talents were mostly buried in functional keyboard parts, and lyrically, I had to delve into the weird and wonderful demands of Cale: 'Sex Master', 'Strong in Reason', songs that made me feel at odds with myself. It was frightening.

After the awe of meeting John Cale had worn off, I really couldn't understand why we were working with him, because he was unremittingly difficult. He was angry and late. We'd always be waiting for him. Then when he did show up at the studio at midday, one o'clock or whatever, after we'd been there a couple of hours, he would poke us with insults or come in with a whip and start cracking it against the floor, things like that. On our first session, he made us swap instruments then turned all the lights off in the studio, telling us he wasn't going to let us out until we'd perfected 'Amazing Grace'. There were times when I couldn't see the direction we were being driven in and that would piss me off. But I think when somebody's that out of it, they don't really know what's going on. He would throw a hand grenade in every now and again just to liven things up, and I think that was a good thing looking back, but at the time I was terrified.

We did manage to rock out, though, with 'First Thing Wrong', 'Get Smart' and 'Out of Control'. We were confused and on a mission, but in our own naturally gentle way. 'Strong in Reason' is a favourite of mine from that album, and 'The Call' was inventive and really showed Gilson off at his finest. Cale pulled in the girl who worked in the downstairs canteen to scream over a few takes; she had no idea how mad he was and neither did we. During one session that never saw the light of day, we recorded a smutty song about phone abuse called 'Deep Cuts', and she embraced the part fully, swearing and giving the mystery caller grief. It was light relief from the eccentricity of Cale. He hated the name Squeeze and wanted us to change it to Gay Guys; that never happened, but that's how strange life was in the studio with John. In retrospect he was a genius. His engineer was John Wood, who kept a steady hand on the tiller, with his lovely jumpers and beard. He came with a polished CV that included Nico and Fairport Convention, not to mention Nick Drake.

Our first album was a mixture of the wilfully weird and pop promises. It was a muddle of two worlds pulling apart; our youth in one direction and our hopes of being serious songwriters in the other. Miles seemed as confused as we were, but the record company embraced the result, warts and all. My favourite song from that album is, of course, the single 'Take Me I'm Yours', which Cale had nothing to do with as he was ill that day. Rather than waste time in the studio, Glenn persuaded us to lay down a backing track with electronic keyboards and drum machines. To do this we had to hire in the equipment and two men in white coats to work it for us. Jools, Gilson and I were concerned at the time, as we felt the song was becoming more about machines than a band, but in hindsight it was a real coming-together of the two.

A&M loved the sound of it and they released it as a single and suddenly we were on *Top of the Pops*. It was fabulous and a dream had come true. I was recognised at the baker's shop, my mum and dad liked me again, I was on the telly with my mates and we got to number 19 in the charts. As soon as we heard we were going to be on *Top of the Pops*, we were forced by the Musicians' Union and A&M to go back into the studio to re-record the track – a farcical situation brought about by union pedantry. The Musicians' Union chap turned up and was immediately taken out for a lunchtime drink by our A&R man, returning to the studio several pints later. By this time, we'd re-recorded the song – albeit a very splintered version – and swapped the tapes, so that the original version was used. This happened every time. The Musicians' Union representative was none the wiser. Or was he? To be an A&R chap in those days you had to really like a drink.

Top of the Pops wasn't at all as I'd expected. It was like being back at school, complete with a headmasterly producer and DJ Peter Powell, who played the role of head boy. I remember heading downstairs to the dressing rooms and walking along a corridor seeing the names of all these famous acts – Thin Lizzy, Tubeway Army, Gerry Rafferty, etc. Jools and I headed immediately to the door marked 'Legs & Co.' to introduce ourselves and try to convince them we were the band that were going places, but when I opened the door we were met with the sight of Bucks Fizz's David Van Day swanning around in a polo-neck jumper and way-too-tight trousers, chatting to the girls. Every time I go to Brighton and pass his hot-dog stand by the Churchill Centre, I look back at that moment and wonder which of us had the better journey.

I bumped into Gary Numan in the corridor and the first thing that struck me was how bad his make-up was – I wondered why he'd bothered with it. I was never a big fan of his, especially when his record kept 'Up the Junction' off the number 1 slot. We also met Thin Lizzy, who we got on well with. My 'in' with Phil Lynott was being able to tell him we'd recently stayed at his mum's Manchester B&B while we were touring, and that I'd had to sleep in the bath due to Gilson's snoring. Downstairs in the bar, the scene was like something from *O Lucky Man!*, with Manchester United footballers, CID officers, the local mayor and some scantily clad women surrounding Phil's mum, who held court all night long. I remember being served beans on toast at four in the morning. It was bliss.

I'd expected *Top of the Pops* to feel inclusive and open, a community of artists coming together in mutual support, but it actually felt like the opposite. Everybody seemed surprisingly guarded and distant during the recording, but things opened up a little once we all headed up to the BBC rooftop bar. Here, the record company plied us with drinks – making sure they also got a few in for the producer – and we hung out with the other acts, while casting glances at various newsreaders and the Two Ronnies. I think we were at a crossover point, where the poppier bands from the Seventies became arseholes because they couldn't quite cope with the youth who were coming up, so they didn't really know how to react. We'd be in a little circle with the record company, who'd be buying us drinks, and we'd just be avoiding everyone else on the other side. DJs at that point had an ego because they were on TV a lot, which was far above their station, so in other words if you weren't nice to them they wouldn't play you on Radio 1. And I found that a trap really – because I didn't want to get to know them but I did want to be on Radio 1. Being on telly lifted the step. I was walking into the pub just waiting for people to recognise me. The feeling of being on TV was a feeling of having arrived, but where? My parents loved it and rushed all the neighbours into the house to watch the programme with them. Being on the radio was now commonplace. John Peel gave us a few sessions live in the BBC Maida Vale studios. Fags were lit and smoked on one side of the mouth as I waltzed along the high street in my blue jacket with a black velvet collar, tripping up on thin air. My dreams of being in a band and taking off were taxiing to the runway. We were now vaguely famous. Storm Thorgerson filmed the band on Deptford High Street (though I've never actually seen the footage) and we were photographed by Jill Furmanovsky, who was Miles's squeeze at the time. It was wonderful. We were being filmed and photographed locally, which made me feel important. We had arrived, albeit on Deptford Broadway in south London.

The record company put up massive posters publicising the album – one could be found in Deptford at the end of the high street. Three pink musclemen pulling shapes. Our faces were never going to sell the album and our reputation in front of the camera let us down. On an early photoshoot, we hired outfits from a costume shop. I was dressed as a vicar, Jools was an egg and Glenn a giant bird. On the back cover of the album we were in our swimming trunks, some eye make-up here and there and a few socks down the pants. On TV we managed to confuse people by swapping instruments. Jools sucked on a large cigar, Harry had no top on; we were desperate to avoid being branded teenage pin-ups. We were rebels without any real cause. Any attempt to mould the band would have been useless as Miles, I'm sure, would testify. One day in his London office just off Oxford Street he gave Glenn and me £500 each to buy some smart clothes to wear on TV. Glenn bought a kaftan and some brothel creepers; I invested in a cardigan (yellow with red triangles) and some brothel creepers too. We swapped a creeper, so we each had one blue and one red. We looked hopeless and not at all like The Beatles as Miles had wished for.

It was all about our songs – and on this first album I'm still not sure how we survived the hand of John Cale, with his constant colds, his brandy-swilling rants and late arrivals in the studio. The *Squeeze* album came out in March 1978. In the racks at the same time you could find *Jesus of Cool* by Nick Lowe, *This Year's Model* by Elvis Costello and *The Rutles* album. Life seemed as it should be. We were making records and we were on *Top of the Pops*. We were flying. It felt like there was a movement afoot: every pub was filled with great new music and the bands from the past seemed to fade away or adapt a newly tailored rough edge. Although I felt like we were part of this movement, I never really hung out with our contemporaries; there was no time. We were busy with promo and radio sessions, loading up the van and getting to the next gig. There was a crest of a new wave but we seemed to surf in the shallow waters of south London and did not venture too much into the swinging circuit of central London or Camden, where everyone else seemed to be gathering. I really loved the feeling of being in a band, rattling our way around every venue that would take us. We played to our strengths, loud and fast. Our first real live break came in the shape of a support slot with the very lively Eddie and the Hot Rods; we played a thirty-minute set each night and blew people away. I still look back on that tour as being the opening of a window. The view was of the future and us being the headliner. But first, America.

Miles had great connections in the States. His brother Ian became our agent over there and a tour was booked. Our first date was in New Jersey at The Lighthouse in Bethlehem on 23rd May 1978. We literally played to one man and a dog. We were forced to play a second set by the owner. The dog left. We went everywhere in a small blue Chevy van with Gilson in the back like a bear with a sore head. Jools was the joker. Glenn played banjo all day long while Harry hung out of the window in the breeze, trying to look cool in shades and no shirt. When you see dogs in cars, they always like to hang out of the window – Harry was a bit like that. Miles took charge of the truck with the gear in it and John Lay, our tour manager, drove us from place to place. In each town Miles would head to the local radio station and demand they play our EP. He worked really hard knocking on doors. Radio over in the US was mostly about 'Baker Street' and soft rock. It was terrible.

We were flying Freddie Laker, we were touring in America, the sunglasses were on and the cameras were out. Real musclemen were joining us on stage; and at the Whisky a Go Go in LA, I shocked A&M boss Herb Alpert by playing in a T-shirt that Miles had made for me that stated, 'I can see your tits, now show us . . .' Yes, that old chestnut. You'd have thought I'd have learnt from that incident on the A40. His wife was not impressed. The whole of A&M were there to see us play at the Whisky that night; we were brilliant, but it had been a long tour and we were fading around the edges. We were going slowly stir-crazy in our Chevy van. The three-month tour eventually drove us all mad.

Touring in those days was compact; we stayed mostly in motels on the edge of town. Glenn, I think, shared with Harry on most tours and Jools shared with Gilson as the rest of us were, I think, too scared. I shared with John Lay. John was a dead ringer for John Cleese with his narrow moustache, and I loved his no-nonsense style at hotel check-in. One day as he was sorting out our rooms we noticed the name of the concierge – Beau Bumgardener. We fell about with laughter and spent the next couple of days thinking up excuses to call him to our room. Silly, but then touring was an extension of school for most of us – and laughter was the raft that kept us afloat through our boredom.

Smoking dope also helped, but American weed was strong and one toke would make my teeth grip together. My eyes would change dimensions; I would stare at nothing for hours and laugh at the daftest things. English marijuana was lemonade compared to this pungent smokestack of dreams. We did enjoy a party as a blob, which was how Jools always referred to our collective self. Once we finished a show, we'd invade the hotel bar or a neighbourhood dive for our entertainment. Best of all was if they had a piano. We'd pretend Jools was blind and raise money for drinks

Dad with his mates tucking into some grub, post-Second World War.

Mum in her WRAC uniform.

Brothers in arms
but not in fashion.

A jolly old Christmas
time at Combe Avenue.

Mum on a mobile phone,
me heading for the moon
and Dad squinting.

My first bike on
King George Street.

A toy bus, an ice cream, a holiday
... and I'm still wanting more.

Sunday lunch, always a
treat, served up by Mum.

Happy days waiting for Glenn to arrive, prior to my early demos.

GUITARIST WANTED

MUST BE INTO THE BEATLES KINKS
SMALL FACES LOU REED HARMONY
GLENN MILLER. FOR BAND WITH
RECORD DEAL AND TOURING

call Chris 858 083

The ad from the sweetshop window:
50p well worth spending.

Windsor Free Festival,
with a man in his underpants.

Maxine in Blackheath Village.

Squeeze down the foot tunnel in Greenwich, me with a whisky bottle.

Jools and Gilson in a Deptford pub.

Me and Glenn looking innocent in paradise. (*Jill Furmanovsky*)

That fateful day when I signed my life away for £15 a week.

as he boogied his way through some Meade 'Lux' Lewis or Merrill Moore. One night in New Orleans we watched in awe as James Booker played Jools into a cocked hat; it was a very dark night in every sense of the word.

The band at this time were joined at the hip, and went from party to party and from bar to bar tripping the light fantastic. We all liked a drink, but it affected us in different ways. With Gilson, alcohol seemed to propel him into another universe. He would swing from being mild as a baby one moment to unpredictable the next. One night we were at a party at someone's house in New Orleans, and rather than leaving by the front door, he decided to throw himself through the French windows, ending up on a balcony below. It was possibly a cocktail of vodka and local marijuana. Sometimes he would turn blue and we'd have to call for medical help. The rest of us were no choirboys either, we also liked a party. I was always really worried about Gilson. Jools was the only one who'd share a room with him, which probably laid the foundations for their lifelong friendship.

I loved Gilson as our drummer and was in awe of his inventiveness and courage, but I was constantly terrified he would do damage to himself or deck me. He did try once. We were both sitting in the front seat of the Chevy van, driving into Cleveland, and I asked him to turn the radio down. He ignored me and the rest of the band, who were pleading with him to sort out the volume, and out of nowhere he let me have it with both barrels. I wanted to cry. An hour later, I was sitting in my hotel room wondering if I could get the phone number for Keith Moon, who seemed like a pussycat compared to Gilson, when he started knocking on the door. I ignored his requests to come in. After several more attempts, he kicked the door off its hinges, walked into the room and hugged me, telling me he was sorry. He was a lovable old bear who sometimes wouldn't be caged.

The tension of that tour and being trapped in that small blue van often made us all boil over; we were mad, bad and dangerous to know, as Jools used to say. Sometimes the heat and the hangovers would get to me. Harry's constant posing often drove us all nuts. There was one occasion when I pushed him off stage mid-gig because he was posing so much, but it was all in good fun. We all signed the plaster on his leg and so did our many new-found fans. Thank God the Sony Walkman had been invented. It kept me happy while soaking up those long journeys. Any detailed memory of this time has been eradicated, but I bet it was a lot of fun along the way.

We became a 'new wave' band when we went to America, along with Blondie, Elvis Costello, The Stranglers and other great bands that had both the attitude and the musicality that punk lacked. We were much more comfortable with that tag. We played endless sets at CBGB in New York, which had become the epicentre of the new wave scene over there. Though the gigs went well and the place was rammed, CBGB wasn't a place I loved. It was in the Bowery and there were always rumours of people wandering around outside with guns. I wanted to get in and out of there as quickly as possible. But we'd play our part, hanging out there or in a bar called Grass Roots around the corner where I would smoke local grass, drink warm beer and play pinball with The Ramones or Television for a couple of hours. We never became mates, though. That's the thing about musicians: when they're together, they don't really talk to each other. We might have crossed the floor of the bar to have a beer with Debbie Harry and Chris Stein, but we never got to the stage where we were sending each other postcards. If you're in a band, you've got to have a sense of coolness about you. And if you're cool and Tom Verlaine's cool, then you risk things freezing up. We might have been in the same class, but we were all too cool for school.

America was so much fun, even in the heat of a small Chevy van. What was not to like for a bunch of young men from south London: enthusiastic audiences, watery beer, long drives and dodgy motels. We were loud and very much enjoying the accolades of respect we would gather along the way. It was all of our dreams come true and I had never been happier.

We were riding the new-wave wave and getting credibility on the back of it too. But Squeeze were always a pop band in my eyes. Of course, I'd never have admitted that back in the late Seventies. Pop then meant Cliff Richard and Gilbert O'Sullivan, and the musical landscape had changed completely from the one I'd grown up with. But whenever I listen to great pop music from the Seventies, I get a warm glow. It takes me back to a safe place, when there was food on the table, sun in the sky and everything was really happy. Christopher Rainbow, Todd Rundgren, Carole King – all voices that dissolved me like sugar in a warm cup of tea.

Back in London, The Bell in Greenwich – a small pub on the edge of a dodgy council estate, outside which Squeeze had performed a short set on Jubilee Day in 1977 – became my second home. It was an afters pub, which meant it closed at 11 p.m., doors bolted, but with us all inside. Most of the drinks were on the house. My tipple would have been tequila sunrise after lock-in and pints of lager up until then. The Bell was run by some shady people and often I had no idea what was going on, what was being bought and sold or agreed to. We were local celebs, though, and just for us to be seen perched on a stool at the end of the bar was enough for them.

A mile away, there was a pub called The Deptford Arms, where we also played a short rooftop set on a hot summer's afternoon. The punters in there enjoyed our company too. The pub was heaving with villains; the gangs from south London would gather there to mastermind bank robberies and break-ins – or at least that's how it felt to me – though our local-hero status kept us shielded from anything untoward. I smoked differently when I was in the villains' company; I could see myself pulling on a tip as if it were stuck to my soul, looking at its ash as it roared into life. I walked with swagger and bravado. I knew I was safe.

Pubs were where I lived. In Blackheath it was The Crown, where toffs, estate agents and villains alike would stand at the long wooden bar. Here I would sit with notorious local criminal and dealer Johnny Edgecombe – he who supplied the gun in the Christine Keeler affair – or talk nonsense all day long with Alan from the City. In The Bell, I hung out with the locals. One of the regulars invited me to go and see Frank Sinatra at the Albert Hall with him, an offer I couldn't refuse. He picked me up from the pub in his Bentley and drove me across town with classical music blaring out of the windows. It was a memorable evening, and on the way home he turned down the Mahler long enough to give me some advice. 'Any girl that wants to marry you,' he said, 'get them to sign a contract. Offer them nothing and you won't be robbed if you end up getting divorced.' At the time it seemed ridiculous, but when I did end up getting divorced some years later I naturally thought of my dodgy friend from The Bell and wondered what had become of him. I'd simply got out of the car when he dropped me back home and never saw him again.

It was also in The Bell that I met Derry, a sweet girl who lived in a block of flats nearby. She loved the band, so I invited her along to *Top of the Pops* on one of the nights we were appearing on the show. But when she asked me to drop her off in Soho on our way home, I discovered she was working the streets for some Maltese pimps. I went back to her flat in Greenwich to ask her mum if she thought this was a safe thing for her to do, and it turned out her mum and sister were on the game too. It was a colourful time.

Punk was still going strong in London and going to clubs was a mission. I once went to the Vortex to see Generation X, who were supported by The Lurkers, Art Attacks and Steel Pulse. Walking down the steps into the club I felt out of place and intimidated. I had been before to see The Cortinas and Chelsea, who we shared an office with at the time, but it was still a big walk. The punk movement felt aggressive and reminded me of my skinhead days a few dark years before. Young drunk wannabes fell about all over the place looking for someone to bump into, shove or spit at. The best I could do was try and blend in, so I went to Boots and bought some safety pins. I attached them to my shirt and swaggered in with my leather jacket hanging open. Billy Idol made a good job of winding everybody up; the place shook to the foundations. I liked his attitude but not the songs, or his pumped-up ego, which he chucked around like a bad smell. The room overheated and soon the crowd was swaying this way and that until I had been levitated without lifting a leg or moving a muscle. It was like being down the Valley at a Charlton game before the nice seats were cemented into place. I left for a Chinese meal, deaf and a little drunk. It was a bear pit of a place, and as much as I longed to be part of the scene, I think I preferred the cosy pub on my street corner.

Maxine came back into my life around this time when she started seeing Squeeze's tour manager John Lay. She had become a young woman, yet those angelic features remained. It was so good to see her again and to have her back in our circle of friends. It could be a zoo, and from time to time chaotic, but it was a secure place nonetheless. Glenn and I were both in new relationships. He had fallen for Jo Davidson, a local girl who lived in a big house on Blackheath, and who'd been to a much better school than us. She made him happy and content, and became a fixture of the Squeeze social scene. She even sang backing vocals on 'Cool for Cats' when we recorded it a little later.

I was now with Mary – Harry's ex-wife – and we went everywhere together, holding hands. She was calm and supportive, enjoyed the same kind of music as me and made me feel special. And as everyone would fancy her whenever we went to a pub together, she made me feel incredibly proud too. Even though she'd been married to Harry, it didn't create any divisions in the band, either in the rehearsal room or on stage. It all happened very suddenly, the hop from bass player to guitarist; we seemed to fall for each other very quickly. They hadn't had a very happy relationship, and before I knew where I was, I was staying at their flat – with Harry in the spare room and me in the matrimonial bed. Harry didn't seem to blink an eye about it; I remember him bringing us tea and toast in bed one day. It was almost as if he knew it was going to happen. It was all very confusing. I think this was my first taste of love and never wanting to leave each other's side, which can be suffocating, but for us it seemed natural. I discovered what a relationship was and I hated to be apart from her. I always kept a diary and it's beautiful to read it now, to see how much I was besotted with Mary. She would write in my diary too. Everyone did. Jools would draw pictures in it from time to time. Both Jools and I were avid diarists. They say if you keep a diary it might one day keep you. Well, we shall see. Reading it now, I see and feel this time of my life as very special. Being in a young band was fun, that development stage can often be overlooked, but for me it was one dream followed by another in rapid succession. I had nothing to complain about.

OLD CHURCH STREET

In late 1978, we started work on our second album. At first we tried recording with one of Pink Floyd's producers, Brian Humphries, at their studios in north London. We managed to almost get to the end of the album, but the record company rightly thought it was too dull. The songs sounded flat, and so were many of the performances. Brian once told me not to touch the recording desk, and hit my hand with his ruler. I was not impressed. So we changed horses in midstream and hooked up with John Wood. We were writing and recording up near the King's Road with John, who'd engineered our debut album. It was another daily cab ride across town, but this time there was loads to do around the studio. Chelsea provided a completely different atmosphere from that of Willesden. After all, Old Church Street was slightly posher than Willesden High Street. All the fashionable shops were within walking distance, I think we made it as far as the café at the top of Old Church Street. John had built the studio with his bare hands and it was his musical version of my dad's shed – complete with soldering iron and wires with boxes everywhere. Here he'd re-corded Nick Drake, among others. It was a very productive place to work, with a nice pub across the street with brilliant cheese on toast. Writing was fast and we were released from any constraints – no John Cale telling us what to do, twisting our creative nipples. We were on a roll; a new trajectory that would gather pace over the next four years.

Cool for Cats was recorded in a few months. Glenn put a lot of time into the arrangements and played most of the keyboard parts too, as Jools wasn't always on hand to contribute – he was in the pub with me. It's an inspired album in many ways and I'm very proud of it. I think of it as our first record because it feels like that to me; it's certainly the first of our albums that sounded how we wanted it. Lyrically, I was scooping up things I heard in the pub, and writing in a dialect – cockney from the south bank of the Thames – that's now almost vanished, 'It's Not Cricket' being a prime example. The songs came quickly; the inspirational tap was on full flow. The music I was hearing on the London pub circuit – Ian Dury, Elvis Costello, Nick Lowe, etc. – was making me raise my game. I knew my lyrics had to be of a high standard to compete.

'Goodbye Girl', the first single from the record, was written on the previous US tour, and when I hear it now, it reminds me so much of Boston – a place I loved to visit. It's the percussion that makes the track, and Glenn and Gilson's genius was to work up a rhythm by hitting bits of metal, empty vodka bottles and the odd tambourine. At first I was uncomfortable about this, and we even recorded two versions of the song – a traditional rock 'n' roll number as well as the more offbeat Kraftwerk-style one. In hindsight, I think it's brilliant. Both versions are. Throughout our career, Glenn has often taken our songs in a direction that at first I'm not sure about. I naturally err towards simplicity. Now I'm older, though, I've realised that much of his talent has been hidden from me by a low-level mist of jealousy. Thankfully that's no longer there.

I wish I had been more engaged with him at this time. I could not convey my ideas in the way that he could, and that often wrong-footed me. It was like a musical stammer but I had no time to learn how to speak my mind clearly. If we had any disagreements during the recording or during a rehearsal, I would simply sulk. I don't remember any full-blown arguments with Glenn at that time. Other disagreements were too subtle and often left hanging like underpants on a washing-line. Sulking was not very grown up of me, but then I had no tools to deal with such a close friendship. For the most part my friendships had all been passing or on one level.

It seems to me that most major songwriting teams follow similar patterns. When you meet, you share the same views and ambitions. You set sail with the band in your rowing boat until someone drops an oar and you spin in different directions. Lennon and McCartney; Townshend and Daltrey; Page and Plant; the Gallagher brothers. We have all followed a similar journey. Luckily our relationship is not as fractious as the Oasis boys'. It's really OK not to agree about everything you do. It's healthy to go and pull in different directions. The tension was often the weight that ended up keeping our friendship balanced, and in those days I needed all the balance I could find. The scales of our friendship were mainly tilted in favour of mutual respect.

The lyric for 'Up the Junction' was inspired by the BBC *Play for Today* episodes I used to watch as a teenager. Those kitchen-sink dramas, written by such greats as Alan Ayckbourn, Dennis Potter and Mike Leigh, appealed to me because I could zone out and go into another world. My imagination could be rested for the time they took to weave their story. Like all of my best lyrics, I wrote the song in one sitting, and Glenn wrote the music on our day off in a motel room outside New Orleans while we did our washing. Miles, our manager, said it would never be a single because it didn't have a chorus, but thankfully we and the record company were more open-minded.

The videos for 'Cool for Cats' and 'Up the Junction' were shot by Derek Burbidge at John Lennon's old house in Surrey, Tittenhurst Park. Both were completed in one day, two versions of 'Cats', and one of 'Up the Junction' shot in the kitchen on our way out the door. Jools and I were keen to get to the pub to chat up the girls from the shoot, but they were off home to their respective pin-up boyfriends. Videos were the new bolt-on to the record, a way to show the song around the world. Our slapstick approach went down well with the BBC and the videos were shown many times on different shows. It was fun making them in those days.

'Slap and Tickle' is one of my favourite songs from the album. It gave Glenn and me another opportunity to do our trademark octave-apart vocal, and the story I put into the lyric was incredibly satisfying for me to write. The song's metre is heavily influenced by Ian Dury.

I'd never heard anyone recite a lyric before he did, and it gave me an opportunity to experiment with an entirely different kind of rhyming couplet. Contentiously, Glenn recorded a rhythmic mini-Moog part, which I was unhappy with at the time. And when we went out on tour to support the album, the mini-Moog came with us. I'd cringe when Glenn started playing it. It was never in tune, and the part would have been much better on a guitar. For a while it became the bane of my life, though nowadays it's very much part of the Squeeze family. I've grown to like its sharp edges.

The original melody of 'Cool for Cats' was much more laid-back and the lyric wasn't anywhere near as good. But Glenn felt the song had legs and asked me to have another crack at the words. So I took the backing track back to my flat on Crooms Hill and listened to it over and over, trying in vain to come up with something that would work. Nothing happened until I took a break for some Welsh rarebit and a cup of Earl Grey, with a bit of Benny Hill on the telly. Watching him perform his comic songs, I was struck by the metre of the verses, the quick-fire lyrics and the vivid images, and decided to try something along the same lines. The words then came quickly, each verse a vignette about the various TV shows that followed – *Wagon Train*, *The Sweeney*, *Minder* and a bit of *Grease*. At the studio the following day, I read the lyric to Glenn and John Wood, and a consensus quickly developed that I should be the one to sing it. I did it in one take. We employed the services of our girlfriends to sing the backing vocals and the job was done.

When the album came out, *Sounds* magazine said the lyrics were sexist, but I was just observing things around me. This was the late Seventies and I didn't really know what sexism was. I was sharing a flat at one point with a girl who worked for the feminist magazine *Spare Rib* and she agreed with *Sounds*. She said I should take a long, hard look at myself and my attitude to women. But I didn't know what she meant. I grew up in a family where my dad gave my mum spending money each week and I didn't know any different. I've always been very feminine-minded and I saw my lovers and female friends as my equals, so it hurt me to think that a woman would think I was sexist. Misogyny to me was what we'd witness every time Squeeze were on *Top of the Pops*. There the DJs acted with grand superiority, and shamelessly exploited the girls who came to watch the show being filmed while they were on set. It seemed that if you wanted to sleep with the drummer from Slade, you would first have to get filtered through one of the DJs on the studio floor. At the time it all felt very friendly and nothing seemed out of the ordinary. Jools and I held our fingers in our nostrils live on TV behind the Hairy Cornflake as he introduced the next band; the producer of *Top of the Pops* told Jools that he would never work in TV again. Jools seems to have done OK.

Now that we'd made a bit of a name for ourselves, touring was much more fun. We played a series of bigger gigs with Dr Feelgood in 1978, then 'Cool for Cats' was released as a single and went to number 2 in the charts. We were beside ourselves. A few months later, 'Up the Junction' came out and also stormed up to number 2. They were giddy times and my feet barely touched the ground, but when they did, I was usually in the pub. Two massive singles and a huge tour with The Tubes got our fire well and truly lit. Success was dribbling into our lives and it felt comfortable to be in the public eye. We were on TV all the time: *Top of the Pops*, *The Kenny Everett Show*, even *Jim'll Fix It*. The only thing I remember about that experience was that it was fixed. A fourteen-year-old girl had written a letter saying she was a huge Squeeze fan and wanted to sing a song with us. So we went on the show and performed whichever hit it was at the time, and she chirped away in the background somewhere then went and sat on Jimmy Savile's knee. We all knew that it was fixed by our record company, but it got us on the telly so we went along with it. And that was that. We turned up late to record *Tiswas* in Birmingham after a long night in the hotel bar, even though the hotel was right next to the studio. We found it hard to show up on time. Chris Tarrant was livid. He seemed furious with us, throwing all of his toys out of the pram. Not a nice look.

Despite selling out the Hammersmith Apollo five nights in a row with The Tubes, my memories of playing in London at this time are all of pubs and small clubs. From Deptford to Camden and back again. It was a wonderful feeling playing in our home city, and taking the stage there, I felt connected to a greater musical movement. It always made me walk a little taller. We were supported by some great bands – The Specials, REM, The Jam, Dire Straits, U2 and XTC – who'd go on to have huge success. We generally got on well with them and there was never any bitterness between us and other bands, apart from with The Jam. They supported us at The Marquee and Paul Weller's dad, who was their manager, was really forceful about them getting the maximum amount of time. They brought their own microphones and all sorts of things, and I think we probably sneered at them a bit and took the piss. But when I watched them I remember thinking, 'Fucking hell, this band are amazing. The songs are brilliant, Weller's a great guitar player, it's just so exciting.' They'd certainly earned my respect, but the next time we found ourselves on the same bill, Weller's dad came up to me and pinned me against the wall. 'Where are our fucking microphones?' he shouted in my face. 'Last time we played with you, some of our microphones went missing. You were the only person who knew they were there.' He was going to lay me out. I had no idea where they were.

We went back to the States in 1979, to support The Tubes in large halls all across the country. Nobody wanted to see us. One night the curtain went up and bottles were thrown. The audience were expecting to see hard rock act April Wine, who were second on the bill. We lasted four songs and retreated to the cold dressing rooms backstage. It was a learning curve.

On one flight to New York I sat next to a woman who was interested in the fact that I had a Nikon camera. She asked me what pictures I took; I said pictures of the band. She was much older than me, possibly mid-forties. We talked about photography and she asked if I would like to meet a famous photographer if I had a day off in the city. We met one day outside the Chelsea Hotel where we were staying and she took me to see a fragile old lady called Lisette Model. We walked her around the block very slowly and talked. Lisette had been a mentor for Diane Arbus, who I adored, so it was a very inspirational visit. I went to see her on later tours too; she was gentle and I'm sure had no idea who I was. She had just had a book released called *Aperture*, which she signed for me. It was a chance meeting that inspired me to keep taking pictures. A hobby that slowly passed, I'm afraid.

Quentin Crisp stayed at the same hotel as us. I often saw him flamboyantly strolling around the lobby. I went to see him read from his many books, all of which I bought and all of which he signed for me. He was a strange-looking figure whose glance could buckle my feelings and make me wonder if I could ever be that glamorous and intriguing. New York was full of such interesting people.

I met Cindy in New York at the bar in CBGB. She was small, thin and funny, like the character Anybodys in *West Side Story*; the tomboy. She showed me around the darker side of Manhattan and introduced me to her friends and to Bob Gruen, the photographer she worked for. The New York scene was great fun. If there was a seedy party to be had, then Squeeze would be there. We'd seek out the underbelly of whatever was going on, and enjoy whatever we found. One night, Jools, Glenn and I went to what was basically an orgy in a warehouse, although as observers it was way too far out for me. There were people screwing each other and doing heroin to eardrum-shaking music while we watched bemused. I ended the night sleeping on a park bench. It was all very appealing to an Englishman who until very recently had never gone further than the Isle of Wight.

New York was the place to be and we were playing all manner of shows; we even played at Lou Reed's birthday party, attended by Divine and Andy Warhol. There were not many people there at all so we raced through our set. Underneath the disco lights of the club I could make out a gaggle of people by the bar, half inter-ested in our performance. New York was as magical as I thought it might be, the glamour of having no money but getting by on the pure energy provided by the people you met late at night in clubs and bars was enough. I would walk everywhere just to involve myself in the electricity of the city; I felt plugged in all of the time, even when nursing a hangover.

I came home from that tour with a New York Monopoly set and some T-shirts and found myself homeless outside The Crown in Blackheath. Mary had booted me out of her parents' home where I had been staying with her between tours. She'd had enough of me being away all the time and she may have had a whiff that the band had been having a very nice time while on tour. I was stupid, but being in a band had its fascinating moments, and being away from home was dangerous.

The following summer we played the Reading Festival, headlining the Sunday night supported by Deacon Blue and the Hothouse Flowers. We were ready to go on stage but Jools was nowhere to be seen, so we went on anyway without him. We were furious. As I looked back at Gilson, I could see Jools turning up behind the stage in his Buick with Mary beside him; he casually got on stage and we raced through the set. At the end, we took a bow. When I looked around, Jools had gone, driving out past security. It was a stylish moment, like a scene in the movie *Grease*. The festival was so different from the way they are today. We had been canned on stage by a sea of very drunk people. Meatloaf had been canned the night before. I hated the atmosphere – it was nothing like the gentle stages of the free festivals from my not-so-distant youth.

Mary was now living with Jools, and I was soon to be married, all in the space of one small year. Cindy and I moved quickly to cement our relationship. It all happened so quickly. When two magnets meet and it's hard for them to be separated, that's what it felt like for me with Cindy at that time, like it had been with Mary before. Marriage was a large part of my family's life; both my brothers had had traditional weddings and now I was following suit. St Alfred's Church in Greenwich was where we tied the knot, and the sun shone as we walked to the altar to take our vows. I was locally famous, so people from the newspapers wanted to come to take pictures; we had a vintage American Buick car to drive away in. I was fresh from the pub across the road and a little light-headed, as was my mother. It was a giddy day all round. Drunk at the reception in my flat, my mother told me I should have married Mary, and then, giggling, promptly fell down the stairs and had to be taken to hospital with a broken ankle.

We spent our honeymoon upstate in New York with Cindy's
parents. Her dad was a gentle soul who ran the local drug store
and her mother was a talkative smiling bubble. We walked in the
mountains and lakes together and really enjoyed our time away
from the electrifying hub of New York. I had found another home
in the Catskills and it felt very different. I was the first in the band
to be married. At the time it seemed like part of my journey, but
later I found out how much it had upset Glenn – it put a wedge
between us and I'm not sure why that happened. Yet he was such
a good best man. It was here where we began to drift a little. All
good friendships have to oscillate from time to time and eventually recalibrate.

Our journey as a band was about to gradually change, although
in a good way. I was married and had all the trimmings of fresh
new relationships as Cindy and I amalgamated our friends, and
the band were young and exciting with records in the charts.
Somehow, during this very busy time, we had to write the next
album, which A&M were gasping for. I wrote it in a month – either
in Cindy's flat, or in Grass Roots or around the corner at CBGB.
In the little time we had between tours, Glenn and I managed to
put together another set of demos. Glenn's demos are legendary,
second only to Pete Townsend's in quality and delivery. I would
hand him twenty or so lyrics, and a few weeks later he'd send me
a C60 cassette containing all these fantastic, fully formed songs.
I miss those days – waiting to hear what might be. The songs we
wrote together shone in demo form, so when the band got hold
of them they could only shine further. I was driven by the demos;
they inspired me to write more and more to impress Glenn. He

always managed to surprise me, though, and often I would have to pinch myself with the joy our songs would bring me.

But then there were the curveballs. The songs with odd changes in them, the ones that would make my toes curl, songs that were just not my cup of tea. But how could I tell him without upsetting him? So I didn't. Sulking is passive bullying and not very nice, but it was my default setting and I never knew any better. Touring was a perfect place to frame a bad mood. If I found I didn't like what was going on, I would isolate myself and keep quiet about my feelings, then dance like a nutcase across the stage. The isolation promoted secret drinking in my hotel room, and all of this together started to silt up the emotional waters. I'd not been taught the art of emotional communication by my parents, so I invented my own, which was primal at best. I was mostly in a good place, but that place tended to be in the pub with my friends. If I could find no friends to take I would take my imaginary ones.

Home life was contained within a steady beat of parties, trips to the pub and driving around in my first car, a white Morris Minor convertible. I was proud as Punch of it. I loved living on Crooms Hill in Greenwich with Cindy. Glenn was in the basement, and Cindy and I were on the top floor. It was such a madhouse, full of music and the odd porno film (thanks to our eccentric landlady, who would rent out the middle flat to makers of 'adult' movies), and it became the new hub for our songwriting. Across the road was The Rose and Crown, up the hill the heath, all around us our friends, who would drop by from time to time. It was a stone's throw also from King George Street where I had been born. I felt warm and happy in that house, and sometimes the worse for wear. But that was all part of enjoying our new-found success.

There were other local bands, such as Stone Cold Sober and The Red Lights, but we were way out in front – we were the dogs. Minicabs home from the pub were a regular event; the new thing was Indian and Chinese takeaway food. I had some money in the bank thanks to PRS, which is money collected from TV and radio play; I was in the record shops every week snapping up all the new releases. Music had become the daily bread I broke with everyone in my world, and my childhood dreams were being achieved.

Because Mum suffered from agoraphobia later in her life, she seldom came to see Squeeze. She was coaxed out once, though, to the Albany Empire in Deptford, and danced with Dad in the balcony – and of course she cried to see her son so very happy. Coming home one day, I gave her my gold disc of 'Cool for Cats'. She was so proud of me, and all the neighbours were invited in to witness the trophy being hung above the TV. (It hung there until Dad died; and now it hangs in my house.) I was on telly. The flags were out on Combe Avenue where once I had been a skinhead beating kids up with my mates; smoking dope with Bob Blatchford and listening to The Stooges and MC5; playing strip poker in the shed with girls and losing happily. I had come home under a cloak of fame. A Rolls-Royce once picked me up from the house to take me to *Top of the Pops* and all the neighbours came out to see me; the only other time fancy motors turned up on our estate was for funerals and weddings. Some years later the bill for the car arrived with my royalty statement, proving that nothing is for free.

Touring was as mad as ever and we all got on extremely well, basking in our own success on various stages and at the corner of many late-night bars. Jools and I almost got arrested again on the

way back from a crazy New Year's gig in Glasglow. We stopped the
van for a breakfast at a Happy Eater. Jools and I tried to order fish
fingers. The lady behind the counter said that they were on the
kids' menu. We offered her £20. She told us that was bribery and
called for the manager. We then offered him £100 for two plates
of fish fingers. He called the police, who turfed us outside while
the band looked on unamused in the van. After our unsuccessful
bid to buy fish finger for £100, we signed autographs for the two
policemen and hopped back in the van happy days indeed.

CROOMS HILL

Argybargy was part two of the *Cool for Cats* album, recorded in much the same way. John Wood was still at the mixing desk at his Sound Technics studio in Chelsea, and he proved to be a steady hand on the tiller yet again. Both albums are classic young Squeeze. Glenn was focused in the studio, playing some amazing solos and holding the songs together. Jools had a song on each album, which I co-wrote with him, and this allowed him and the band a chance to show off their musical roots. Glenn and Jools were the band historians when it came to rock 'n' roll. They knew every song on every jukebox and together they ignited many a quiet bar. I watched from the side and wished I had the talent to amuse in such a wonderful way. Writing with Jools was slightly different to the way I wrote with Glenn – I would hand him some lyrics handwritten on A4 paper and he would present a song in the rehearsal room rather than demo it.

John Bentley had joined the band on bass. He turned up late for the auditions – we'd already chosen someone to replace Harry, who we'd had to let go – but John insisted we set back up and let him have a play. He got the gig and we were off on another twist in our tale. John was fun to have around and got on well with Gilson. Recording proved very simple with our new rhythm section – Gilson was always so inventive. John was from Hull and enjoyed a wicked sense of humour; he had the gift of the gab and fitted in so well with our band. He played with great confidence and was creative. He looked like Dudley Moore on a good day and dressed well, though mainly in the same clothes. He liked small joints and the ladies, who loved him too. He was a handsome chap who played without having to look at the frets.

The record company seemed happy enough with the two hits to come from the LP, 'Another Nail in My Heart' and 'If I Didn't Love You', though I've never felt attached to the former. Like a lot of lyrics on that album, it was written quickly and has its roots in the constant flow of verses and choruses I was forced to pro-duce rather than in me unearthing any deep emotional thoughts. Glenn had this idea of having a guitar solo rather than a second verse, and he worked long and hard at getting all the notes in the right order. It was the correct decision. 'If I Didn't Love You' is my favourite track on the album. The line 'singles remind me of kisses, albums remind me of plans' comes from the days when I used to take girls up to my room at Combe Avenue and put on records with long running times, to give myself enough time to get my arm around them. 'I Think I'm Go Go' was the first song I'd written about travel – it mentions a New York radio station and references my time in the city. 'Vicky Verky' was a continuation of 'Slap and Tickle'; in some ways, it had the same sort of characters, a similar metre and a beautiful melody by Glenn. 'Pulling Mussels (from the Shell)' was inspired by going on holiday as a teenager with my next-door neighbour, whose dad had an Austin A40. We drove down to a caravan park near Margate and saw The Small

Faces play in the local social club while we were there. Lyrically, I tried to imagine how Ray Davies would write a song about this most English type of holiday, and the words came quickly and easily.

I still love the *Cool for Cats* and *Argybargy* albums, but I hate both record sleeves. With *Argybargy*, we were left to take the group photo ourselves with a foot switch; we all took turns pressing it. On the one hand, it does represent the band as we were at that time – a bit lively, a bit mad. But on the other, it was very rough around the edges. I suppose we were too. We were seeing less and less of Miles. His younger brother Stewart – once the drummer in Curved Air – had formed a band back in London called The Police, and Miles was grooming them for success in much the same way as he had the young Squeeze. They recorded at Surrey Sound, they signed to A&M, they recorded hits and toured America following the same route we'd taken. There was a theme. I'd even been present when the band had been auditioning for a singer. Sting turned up and I told everyone he couldn't sing for toffee. I was wrong, obviously. Greater involvement with another band didn't stop Miles sending us off on tour to Australia, though.

My daughter Natalie was born just before we went; I got the news that Cindy had gone into labour while we were doing a Christmas gig with Madness and The Specials in Birmingham. Miles had kindly installed a phone at the side of the stage for me and it rang just as the audience applause was dying down. I leapt into a waiting car and the driver raced me down the M1 to London. By the time we got to Kilburn, I was gasping for a beer, so we did a pub crawl down the Edgware Road, making it to the hospital in Lewisham, a little the worse for wear, just an hour before Natalie was born. Later that night, Gilson turned up at the hospital with a McDonald's and a bottle of whisky to help me celebrate fatherhood. I was so happy to be a dad. Even through all the alcohol and hamburgers I'd consumed, I could see how beautiful Natalie was, and over the next few days I puffed up with pride whenever her name was mentioned.

One minute I was telling everyone how amazing my life had become and the next I was being handed my plane tickets. Cindy being pregnant had been a wonderful time; the expectation of birth and the slow realisation that I was going to become a father were something else, taking me away from the band and the journey I was on. That whole year was emotionally draining and in some ways I needed the tour to steady the internal ship. That was the nature of my life at the time: tour, album, tour, album.

Australia was one of the first straws to start bending the camel's back of my marriage. At first, Cindy coped really well with me being away, because she knew that was what I did. It was like she'd married someone in the merchant navy. She had a great group of friends around her in south London, including Jo Davidson, who stayed by her side, but it must have been hard because her parents were in New York and I was away on the other side of the world, separated from my new family by travel, the band and the pub. We were on such a roll at this time that it was difficult to focus on both my lives at the same time. There was the success I needed to chase, but equally there was a wife and child I needed to be there for. Australia was a long way away from Crooms Hill, where Cindy and I had made our nest with Natalie. Once in Sydney I hit the Pernod to numb the feelings. I had no idea what day it was, or for most of time where I was. It was summer down there and it was hot – too bloody hot for me – and I slowed to a drunken crawl. We were treated well, the crowds were great and we met some good people to party with. On a rare day off, we went out on a speedboat, and I tipped some cans and sat in the sun. Back at the hotel that night, the pain started to cripple me. I was red like a crab. I resorted to covering myself in calamine lotion and wearing my pyjamas everywhere I went, including when I was up on stage. I could hardly stand. Gilson could hardly stand either, but still managed to surf on top of a car in the hotel car park.

Melody Maker came to review our quest, and asked us what we thought of Australia. Tactfully, we said it was shit. We never went back and the hits over there dried up. One of the most memorable shows was in a small coal-mining town called Wyella. It was an hour's flight in a small plane. After the show, I made the mistake of getting stoned, and then got into the plane with the pilot who had been waiting for us. Once up in the warm night air, Gilson asked how long he had been flying; he told us he had just got the all-clear after a recent heart attack. At this point he could not get through on the radio to the control tower at Adelaide. He said the only thing we could do was quickly land so that he could call from a phone box, but the lights on the runway were on a timer. We'd only just made it down to the ground when they went off. I was so scared that I was ready to die while holding on for dear life to Jools's arm.

I was never home, and home began to crack. We were being worked hard by our agent, our manager and the record company, but what else was there to do? This was my journey and no destination had been programmed into the sat nav. We all wanted success at whatever cost, even an emotional one. Touring the album in America was hard work but so much fun. We were young and full of beans, all sorts of beans. We had a tour manager called Mike Hedges who always called us before a show with his catch-phrase 'last pisses and shits, five minutes'. He was a barrow boy from south London and gifted with the gab. He once walked us on stage in New Jersey and in the corridor was a smartly dressed elderly gentleman. Mike pushed him out of the way. While we were ploughing through the set, Mike head butted the guy, who just turned out to be the Italian owner's dad. We came off stage and Mike hid in a guitar trunk. We were all in towels when three big chaps burst in wanting to kill him. I was shaking with fear and chucked a can of beer at one of them, which bounced off his chest. We legged it out the back door into Miles's hire car and into the city. Our gear was impounded and we lost the fee. Mike was wheeled out into the back of a van inside the case. It was a close call, a brush with the local Mafia. Touring was exciting and nerve-racking and it was our way of life.

Back in the UK one night we had an unplanned meeting in a hotel bar that set us off in another direction entirely. Elvis Costello was performing in a town near where we were playing in Malvern when we bumped into him and his keyboardist Steve Nieve – who we knew from days of yore, gigging around the pubs of south London. We lined them up, talked shop all night and tried our best to solve the world's problems. It was good fun. Being in total awe of Elvis, I was all ears and hung on his every word. To me he was the lyricist of the time – the king of retort and pun. Jake Riviera, Elvis's manager, told us we were brilliant, but latched on to how tired we all were and asked us why we weren't doing more as a band. Jake was a colourful person who stood up on imaginary hind legs when making his point. He was like a corgi, snapping and barking orders and ideas. I was impressed. He shone a light on our journey that would turn us upside-down. He was inspired and full of great ideas; he cared about music and knew how best to rule the world.

This new world, as it turned out, wouldn't include Miles or Jools. We parted from Miles and went over to west London to Jake's offices, where lawyers were employed to look over our previous contracts and sort out a severance. Miles was furious and kept calling to say it would be a massive mistake, one that the record company would not entertain. He was welcome to clutch at straws as we marched on regardless. Unlike Miles, Jake had an impressive record collection which spoke volumes to me about his passion. If they had been cars, Miles would have been a Reliant Robin and Jake a Corvette: Jake had tons more class and style.

Meanwhile, back in south London, Jools called us all in for breakfast at a café in Blackheath, where he broke the sad news that he was going to leave the band. He would stay with Miles and record on his own. My throat became dry and I felt like bursting into tears. It was like losing a finger. We sat around in the café patting each other on the shoulders, but Glenn seemed completely let down and left as upset as I was.

Jools was swiftly out of the door and on to the next thing. He had plans that he may have been weaving for many months before. In my heart I wished him well, although I was devastated. I felt I'd lost a really close friend. I didn't see him for a long while after that. Jools and I were both lads and wanted to be in a gang. Gangs had been a huge part of my life pre-Squeeze, and when the band first got together I was looking to form a musical gang

– inspired by The Small Faces and The Who. Jools had the gang mentality so I'd hang out with him, sleep round at his house, write the odd song with him, get arrested with him. On tour, we'd be the first people to call each other in the morning and would go for breakfast or just hang out. Miles had seen something in Jools that went beyond playing keyboards in a pop band. He'd already become our spokesman on stage after Miles had come to one of the gigs and said, 'No one's talking on stage. Jools, why don't you do the introductions because Glenn and Chris don't want to do them?' So Jools would get the microphone, introduce everybody in the band and just start talking and be the entertainer. He was a natural, like the ringmaster in a circus tent, and he was always very funny. Miles saw potential in that, and when TV came along, he took him to *The Tube*.

Back at camp, Jake Riviera had an idea. Ex-Ace and Roxy Music keyboard player and vocalist Paul Carrack was free, and Jake thought he'd be a wonderful addition to the band. Paul was managed by Jake, so it all fitted together nicely. My tears soon dried and we went into Nick Lowe's basement studio in Shepherd's Bush to rehearse with Paul. Suddenly it was 'Jools who?' Paul, or PC as we all called him, was confident and always in good voice, an ardent football fan and a dear friend, who I shared a room with on some US tours that followed. He was a family man, and the warmth of his company glowed brightly. I loved being around Paul, as he was dry with his humour and always up for a good night. He was an inspiration to be around.

Elvis, Jake, Nick and Paul became part of my new gang. We were all in our mid- or early twenties – hanging out, recording, writing and being in bands. We went to the same parties together, we toured together and hung like bats off each other's ceilings talking nonsense for days together. It was fun all day, and at night things got even better. Jake would call the shots, and you could see how Stiff Records must have been in its heyday, full of wild, exciting moments. I was always over at Jake and Toni's house in Chiswick for dinner, or with Elvis and his wife Mary at theirs. Nick would meet me in the pub, so long as it was local, while Paul was more of a home bod. It was great.

Nick was married to Carlene Carter, daughter of Johnny Cash; she was so much fun, and very generous. We had some great nights together and Cindy fitted right into the American-girl, let's-all-have-a-good-time vibrations. These loud nights scared me sometimes, as I couldn't keep up. Cindy and Steve Nieve's wife got on really well, and to be around them was to be within spitting distance of madness and dizzy drunken conversations that went on all night long. None of which I could understand. Steve and I became close friends, I loved his playing and we had both become fathers at roughly the same time. We even tried writing together but couldn't get past the manual on the complicated Fairlight computer we had borrowed. We were also exceedingly happy on good red wine and other nonsense.

One night, Elvis surprised me by asking if I could write some lyrics for a song he had called 'Boy With a Problem'. I was stunned. I went home and kept playing the demo on my cassette machine, trying urgently to come up with some words that would knock him out. Elvis liked the lyric I delivered, and though he made a few changes, the version he recorded was mostly mine. This was a milestone in my life for which I'll forever be grateful. Elvis has always been such a generous friend. He gave me a guitar when he knew I was on my last hundred quid, he invites me to his shows, and we email from time to time in a novel exchange of 'How's it going then?' He is a pedigree, albeit long-distance chum.

Cool for Cats and *Argybargy* were ships in the night, gone and behind us, though the hits from those albums will follow us for the rest of our lives. It was an intense time, and it had to be; you only get one shot at the target, at least that's how it seemed at the time. Elvis had 'I Can't Stand Up for Falling Down' in the charts, Madness had 'Baggy Trousers' and The Nolans had 'I'm in the Mood for Dancing'. The Police were number 1 every week with quirky videos of them hopping about on recording studio desks. They could afford to. Everyone was gearing up for the future. We were content, however, to keep it simple. We just wanted to record great songs and enjoy our life of constant touring around America and Europe. We were up all night and all day; we were burning every candle at every end and having loads of fun with our new mates.

Nick Lowe was great to work with and we never messed around. We would bang it down, as he used to say, then head to the pub to celebrate. Jake's idea was for us to record a four-sided album: Nick Lowe would produce one side, Dave Edmunds another, Elvis Costello and Paul McCartney the other two. Sadly, it never got off the ground. More cab rides across town – this time to Acton, where we spent six weeks writing and recording the album in Eden Studios. We started at 11 a.m. and finished at 10 p.m. most days, with salads and light meals supplied to keep us trim and healthy. I enjoyed the regime Elvis dished out. Cider but no lager, as I recall. At home, life was as you might expect for a young father, full of baby things and early-morning calls. Hangovers and kids didn't mix. But for the most part, I was on alert; I knew this record had to be good and we had to be at the very top of our game.

We cracked on at a furious pace with one take after another, each song tenderly looked at and devoured by Elvis and Roger Bechirian, who engineered the sessions. Glenn got on well with Elvis and I was still in awe of his work, so every time I handed him a lyric it was like giving it to a cute teacher I fancied at school. I was inspired like never before; I was up all night picking through every pun and each story. I really enjoyed the challenge of writing the album and both Glenn and I came up with the goods. We were very much focused on this new-found grown-up way of working. Elvis provided the umbrella of credibility beyond that of our own.

During the recording we got the sad news that John Lennon had been shot. We downed tools and stood stunned in the pub at the end of the road. Friends were invited over to the studio where a mass expression of appreciation and disbelief took place, it was so devastating. The next day we picked up sticks and rolled on with the recording. That was a very powerful day for us all.

We'd had 'Tempted' up our sleeve for a while. We'd already recorded it, with Glenn singing, for Dave Edmunds. Unfortunately, it sounded like ELO and not like Squeeze at all. Elvis thought Paul should sing it, so we went into the studio and nailed the track in one take. Glenn looked shell-shocked, but was man enough to admit that Paul really could sing the song better than he could at that time. Elvis arranged the song and played the guitar riff, and provided backing vocals with Glenn, while I sat around eating salad and jotting down lyrics, content that history for Squeeze was being made. The whole process of the album was never to be repeated. It's by far the most complete album we ever made, from the genius 'F Hole' to the sublime 'Labelled with Love'. Elvis's bass player, Bruce Thomas, came up with the title *East Side Story* – and it fitted Squeeze like a glove. The sleeve was arranged by Barney Bubbles, who was out there with the fairies but in a beautiful and inspiring way. Chalkie Davis was taking our pictures. What more could we ask for? We were surrounded by genius.

Jake had another great idea, he was full of them. Two bands on one bus going around America together, taking over the world; a magical mystery tour across several states with nine band members, Jake, a tour manager, a driver, an accountant and a security man. Elvis Costello and the Attractions supported by Squeeze. The tickets flew out the door and we tore up every town we went to. For the first week it was like a holiday; there was loads to drink and marching powder, the hotels were top notch and we wanted for nothing. Backstage, our world was exclusive and good-humoured; there were many jokers in the pack. Steve Nieve and Elvis's drummer Pete Thomas were like Pinky and Perky, up all night on invisible strings playing jokes on everyone. Elvis and Glenn were more serious and looked mostly in opposite directions. The bass player was Bruce Thomas – otherwise known as the Rhino – who was always in a bad mood. His Fender bass would often take flight across a crowded stage, hurtling mostly towards Elvis. Gilson was under lock and key, John Bentley was having lots of fun and was very Dudley Moore-like. And me? I was knocking about the bus in search of the next beer, a bottle opener or some headphones to avoid the madness with my Walkman. Jake sat at the front of the bus reading a restaurant guide. This was thick with places to stop for a meal, none of them any good, but we gave the book quite a thrashing. We drove off route one day for some Welsh rabbit – this turned out to be a plate of melted Kraft cheese with ears cut from a slice of white bread. We were not amused. Another stop-off was to Buddy's Ribs, a rib joint at the end of a runway at the airport where Buddy Holly took off for the last time, or so the guide led us to believe.

Jake was great at organising events for us; it was exciting and hard to keep up with, but we all did our best. Touring on a bus filled with mischief was something I hadn't bargained for. It taught me so much about the dawn, the bars and dark corridors in hotels, and about how touring really should be: full speed ahead until you pass out. And then some. During one journey from New Orleans, we were stopped by the Ku Klux Klan, who got on the bus with guns to look for donations. We were in our bunks and stayed there until they got off. The tour rolled on and our shows got better and better, apart from the fact that we were mostly chasing hangovers.

A&M were on tenterhooks. They didn't think they liked Jake or the way he managed the band, and I saw a telegram (yes, they were still being sent in 1981) from the label's co-owner Gerry Moss saying: 'Avoid Jake Riviera; he is rude and is mismanaging the chances of this album being a hit.' What did he know? In San Francisco that year, Mr Moss was waiting for us when we came off stage. Jake asked him what the B-sides were called on the singles we currently had out, then grabbed him by the nose and dragged him along the hall away from the dressing-room door. Brilliant. After the same show, Jake took me aside and asked me what was so fascinating about my shoes. I was lost for words. 'All you do on stage is stare at your shoes,' he shouted. 'Look at the fucking audience. Pick a girl, smile at her and the connection with the crowd will be made.' It was a great tip.

We had another number 2 single in the UK with 'Labelled with Love'. We were back on telly again and I personally felt reignited. We had a new manager, a new keyboard player and some great plans for the next album, for the next year and beyond. Videos were starting to take shape as MTV was creeping around the corner, and more and more record companies were investing huge sums of money to get bands seen by a wider audience. True to form, however, we had Barney Bubbles push some mops around a flickering screen for our single 'Is That Love'. Jake told us not to chase the MTV rainbow; we were never going to be Duran Duran anyway.

I had made it, whatever making it was. I seldom had the time to go and see my mum and dad – and when I did, I just went to the pub. Life was good. I was famous for fourteen and a half minutes and I wanted to make the most of it. Hanging out with local villains, being large at parties. I was on the dial, and drink and drugs took centre stage, though in a secret and private way, behind closed doors. My nose became over-familiar with the toilet seats in public loos; pub car parks and lay-bys in country lanes were new places to swig beer and sleep. Anywhere but my own home with my wife and daughter, or my mum and dad's house. By the end of 1981, we had been on tour for months, and in a short break in August Paul Carrack left the band. Like Jools before him, he had other fish to fry: a record with Nick Lowe and Carlene Carter, solo albums and a path into his own future. It was very sad the way he left so abruptly, but I understood why.

He went on to form a band with Nick and I became one of their biggest fans. Meanwhile Jake turned up with a massive contract for us to sign – we didn't, and he resigned, spitting feathers. Our original contract with him had been verbal, but we'd just had a hit album and he understandably wanted to get the financial side of things nailed down. He wanted us to use his lawyer to go through the contract, though, which was a big problem for us, as we were only just becoming aware of what we'd signed away to Miles. The lawyer he kept pushing on us was called David Gentle, who'd been a fixture at all the festivals we'd played at when we were younger, and it just didn't smell right to me. Jake put us under pressure and didn't want us to take the contract anywhere else; he kept saying that we could do it all in-house and save money, but because we'd had our fingers burnt with Miles, we were being really careful. It was never easy and sadly we went our separate ways. Jake had inspired us to look at our deal with Miles in the first place. He was right to point out what a rum deal we had signed up to. I'm grateful that he helped point this out to us. He never took a penny from the band in all the time he looked after us.

Glenn and I decided to take Miles Copeland to court with the help of my brother Lew, who was passionate about helping us find some justice and recompense. Our original contract with Miles signed away the rights to all of our songs, masters and copyright, never to be returned. His company owned 50 per cent of my words and Glenn's melodies for life. We had been completely taken in by everything Miles had told us. Everything in his contract was cross-collateralised, which is totally illegal now, so if we didn't make any money from the touring but did from the publishing, one would pay for the other. Miles knew we'd sign it because we were young, we didn't know any lawyers and he was promising us fifteen quid a week each, which seemed a great deal to us at the time. That was fundamentally wrong and you couldn't do it today – you'd get banged up for grooming a young band in such a way. He had really taken advantage of our naivety. Just as we were about to go to court, we had a call from Miles asking if he could come over and see us. He wanted to avoid the hearing at all costs. He came to Glenn's flat in Greenwich, and we sat and asked him questions that were neatly aimed at getting him to reveal the truth about how much we'd really made and how much we were owed. Behind a curtain, on the window ledge, was a microphone; in the next room was a reel-to-reel tape recorder to slowly gobble up each word. Miles's father, the ex-CIA head, would have been proud of us. We did resolve the case, but were none the wiser or wealthier. My brother Lew and our very talented young lawyer James Harman worked so hard on that case, and in the end we were all relieved just to close the door on a chapter that was fairly painful and somewhat costly.

Paul Lilly was our manager for a brief period while all of this was going on; he was our sound engineer and had convinced us he could do the job better than Miles, which he could. My mum could have done a better job. He got us to invest our money in a PA company; it was an odd thing to do, but it helped us with our tax situation at the time. Paul was gentle and kind. He opened an office in Greenwich Market and employed Jayne Homer to be his secretary, poached from the offices of our record company A&M. She is still with us today. He took on management of Chris Rea and left us behind when Chris hit the European jackpot, a number 1 record across the board. Managers were beginning to really annoy me. There seemed little loyalty. Either that or we were becoming harder to handle.

We were high, then low; a band collectively experiencing bipolar mood swings. Somehow we pulled things together to write another album. *Sweets from a Stranger* was a dark album to record; that's my view. We started it with legendary producer Gus Dudgeon, widely credited for making Elton John a worldwide star, but we replaced him with Phil McDonald, formerly The Beatles' engineer. We tumbled into Ramport Studios in Battersea, owned by The Who. Phil dined out on the stories over expensive dinners late at night. He was calm to work with but never really lit any fires. Don Snow was now on the revolving keyboard stool, and we rolled up our sleeves. Don was impressive and could play most instruments; he was a very funny man who could imitate anyone, but he had another side to him that I could never read, and neither could he. He was up and down with his moods just like I was; together we oscillated like valves in an old radio. Gilson was becoming darker and harder to read too. He constantly turned up in a foul mood and seemed disconnected from the band. And by this time he and Glenn had built up huge resentment towards each other because Glenn would try to tell Gilson what to play, and Gilson would kick against it. It was miserable.

The best song on the album was 'When the Hangover Strikes', on which Glenn surpassed himself melodically. It's a crooner's song with fantastic chords, worthy of Sinatra. I was very proud of my lyrics too. The record company glazed over, but put out a few singles. 'Black Coffee in Bed' was too long but did get some plays on the radio after a brutal edit. Record companies back then were in the habit of playing with your art without you knowing about it. We first heard the new version of the song when a promo cassette arrived through the post. It was hilarious and very, very wrong. We were livid. Elvis and Paul Young dropped in to sing on 'Black Coffee in Bed', and that was the highlight of the recording for me. Paul Young was topping the charts at the time and was in fine voice, and with Elvis there too we sounded like The Drifters. It was a friendly afternoon filled with back-slapping banter, but I felt like I had fallen from the lyrical challenges of the previous album and had delivered some lazy writing. I was not on my game and had gone backwards into a safe but untidy mind. It seems like a dark album to me for so many reasons, not least because I was still mourning both the loss of Paul Carrack and our management situation with Jake. I felt lyrically homeless.

Our new manager, David Enthoven, who'd previously managed King Crimson, T. Rex and Roxy Music, had his work cut out for him. He was introduced to us by someone at A&M, and our first meeting was at the Greenwich Theatre, right across the road from where I lived. David had been schooled at Harrow and could not have been more different from us, but his warmth and ambition shone through his wicked smile and straight talking. After the album he came on the road with us and soon became a very good friend. He was so much fun and mucked in wherever he could. Like us, he enjoyed a drink and a game of cards; we toured well together. He was gentle with everyone and enjoyed the slapstick camaraderie of touring life. I was once invited to his country house, where he lived with his wife, heiress to the Wills cigarette dynasty. On a winter's walk, all wrapped up, David would eat raw beef from a bag like he was eating sweets. We were both mostly drinking fine wines and blowing things up our noses while sitting by roasting fires eating very little and talking bollocks.

David talked us into a 'greatest hits' album and we added a new track called 'Annie Get Your Gun', which was recorded by Alan Tarney, who was famous for the songs he'd written for Cliff Richard. Alan put Squeeze into a computer and recorded the song without us; we came in to sing on top of the track. Gilson added some drums and moaned all day long about how technology was stealing his job. 'Annie' made the radio and to this day is still always in the set. Lyrically I have no idea what it's about. It was a strange marriage – Alan and Squeeze – yet somehow I think it really worked.

Touring went on and on, and on a train en route to Paris from Hamburg, Glenn and I decided the band sounded tired and agreed it was time to close up shop – a rare coming-together at this point in our relationship. It was like a black-and-white movie. I was looking out the window and so was Glenn; we just came to the same conclusion right at the same time.

We were both knackered, Gilson seemed beyond reach and our keyboard seat could not take another swivel. As a band we no longer seemed like a unit. It felt as though we were winging it. The break-up was a mixture of exhaustion and sadness because the constant touring had taken its toll on Gilson more than the rest of us. I felt helpless around his drinking and, although I didn't know it, mine too. Little did I know that I was to follow in his footsteps – in a gentler and more devious fashion perhaps.

I didn't really know what I might be saying goodbye to. It had been such a magical ride, from the first time I met Glenn in 1973 to that day on the train in Hamburg. I had no clear idea of where we might go from here, but as ever, I had no fear about the future. Stages had grown from the corners of pubs to Madison Square Garden; we had come a long way.

Glenn and I kept it all under our hats until the last show of the year, at the Jamaica World Music Festival. We told the band just before we boarded the flight out there. Perfect timing. Gilson and John were furious, and though Don took it in his stride, he was angry too. Sitting behind us on the flight was Rick James and his band, and mid-way through the flight Rick got up and walked into the cockpit, which was only partitioned off by a curtain. As he stood up he lit up a huge joint, and as he disappeared in to see the captain I felt the blood rush round my body ridiculously quickly. I could almost feel the pilot getting stoned on the fumes and flying the plane into a mountain. I watched as Rick walked back into the front of the plane where we were all sitting, a massive grin on his face. I looked out of the window hoping for the best.

I once saw a film of us playing at that festival, and I could see in me a person who was stoned out of his head, playing the wrong chords to the wrong songs, dancing about like there was a nest of spiders in my pants. My head was all over the place and I could not wait to get home. And right after we came off stage, I headed for the airport and boarded a plane home.

It had been a great festival: The Beach Boys, Yellow Man, The Grateful Dead, The Clash and Aretha Franklin; racing crabs on the beach with Joe Strummer; smoking joints in a rowing boat at the back of the stage; falling asleep to Jerry Garcia sweetly playing 'Dark Star'; dancing to Peter Tosh. Not a bad way to say farewell. Jamaica was the oddest place to be at that time; we were completely distant with each other and gone from the band feeling in so many ways. The hotel we stayed in was on the beach: to get a phone call to England you often had to wait several hours, the connections were that bad, so it felt very isolating to be there. Cut off from the reality of home and living in this tender world of impending separation and doom, I had no idea what was going to happen next. After the tour, Gilson became a cab driver, John went to live in Cornwall, and Glenn and I went into partial obscurity for a rest. David stepped to one side, taking my brother Lew with him as his accountant, which I was very happy about. I went home and trod water for weeks on end, contemplating my future. By the end of 1982, I felt as though I was suddenly in a forest. There were shadows and fallen trees, and I had only sunlight from gaps between branches to guide me along the way. David Enthoven was there too; I could see him ahead of me. He had come along to pick up what was left of Squeeze – and what was left was a singles album and Jamaica. He did his best with what he had; we parted ways; it was all amicable.

TOYS HILL

Cindy and I were living in the country when she became pregnant again. I was over the moon. My son Riley was born at Pembury Hospital in Kent, and as I held him for the first time, sitting alongside Cindy's mum, who'd flown over from New York for the birth, I felt so proud. I was a father again, and this time to a boy. He came out of the sunroof because of some complications, which meant that I had first cuddles. Afterwards I headed straight to the pub to wet the baby's head, then drove home with one eye shut and the other peering out for oncoming traffic.

We were happy out in the sticks with our little family, albeit in an isolated way, though Cindy enjoyed it less than me. I'd become firm friends with the photographer Chalkie Davis and together we would enjoy the country life and go for long walks to Toys Hill where there was a nice pub and Winston Churchill's old house, Chartwell, which was close to my home. I loved Churchill and his colourful paintings, his wall-building and chair designs, but I drew the line at his cigars. Fine wine and champagne were on my radar – I was at Berry Bros & Rudd most weekends stocking up on red wine and sometimes sherry. It was a fine way of keeping out of harm's way and from working on any new songs. I was

Burlington Bertie. 'Tempted' and Jake Riviera seemed years ago. I wrote by night and slept by day; I snorted and drank my way from one month to next. I was not of this world and it terrified me, but it never stopped me. Squeeze was behind me now and it was time to smell the roses, but my nose was constantly too blocked up.

I was not missing the treadmill of recording and touring, the headaches of management changes and keyboard players coming and going like wasps. I was enjoying my time in the Weald of Kent. Home was a place people liked to come and spend weekends, parties were many, but I felt increasingly lonely in my own skin. I was unsure as to why. It just might have been the drugs catching up with me. At one of our wild weekends Pete Thomas and his wife Judy came to stay. They slept in the loft with the electric radiator on full. Six months later I went up to get something from a case; the heat was overbearing and the flies were swarming about in wonder. Our electric bill literally went through the roof. All good fun.

Glenn and I worked on *Labelled with Love*, a musical that ran for three sold-out months at The Albany in Deptford. We had been approached by writer John Turner with a script; it seemed like a great idea. It came completely out of the blue and woke the sleeping giants in us both. The experience of having our songs sung by other people and watching them weave a story from one to the next was inspiring. The show had a weak plot but it was a happy one, unlike most of my songs. And being there backstage each day was incredible. I was Andrew Lloyd Webber on Deptford High Street. The shows kept me from the darkness that was falling slowly about me. The reviews were really positive and the cast, including Alison Limerick and Danny John Jules, were beside themselves. A review from one paper said, 'Tim Rice, who knows a thing or two about musicals, was in the audience the night I went, checking out the competition. He will not be the only writer looking over his shoulder at a theatrical career blossoming in this unlikely corner of London's dockland'. I wish it had travelled up to the West End; maybe it was too scruffy for the larger theatres. Most of the songs came from the *East Side Story* album so there was a thread there, one I had not seen. Now it makes sense to me, there is a narrative within the songs on that album and on stage it seems to work.

One night at an after-show party, Glenn walked down the stairs to dance with Pam the wardrobe lady. I had not seen Glenn want to dance since the early Seventies. I watched from above and knew I wouldn't see him again for some time. She was attractive and danced like she was in a Sixties hippy movie. They looked entwined in boogie wonderland. It was awkward for me as I was not in her good books. At one of the rehearsals she'd laid into me for supposedly being sexist when I'd asked her if she'd mind sewing a button back onto my jacket for me. 'What the fuck are you asking me to do that for?' she yelled at me, in front of everyone. 'That's not a woman's job. You should be able to do it yourself, you're a grown man!' It was a fair point – even though it was delivered in such a horrible way. With wonky buttons on my tweed jacket I did try to like her but she always seemed to pour her words over me like they were hot tar; all it needed was for me to add the feathers, and I was good at that.

Pam and Glenn became inseparable; they were a really, really tight couple. I could not get a cigarette paper between them. And part of me wanted to applaud that but there was something suspicious about it for me. I just didn't trust Pam because she wasn't the sort of person I could warm to – she seemed cold and wouldn't engage me in conversation unless it was something to do with her or Glenn. So I felt excluded. It was a wedge between us, particularly when I discovered he'd started taking heavier drugs. I was scared for Glenn. One day I picked him up in my car and he said, 'I'm getting married to Pam. Will you be my best man?' I felt as though I was picking up a red-hot poker. What could I say? This was somebody I dearly loved – despite our differences – and I didn't feel I could say no, even though I knew I wouldn't do a good job or be able to come up with a convincing speech. I'm ashamed to say that at the wedding I simply couldn't think of anything to say, so I gathered the courage to get up on a table in the back garden of Glenn's house, said a few words and left as quickly as I could. Not very nice of me or supportive but I was trying to understand the situation from a very lonely place. They drifted from my radar for several months and even went to India, coming home with, of course, a sitar. I was drifting too, but I never got as far as inside my head which was a bit like India at the time.

Another manager came and went – a very mature Shep Gordon, complete with a different Hawaiian shirt for every day of the year. He had hoped to sign Squeeze but settled for Difford and Tilbrook as we both thought we should change our identity and respect the past. Glenn was very careful to make sure that we didn't use the name Squeeze without the primary members being present in the line-up. Shep was good friends with Gerry Moss – the 'M' in A&M – and for a while he and the dangling carrot of his impeccable connections re-energised us. His Muttley laugh was infectious and his humour uplifting, and I really liked his company even if he did spend most of his time out in LA or Hawaii.

With Shep guiding us, we recorded the *Difford & Tilbrook* album with ex-Bowie producer Tony Visconti. It was like being in a school play – I felt shy and out of place all the time. The songs had little power and never tickled my scales in the way Squeeze did. We were strange fish. Glenn grew his hair into a long, flowing mane and I grew an appetite for cocaine. The two of us had drifted apart and didn't speak a word to each other during the entire recording of the album – we very rarely even threw each other a glance. Glenn would wander in and out, and I developed an uncanny knack of disappearing just before he turned up. Tony Visconti thought he was signing up to record the new Lennon and McCartney, but that was not to be and it was frustrating for everyone.

Musically Glenn did a masterful job of arranging those songs, because they were complicated. 'Love's Crashing Waves' was about as commercial as we got on the whole album. And that pissed everybody off, particularly Shep, who wanted us to be as big as Squeeze. Despite this, off the back of this period Glenn and I signed a healthy publishing deal with Steve Lewis and a young Richard Branson at Virgin. I remember meeting Richard; he appeared nervous, and eye contact was not something he seemed to do. I chased his face around the room but he kept hiding from me. Maybe it was the amount of money he was about to give us. The album in retrospect has some genius moments: 'Hope Fell Down' and 'On My Mind Tonight' are musically so sublime. Lyrically I think I might have been coasting but I'm proud of what I coasted with. The album is a rare treat for our fans, it's always so hard to find online or in record shops. Debbie Bishop, who starred in our musical at The Albany, sang some lovely parts on the record, a great contrast to Glenn's voice, and mine.

With money in the bank it was time for Cindy and me to move back to London, and we moved from Toys Hill and bought a nice big house on Lee Terrace, on the edge of Blackheath Village. My parents were well impressed with me: I was in a posh house on four floors with hundreds of windows to clean. The country had been a field too far for Cindy, and she'd felt isolated when I was away working or up in London taking meetings. The move back was good for her. I also treated myself to a jaw-droppingly cool black Jaguar MK11, hand-built by a company in Coventry called Vicarage Cars. It was my pride and joy. Sadly the taxman came and the car had to be sold to pay the bill, but just for a few months I was that rock star with a rock-star car in his garage. Glenn and Pam bought a massive house in Blackheath not far from ours. They had two huge black poodles and lived a surreal, almost prog-rock lifestyle.

At that time, I was doing everything I could to look after myself and not be controlled by Pam. Imagine my disbelief when I turned up for a video shoot one day to discover she'd made all the clothes. She thought we'd look good in eighteenth-century frock coats. It was curtains for me. I went to see my designer friend Scott Crolla, and he and I went to Heal's, where we bought some fabric and he made me a suit. It really was curtains – nice flowers on a bright-blue background. Splendid. It must have hurt Glenn's feelings that I wasn't signing up to what his wife was going out of her way to do, but I didn't have the ability to communicate my feelings at the time. I just went into lockdown. I was still smarting from Pam's request that I send her all my new lyrics so she could edit them before passing them on to Glenn. I felt suffocated by her needs. It was not her fault, it was a time and place that invited bad behaviour and misunderstanding. I often wonder which direction our career might have taken had Pam not come along.

The record company got us on *French and Saunders* with the song 'Wagon Train'. It was a comedy show and uncomfortably I think we fitted right in with this rather weak song. It opened up a few doors and we were asked to write theme tunes for two TV shows, *Father's Day*, which we got Paul Young to sing and *Girls on Top*. We were sort of in demand.

Looking back, 1982, 1983 and 1984 were odd years that were muffled by introspective soul-searching. We were serious writers with serious faces, but we were losing our connection as people. In New York, while touring, we went to hang out with The Sugarhill Gang at their studio in New Jersey; this was one of Shep's ideas to get us involved with the upcoming East Coast hip-hop scene. Doug Wimbish and Skip McDonald played bass and drums like I'd never heard, and being in the studio with them was a powerful experience and such a great twist to our journey. We cut a few songs and made good friends with Eric 'ET' Thorngren, the studio engineer. We could have made an album there and turned a corner that might have taken us into a different league. But that never happened, instead we went on tour with a bunch of white, middle-class session musicians and painted ourselves into a very white-sounding corner. Imagine if we had made a record at Sugar Hill; it would have been so cool for us and I always feel robbed that it never happened. The good news was that ET helped finish off our album when Tony's mixes were very sadly rejected by the record company. He flew over to London and patched it up in the best way possible. ET and I hung out together and became close friends. He loved my Morris Traveller and called it a Tudor car because of its woodwork.

I had a soft spot for Shep, but Glenn and he didn't always see eye to eye. Pam got in the way. I'm sure she meant well, but her over-protection and fussing about the running of the band's affairs led Shep to cup his hands and say goodbye. Shep never commissioned our work. I have always respected him for that and for many other personal reasons too. Managers came and went in our lives, and he was one of the good guys.

LEE TERRACE

After the darkness of the *Difford & Tilbrook* album and the tender high of the musical *Labelled with Love*, I was lounging about in an empty field of inspiration. Early in 1984, Jools called Glenn and invited us both to play a charity event with him and Gilson in the Northover pub in Catford, where it had all begun ten years earlier. We agreed to this one-off and without any rehearsals played a blinding show in front of a packed pub – and Miles who was there with Jools. The magic on stage was so amazing, like old times; the electricity of our songs oscillating between these great musicians was food for thought.

We all called each other the next day to see if we could get back together. Jools, despite his new-found astronomical fame from *The Tube*, was onside, but only if Miles could come back as our manager. Miles got in touch and said, 'Look, I can make you a great deal with the record company if you're serious about going back out on the road. I can get you a merchandise deal and an uplift on your deal at A&M.' For me, it was the devil we knew. It was difficult to be around Miles at first but his John Denver smile soon had us all back in his rocky mountain ways. The Police had sold millions of albums so his star was at its highest, and he could use this to open more doors for us. It sounded good to me.

Squeeze were back. The dynamic, however, was odd. Gilson had sobered up and at first I couldn't get on with his new way of life, despite being full of admiration for him. Jools was always on the telly; his profile was enormous, thanks to being on Channel 4 each week. For some reason things didn't click with John, so we asked Keith Wilkinson, who'd played on the *Difford & Tilbrook* album, to join the band. He was a tender and precise bass player, and a kind person to tour with, but Miles thought his baldness was an issue and tried to get him to wear a hat. Not so kind. Miles chewed strips of paper that he constantly pulled from notebooks, and somehow the flame was relit.

Glenn sent me the first set of demos in the post. There were some real gems in there, 'No Place Like Home' being one of them. The tape contained re-workings of some songs we'd recorded before, but the newer stuff sounded inviting. It was a progression from the lonely Difford and Tilbrook days, but at the time I thought only by a few degrees. For my part I think lyrically I was not firing on all cylinders and I'm sure that didn't help Glenn find new inspiration to work with. However, the songs were good enough to open the door into our first album in a few all-at-sea years. I was writing about the tragedy of exhausted home life and the old chestnut alcohol and its effects. The domestic masterpiece on the record was 'King George Street' with more lyrics and chords than you could shake a stick at, it was brilliant. It's not one that gets many call-outs from the audience which is just as well, it's a fistful of chords. We met up with record producer Laurie Latham, who'd recorded *New Boots and Panties!!* with Ian Dury and the Blockheads and who was keen to work with us on a new album. He'd scored tax-exile status, though, which meant we had to work outside of the UK – so we went to Brussels. Dog shit on the pavements, nouvelle cuisine on the plates and cocaine in my pocket; it was an inspired choice. Prince's 'Paisley Park' was on constant play on my Walkman; life seemed oddly optimistic. Brussels was a beautiful city to walk around (if you could avoid the dog shit), but there was no real nightlife – just the studio. The best place to eat was the Indian Pont De Indes, I think I went there most nights for a curry, a table for one in the corner.

We recorded there for about a month, with Jools flying in and out of Newcastle, where he was shooting *The Tube*. He was the big young TV face of the time and we had to share him, which was fine. At least for me. But the recording dragged on. Laurie was slow at making things happen – he pored over the sounds endlessly. Laurie and I got on really well, and we once hired a Mercedes to nip down to Switzerland to see Paul Young (who he had produced) play. With some bat food in my pocket and plenty of red wine, we raced across Germany, stayed one night and raced back the next day. It was so mad but fun. I loved to drive, and to drive fast, but I excelled on that occasion with the added weight of a nasty Swiss hangover.

Miles was asked by Bob Geldof to contribute bands to Live Aid, the biggest stage ever, and he chose to put Adam and the Ants up for one of the opening slots. We were dumbfounded that we hadn't been asked, and when we watched the event on TV, that was all we could concentrate on. Sometimes Glenn was hard to reach but I must have been impossible. We were at different places together. I was isolating and deeply out of touch with my marriage back at home, where I never seemed to spend any time, and things

were rapidly falling apart. Despite all that, Cosi Fan Tutti Frutti is a
good album with some very fine moments, 'I'll Never Go Drinking
Again' being one of them, written after some nasty hangovers. It's
the most dated of our records, though; it sounds very much of its
time. With hindsight, it was a stepping stone to the album that
followed. Maybe we'd gone into the studio too soon.

We toured when the album came out and poor old Jools had to
constantly fly in and out on Concorde; his head was all over the
place. Pam also came on tour with us and immediately annoyed
Robin, the bus driver, by turning up with hundreds of hat boxes she
insisted he find space for. I remember her falling out of her bunk
one morning, and hearing the 'oof' as she hit the floor. A curtain
opened on the bunk across from me. It was Jools. We looked at each
other, closed our curtains and went back to sleep. Gilson put a copy
of the Alcoholics Anonymous Big Book in my bunk one morning. I
was interested, but not enough to start reading it or stop drinking,
though I was secretly inspired. Gilson was clean and serene and
wonderful to be on the road with. How times had changed.

My house on Lee Terrace at the edge of Blackheath Village
became a real party house. On one occasion the actor Keith Allen
arrived completely naked with his girlfriend to play endless board
games and drink wine by the caseload with me and Cindy. It was a
nutty night, and I remember wearing an all-in-one velvet romper
suit that was modelled on one Churchill once owned – I had two,
one in blue and one in green. It was high times and money wasn't
an issue, so getting Scott Crolla to make my clothes seemed as
normal as ordering Jaguars from eager salesmen. I wasn't having
much luck with Jaguars, though. One blew up on the M6, but as
Jools was with me, the AA were only too happy to tow us all the

way to the stage door for our next gig. It was replaced by a new model, which also broke down. I wasn't far behind.

At the end of 1985, I went to see my mum one Sunday and she had a brown mole on the side of her head. She said it was nothing to worry about, but she had tears in her eyes. I spoke with my brothers, who were also concerned. Mum was reluctant to go to the doctor. We managed to get her to see one eventually, when the mole had got much larger, and he sent her to Guy's Hospital for a check-up. The results came back: she had cancer. We felt the stunned silence of the word as it entered the family vocabulary. It was like a shark that chases you around in shallow water until you're forced to give in to it. Mum cried, and as her hair started falling out from the chemotherapy, she cried some more – a lot more as she saw her beauty fade away, melting like ice on a spring morning.

Cancer mixed with agoraphobia, brandy, sleeping tablets and anti-depressants made her life too difficult to handle. She was taking a tray of pills each day, and she did little but sit by the fire and pray, sip from her glass or sleep. It was shocking to watch, but I dulled the pain by drinking and managed the grief with regular visits to the local pub with Jools's dad, who had become a close friend. On the last Mother's Day of her life, I visited her with my very good friend Barny after being in the pub for most of the day. 'Oh God, it's Mother's Day!' I remember saying as we came over the heath. I went into the off-licence and bought her some cherry brandy – God knows why. I knew she wouldn't like it. By the time we got to the corner of the street, the bottle was three-quarters empty. She laughed and we finished off the rest around the chair that had become her throne and soapbox.

With a few whiskies she was lucid and funny with it. She did drift in and out of herself, but she managed as best she could with the inevitability of cancer. She took to her bed from time to time and visits to see her revealed a scared and retreating mother figure; this woman who had once held me in her arms, baked cakes and prayed for me with such emotional strength. In December, when she went into Greenwich Hospital for another check-up, my dad, my brothers and I gathered to have words with the doctor. Through the glass we could see Mum sitting upright in bed. He told us she had about two months to live. He then left us to talk to her about it and decide what we should do. Nothing. There was nothing we could do. She was leaving us and we were unequipped to deal with it. I flew to New York for a TV show that night, but when I tried to board the plane, I was so drunk I cried and fell over. The pilot came to talk to me, and in the end he up-graded me to first class. I sat next to a nun and fell asleep on her shoulder. Ever since then, flying has been a major issue for me.

That Christmas was Mum's last. I went into the intensive-care room feeling numb and hungover. We were a long way from the cold stones of the Giant's Causeway and prayers in the sea breezes. She was praying, though, and I remember her saying prayers for me, for my kids, for everyone except herself. I left and sat in a waiting room, and a few hours later my brother and father appeared to tell me she'd gone. It was a cold moment. The clock stops when a parent dies and you wonder where on earth time has gone and why you've been robbed of their love. Suspended in shock, we fell to our emotional knees.

No more jelly cubes, no cake, no mother's love. Just the wonderful memories. She died on New Year's Eve and we buried her on her birthday – 10 January 1986. It was a big funeral with lots of policemen there, loads of people from the church, and friends from far and wide – even Mum's sister from Ireland, who could hardly walk due to multiple sclerosis. It was cold and I was trapped inside my head and my heart, but my brothers and my father held me and loved me. It was so grim saying goodbye, yet that's what we do until it's our turn to be lowered into the ground.

The wake was at my house – a home she loved so much yet seldom came to. With tears in my eyes, I raised many glasses of vintage brandy from Berry Bros & Rudd. I was the pop star with too much money; she'd have been proud of me tipping them back. Dad soaked up the compliments and looked totally lost for the first time in his life; the war was over and the cancer had won. He looked defeated, like we all did. He tore into some old jokes and sang a little on his way out of the door, back to the house in which he had lived with the girl of his dreams for all those years. He loved to be alone, but this was different.

My connection with Mum is a sum of many parts – a bit of this, that and the other. A bit of the Irish, too. When I pick my nose, I think of her. When I laugh, I laugh like her. When I worry, I worry like her. She'll be part of me forever. I miss my mum. It would be so great to go around and see her; to smell her roses and introduce her to my beautiful wife Louise, the love of my life, and all the children. But it's so long ago, I can hardly even access the feelings of her death. I was numb then as I am now. Not because I didn't love her, but because time has iced over each image of her – just like the icing on one of her cakes.

A few months after the funeral, Dad's next-door neighbour Mrs Jones started to invite him in for his tea; her husband had also passed away recently. The two of them became very close and my mother would have been turning in her grave with jealousy, but she had no reason to, Mrs Jones was just being a good neighbour and Dad was happy to accept her company. I'm sure it never went any further than tea and a read of the paper over a few glasses of sweet white wine.

After a month or two it was time to get back in the studio, this time to record *Babylon and On*, which we started working on in late 1986. It took months to record and cost us a fortune. Glenn and I wrote together in the same room for the first time and 'Hourglass' was the result. Oddly I think that was Pam's idea. We had a lot of fun writing it, but it didn't feel very natural. It was like being on a first date, slightly awkward at first, but then we were in with the tongues. My favourite song on the album is 'Tough Love' because it tells the story of someone with a drinking problem who's in a volatile relationship at home. It was a reflection on the reality I found myself in. Glenn and I sang it together in our trademark octave-apart vocal, like we had all those years ago on 'Take Me I'm Yours'. It's a sound like no other.

There was yin with our yang. ET Thorngren, who Glenn and I had met in New York at Sugarhill, made the album sound fresh and original by keeping things as simple as possible. We got on really well together, though I never knew how he managed to drink so much alcohol and smoke so much pot while still mixing the songs with such clarity. He was a dead ringer for Jack Nicholson, and when he burst into a sweat sometimes he would have the ability to scare you with his goofy smile. He was full of love and so brilliant at his work.

It was a time of excess. I spent my way out of the emotional darkness by prising open some strange and wonderful personality malfunctions. It was pretty good fun. We had run up bills of about £100,000, but it didn't sound like it. We filmed three huge-budget videos for the album, and even managed to win an award for the 'Hourglass' one. That video, a two-day shoot in a studio on the Thames, directed by Ade Edmondson from *The Young Ones*, with a large helping hand from Jools, was amazing. We dressed as babies, we dressed as lords and had a bizarrely built set realised mostly by Jools. The cost was enormous, one we would never repeat again. It was great fun playing around on set and being lads for the first time in many years; everyone seemed at home and at ease with being back in the band. I thought it would last forever. A follow-up video for *Trust Me to Open My Mouth* was shot on the Old Kent Road in a warehouse. A huge mouth had been erected, and we played inside. The song lacked the chart success of 'Hourglass' but it provided another great big moment of happiness as we danced around giant tonsils.

MTV was the thing to be on and we were on it all the time, along with Sting and Dire Straits, Duran Duran and the other all-male bands that wore make-up. On the screen we had none of the seriousness of some of our contemporaries – thankfully. Our childish take on life served us well and kept us apart from the pouting pencil-thin bands that filled the MTV screens across the world with their well-tailored collars sticking up.

'Hourglass' was a hit in America and it charted in the UK too, and we were soon back out on tour. In the States, we sold out Madison Square Garden twice and did huge arena shows with all the trimmings. We flew out to the US on Concorde with a *Mail on Sunday* journalist, David Thomas, to show him and the UK how big we were in America. We had a New York radio station invite fans out to JFK airport to meet us – with the carrot of them getting a mini CD and a one-off single available only on that day. We landed giddy with free champagne and BA gifts, and as the doors opened we steeled ourselves for the forthcoming Beatles moment on the tarmac. But when we looked outside, there were only about twenty people milling around in the cold. How we laughed. We were rushed off in a limo to the hotel for a stiff lie-down.

Touring then was in plush hotels; we had fake names on check-in, nice food – we'd discovered sushi – smart tour buses with big screens, good-looking fans with long legs, and comfortable seats on aeroplanes. America was all about limos and trucks, and backstage knees-ups. The stages were bigger than we were used to, so we asked our crew to help us fill the blank spaces. Our tour manager also worked for U2, which was how we ended up with a set that had steps on each side of the stage, leading to a walkway that crossed over Gilson's drum kit like a bridge. It worked fine for Bono to race up and down these during U2's long instrumentals, but for Glenn and me it was ridiculous. I ran up the stairs for the first time during 'Pulling Mussels (from the Shell)' and by the time I got to the top, I was already due back at the microphone to sing the chorus. I was out of breath, hungover and lacking in any stadium-rock nous. Glenn tried it once and also got stuck during a solo.

Though it was wonderful playing those huge venues, I felt a bit embarrassed most of the time. On big stages, road crews have often made the mistake of setting Squeeze up wide apart, but we're not that kind of band. We need to be close together – like

The Beatles at Shea Stadium. Touring was getting out of control again and I began to feel the strain. I was the distant one, still finding it hard to communicate my feelings in a manageable way. Our tour manager made us come to his hotel room in LA; he sat us down and asked us both to speak our minds. He was metaphorically bashing our heads together, but nothing much was being said, and within the hour I was back up on the roof in the pool with a cold beer. It was painful, yet on stage I'm not sure anyone would notice the brick wall that I had erected between us. I never crossed over to his side of the stage. Roger Waters had nothing on me when it came to building walls. I feel so sorry that we never got to share those touring moments from a healthy place. We missed each other from my inability to come out of a self-imposed sanctuary.

Being in New York at this time was a cocktail of very late nights and heavy heads in the morning. The Limelight club was my den of iniquity and often I found myself behind a red velvet rope at the end of the club with other celebs of the time: Daryl Hall, John Oates and other bods with big hair. One night the guitarist from Def Leppard joined me for a beverage. He had his arm in plaster, so I asked him if he had played a minor chord. He didn't see the funny side of my off-the-cuff quip and left me to my laughter. Other nights I danced like Woody Allen on the dance floor chatting up New York ladies, none of whom took the slightest bit of notice of my over-engaged swinging of the hips. Their loss. New York was limos and record company visits, club nights and bigger stages like Meadowlands, a massive venue for Squeeze. I was swanning about with an American Express card, a nice suit and a record on MTV.

Back in London after the tour I was asked to help organise Sport Aid on Blackheath, a fun run inspired by Bob Geldof. It was nice to be asked but I was welded to my stool in the pub most nights and was not a natural runner. I did some small preparations, I got some nice trainers, and headed out onto the heath. On the big day Jools fired the starting gun and off I went with about 10,000 runners behind me. The route took us through Greenwich Park to the *Cutty Sark*, where Simon Le Bon's catamaran *Drum* would meet us at the jetty. I was told there would be a big photo of us all on the deck. Bob, Simon, Paul Young, Sting and others. However, *Drum* pulled away before I could get my foot off the jetty. My foot starred on the front page of the *Daily Mirror* the next day just out of shot. The best bit of the run was getting a lift on a friend's motorcycle down through the park.

Squeeze supported U2 at Croke Park in Dublin. It was one of the most exciting shows I've ever played at – like being back at the Charlton Athletic football ground in 1973, watching The Who. Thousands of people were there, and so many of them sang along to our songs, especially 'Labelled with Love', which is a pub sing-along favourite over in Ireland. U2 blew us away, though. They knew how to fill large stages; we never looked comfortable in such a setting.

I was big on cocaine and hung out with all the right people on tour; the tour managers who carried and the dealers who came to our hotel rooms. One of these, called Gig, was tall and had a runny nose; he would treat me to lines of cocaine longer than most coffee-table tops. I would shake and feel good for about an hour, then fade fast only to be propped up by vodka and red wine. It went around in a circle day after day. We also had a tour manager called James Sliman who blow-dried his hair. I thought it was weird at the time. I loved James: he knew everyone and where to go and be seen. His voice was deep like a native New Yorker from a Damon Runyon story.

We were back on tour, back in the charts and back in debt with the record company. The result was the follow-up album *Frank*, which came out in 1989. It had to be made on a tighter budget than we were used to, so we went into a studio on the Old Kent Road called The Chocolate Factory. It was funky and inexpensive; it had ants crawling from the faders on the mixing desk. ET was dumbfounded by this and complained all the time. Glenn argued that by saving money we would benefit in the long run – and with the cash we saved, he started to build his own studio in Blackheath, which was a smart move. No more expensive sessions in New York or London, and videos with silly budgets. It was time to tighten the old belt. Except that I had no belt to tighten. I was broke. My marriage to Cindy was over. I was away, she was a single mother at home alone; we didn't talk, we argued. We'd moved from the big house on Lee Terrace to the White House in Kidbrooke. A new house, but the same old feelings and resentments. Whenever I came home, there'd be conflict because Cindy would be lonely and I'd be high from being on tour. We'd paper over the cracks with parties, where in my view we'd become competitive with our drinking, but generally I wanted to recuperate.

Cindy and I were very close when we met, but by the end we went off in different directions. Natalie and Riley were such great kids and I loved playing with them and being there when I could; they lit up my life and I was so proud to be a father. But I found it difficult to get my head around fatherhood when I was always about to be whisked away on tour. Home was very much a place to put down your bags, fill the bath with children, pack and then leave again. It was a warm place and I think the kids had fun growing up in the houses we tried hard to keep happy for them. I remember leaving and seeing them at a window on the first-floor landing that looked out onto the road. I sat in my car and cried as they waved with such bright rosy faces. They had no idea what was going to happen, and neither did I.

Divorce from Cindy made me a shard of my former self. In court the judge deemed that because the singles album had sold so well, my income would always be roughly the same. He never saw the sales of *Difford & Tilbrook*, a very different picture. On the steps of the court by St Paul's I broke down, in my head singing 'Feed the Birds', in reality on my way to the bankruptcy courts next door. A tax officer present at my hearing asked for my autograph. I was twisted in knots. Divorce can be brutal. It wasn't anyone's fault. It's very difficult to be the partner of a musician – it's like being married to a submariner. There's very little time to have a relationship in a meaningful way and when I did come up to surface I was lost inside my own head.

After the split from Cindy, I went seamlessly from one relationship to the next. Heidi was a wardrobe mistress on the *Babylon and On* tour, and when I'd first met her I hadn't fancied her at all. I thought she was hard work and not at all friendly; in any case, I thought she was seeing one of the crew. But one night in Philadelphia, reeling from the final death knell of my marriage, I got so drunk that I ended up in a swimming pool with two beautiful women and a large bottle of Vodka. Heidi pulled me out, took me upstairs, brushed my teeth and put me to bed. One minute I was Jon Bon Jovi, the next I was Eric Sykes. Heidi was twenty-one and lived in Chiswick with her mum. Her father she never saw; he lived in Essex. I met him twice. He was a keen drinker and cigar smoker, and he gripped my hand so hard when shaking it that my ring cut into my finger. I never liked him very much. Her mother was fun; she balanced out our disagreements and floated between us sweetly. I really liked her. Our early courting days were spent mostly on two tour buses, she on the crew bus and me on the band bus. We got to see each other at the shows at least. Back in the UK we never had time to court in the old-fashioned sense, we just moved right in together to my flat in Wapping above the River Thames. We had amazing views of Tower Bridge to one side and to the other a building site that would become Canary Wharf.

Frank was a fun album to record, and the songs were more earthy and more like the Squeeze of 1979. ET Thorngren saw to that. Glenn pushed me to sing more, so I bagged myself two songs – 'Love Circles' and 'Slaughtered, Gutted and Heartbroken'. It had long been an issue for me to sing on the tracks. Glenn was the best person for the job, the storyteller; yet he'd always been a great advocate for my singing. It gave him a breathing space on stage, but I had little confidence and always felt in his shadow. The way he writes is so structured melodically and it's difficult to sing. The tunes are written for him and mostly him alone. The high point of the recording for me was how Jools played the piano; he really became part of the band again, even though he was still on TV duties from time to time, and I felt like we were making music together as one. One of my fondest memories of the album was the sleeve. Our art director Rob O'Connor wanted to put a drawing of Frank Bough on the front cover, but the art department at the record company could not see why. There was a lot of scratching of heads. We ended up with a tortoise on the cover. We loved it and thought Rob was a genius, which he is. The record company sighed deeply into their gin and tonics. I love the album. It's so honest and was refreshing after a few years of much knob-twiddling production.

Glenn and I get on well during promotional tours, which can be gruelling. We seemed to bond in interviews while talking up our songs and our band. Some of the tours around the *Frank* album meant flying every day to different cities in America. A morning radio, an afternoon of press and more radio on drive-time. Glenn supported my tiredness and my fear of flying in a very patient way. To get through the flying I would drink vodka for breakfast just to get on the plane. The promotion for the *Frank* album was the most exhausting I have known. Glenn is a master at being positive and often leads the conversation. People tend to ask Glenn questions before they come to me. It must be my face. He handles the property of conversation better than me, although we share in the spoils of self-congratulation like pros. Playing songs in this situation drives me nuts sometimes, early morning radio being the worst. Poor Glenn has to sing for his breakfast, and I strum away in support. I'm not that good before midday at the best of times. Never the lark, more of an owl.

Frank was followed by a live album – *A Round and a Bout* – in 1990. It was recorded in Newcastle, which was now Jools's second home. But it wasn't long before Jools left the band again for more

TV, and his big band albums and tours that followed. Glenn was livid with him for leaving the band again. I didn't see it coming, but was respectful of his needs to plough his own fields. After all, his musical landscape was yielding a very nice crop of its own. He wanted to concentrate on his solo career again and didn't need to be in Glenn's shadow or mine, and I totally understood how he felt. Naturally, I was sad to see him leave. His parting shot was an inspired piano solo on 'Peyton Place', a one-take, breathless piece of playing. It's pure genius.

Heidi fell pregnant very quickly and I was beaming with pride, yet nervous about becoming a father again. I planned to tell Natalie and Riley over a Chinese meal. I was sweating and trying to time the whole thing right. I did not want to upset them or make them feel awkward around a new branch on the family tree. I stumbled my words out just as the main meals arrived at the table. Nat was beaming with smiles and Riley wanted to know if he could eat the ornamental carrot.

Even more work fell into the band's laps; a summer of shows at universities came into the calendar, easy shows to do and fun. We were playing a show at an Oxford college ball, supporting the band Imagination and off to one side was a pit for mud wrestling. A typical night out for Oxford wallahs. Don Snow was back in the band on keyboards, but he had changed his name; this time he was called Jonn Savannah. It was an interesting show: a May ball, everyone swanning around in ball gowns, the men in dickie bows. At the sound check, Jonn stayed behind while the band went to catering, the most important part of any show. Glenn had kindly asked him to take a guitar solo in a new song on stage that night. At the point at which this happened, all the lights swivelled around to illuminate Jonn in mid solo, face grimacing, with the notes being eagerly ripped from the fretboard. My jaw dropped. I took my hat off to him for missing a great bit of catering to have the lighting guy work on his new routine.

My phone went as I was hanging around backstage after the show. Déjà vu. Heidi was in labour and on her way to hospital. I jumped in the car with a six-pack and a bottle of wine, and hurtled down the motorway to her bedside at the Ashford hospital. By the time I got there, things had calmed down and she asked me to go home and come back the next day. I headed back the following morning a little the worse for wear, and at 2.30 in the afternoon was rewarded with the wonderful sight of my new daughter Grace. I was beside myself. She was angelic and made me so proud. In the corner of the room was my shortwave radio. I could hear the gentle sounds of Wayne Shorter playing the song 'Misty For Me', a heavenly backdrop for the birth of my daughter.

Home now was a farmhouse in Sussex, one I could ill afford. I was living beyond my means. Within a year it was back on the market and this time I was seeking rented accommodation. I found the perfect place, Old House Farm, near Rye; it was huge and cheap to rent. A rare bit of luck, you might say. Six bedrooms, outbuildings and 650 acres of land. It needed work, and Heidi did not shy away from that. It was £600 a month. Imagine. Natalie and Riley came at weekends to enjoy the countryside, the fields I'd put myself out to graze in to get away from my past and the sadness of a broken marriage.

Our neighbours in Sussex were Paul and Linda McCartney, and ever since we'd moved in I'd been concocting plans to pop over to borrow a cup of sugar. Then one morning Linda invited us over for brunch. We took Grace with us, and Paul was very gentle with her – even dancing with her at one point. He played us a new song, 'Real Love', that he and the remaining Beatles had recorded with Jeff Lynne over an old John Lennon demo, and it sounded amazing. Then we sat down to a meal of vegetarian sausages at their small kitchen table. I really liked Linda. She even suggested that Paul and I should sit down together and write some songs, but Paul was more guarded about the idea and the moment passed. We stayed friends all the time we lived near Rye, and got together many times until Linda passed away, which was heartbreaking.

Despite my money problems and the fact that my drinking and drug-taking was spiralling out of control, being in Sussex felt good to me. It was my home; it was where I felt at ease. But *Frank* had confused the record company – there was no 'Hourglass' to send to radio, no hits or videos for TV, and it sounded slightly flat. So we were dropped. We'd been back together for five years, we'd had another good crack of the whip, made some money on the road, broken MTV, broken a record company and were about to break another.

Miles got us a deal with Warner in LA, who at the time seemed excited to have signed us. A lot of record-industry people in the US have a soft spot for Squeeze, as we're the absolute antithesis of American music. They see us as being a bit like The Kinks – a picture-postcard version of Englishness. Lenny Waronker, the label's president, called us personally to ask us to come to the States to record. And producer Tony Berg, who'd worked with Public Image Ltd, flew over to London to hear the new songs we'd written. I liked him immediately. He looked like Cliff Richard from the side, he played guitar incredibly well and was an all-round nice chap. At Warner's request, the band flew to LA to record at Tony's house. I didn't want to go. There was too much to leave behind, and I was enjoying, if that's the right word, my drinking.

When the band decamped to LA, I didn't deal with it well. We moved into a rented house in Hollywood, and after the first night, I moved out. I wanted to be alone. The idea of being in a house with the band terrified me at that point. I couldn't contemplate the idea of partying with other people; I wanted to do that on my own. I was at the end of my drinking and drug-taking days, and there was no let-up. I'd start on Indian lager (much stronger than the American brands) in the afternoon, then move on to vodka and tequila, and finish early in the morning. There was no moderation with cocaine either. Whenever it ran out, I could get more. I never did more than a gram a day, but that combined with the drinking made things mental.

I moved into a small apartment and the rest of the band stayed put. Glenn was very upset about this, but because of my state of mind I'd no idea how he or anyone else was feeling. I didn't really know how I was feeling either. He saw the album as a new beginning, but because of our lack of communication, nothing was ever said. I wanted to be at home, but I also wanted to record the album. I was no good to anybody. My apartment became a den and the curtains were drawn most of the time. It was my bat cave. Back in the UK Rob Dickens, the head of Warner, very helpfully wrote to his American counterpart warning him they had made a massive mistake signing Squeeze: we were washed up, he said. I met him in a lift one afternoon. He stood by his word which I guess shows how much he cared about our music. We ploughed on regardless.

In a break in the busy recording diary, I flew home. Maxine and I had drifted in and out of each other's lives over the years, but each time I saw her my heart was lifted. In 1990, that same heart broke when I heard she had cancer. She was so young. It was so wrong. I went to see her in hospital, and there she lay with this horrible disease that had taken her face and turned its palette into one of smears and dark colours. We were all so shocked. She came out of hospital some weeks later and went to a retreat in Spain, where she did some focusing work on the cancer, determined not to be beaten by it. She was strong and that has always inspired me.

She got better, and then she got worse. I called her and she invited me to Benenden for afternoon tea in the garden. Her face looked bruised but her spirit was glowing. She had her back to the setting sun, and all I could feel was the love I'd first witnessed when we met outside The Three Tuns all those years ago. She drew breath and gave me a gentle lecture about my life. I sat there with my scone and my Earl Grey tea while she told me I should consider some sobriety. She had become worried about my drinking. She told me to spread my wings and try to write songs outside of my partnership with Glenn, which I'd never really thought about. We talked about my relationship with Heidi and how it might have become volatile. In reality we were as bad as each other. I'd fucked up so many things and hidden behind the bottle. Maxine picked it out like a pearl from an oyster. There was no way I could avoid the inevitable. That afternoon my life was turned on its head, and I had plenty to think about on my way back home.

Meanwhile there was a record to make. The recording at Tony Berg's house and at Real World in Bath was sporadic but brilliant. We had no keyboard player at this point, so we trimmed down to a four-piece and we sounded tight. Steve Nieve did come in to play some sublime keyboards on the album, and I hoped he might join the band, but he was on Costello duties. The result, Play, is one of my favourite Squeeze records, with more than a few songs I found utterly mesmerising when I first heard them. I was writing dark, confessional songs, and when I heard Glenn singing them, the hairs would stand up on the back of my neck. 'Letting Go' is one of the best songs Glenn and I have ever written; its chord changes are beautiful and clever. I always feel a deep sadness when I hear the song, it's so attached to a very personal emotion with me. 'The Truth' says everything about how I was feeling then, and it hurts to hear it. And 'Walk a Straight Line' is inspired. Its opening line – 'I need some help' – was me reaching out through a fog of people I knew well but had pushed away to the point where they'd become strangers.

These were dark days indeed. I'd always felt that Glenn and Tony were more than a match for each other, both headstrong and constantly creative. The yin and yang of the recording sometimes felt strained, but I was in the shed at the end of the garden tuned into my Sony shortwave radio, listening to the war in Iraq unfold on the other side of the planet. I was drinking and distancing myself from Glenn and everyone during the recording of the album, and not being very useful. I was fried then refried. I had no real idea what I wanted apart from to go home. I binged on cars and gadgets, and became insolvent again. I couldn't pay my tax bill and things were starting to be repossessed back in the

UK. One night in LA I went over to see Nick Lowe for some light relief; he was in town with his new band Little Village. I loved his company so much. We drank at his hotel bar and laughed for hours, then I attempted to drive back to my place. I could hardly see and drove the wrong way down the freeway before getting lost in a dodgy Latino district. I was then chased by some Mexicans in a car and somehow lost them along a dark road in an industrial estate. I went to bed, woke up and thanked God I was alive. It was a close call.

Most of the *Play* album is pure art; it's as deep as you want to go. It was never pop, never what Warner wanted. The album came out in June 1991, and by August we'd been dropped by the record company. We were not the Squeeze they had signed, and it all went sideways. Despite Miles re-signing us to A&M just a couple of weeks later, we were on a downward spiral. The record company were hungry for a classic Squeeze album, but the best we could offer them was another greatest-hits package. It sold thousands and kept the bank account out of the red for a few more years.

We did a US tour in support of Fleetwood Mac. It was a disaster – no one wanted to see us, and we played to almost empty venues. The Mac were in another world; they kept cancelling shows all over the place, pleading illness, though we all felt it was more to do with cocaine psychosis. Our equipment was in their truck, so we had to just hang around until they felt like playing again. Nice venues and catering, but that was it. As ever when I was away from home, hotel rooms had become safe houses for my dull head and insatiable thirst.

Glenn and Gilson were never on the same sheet of paper; they often fell out over drum patterns and tempo – the usual pulling and pushing between writer and drummer. The two of them rubbed each other up the wrong way, particularly in the second phase of the band. On Glenn's demos, he'd use a drum machine to lay down a very precise rhythm track. He'd play them to the band and Gilson would grumpily say, 'Well you might as well get a fucking drum machine then, if that's what you want. You obviously don't want a human being.' When Gilson did get into technology and started to try to bring it into the band, he fumbled and wasn't very clever with it – it just wasn't his forte. And that used to frustrate Glenn. So he would take over, and that would create more tension. When we played live, I think Gilson would do things on the drums just to wind Glenn up, because he knew he couldn't do anything about it. I'd listen, knowing exactly what he was up to. He'd play a double-bass drum part when there wasn't meant to be one, or he'd put a flam in where there was no flam. You could see him looking daggers at Glenn's back as he was singing. Invisible sparks would fly around the dressing room; it was not a very nice atmosphere. Gilson, however, was the genius behind so many of our songs. His inventive patterns live proudly to this day. I felt for them both, but had no way of expressing my views.

Gilson was lured away to play with Jools's Rhythm & Blues Orchestra, which was a smooth move for him to make. I was sad to see him leave the band, as he'd inspired me to think about things in a different way. He'd sobered up and was a different person from the one that used to scare the shit out of me each night on stage. He was tender and in repair emotionally from the demons in his life. It touched a nerve with me and I'll always thank him for that huge inspiration. I loved Gilson like I had Jools, so when he left the band the sadness rippled deep into the well, the dark well that was almost dry.

REHAB

The first time I remember experiencing high anxiety was when the band were in New York in 1987. We were signing albums in a record store. I'd been up for a few nights on the cocaine and was feeling more than a little worse for wear. My mum had died the year before and I was dealing with my grief via a constant intake of fine wines and white powder. I felt overcome by the number of fans in the room, but I did my best to stay focused until the line of people had trickled down to one or two. Then I legged it to the hotel. I raced up to my room, ordered room service and lay on my bed. The red wine arrived with two chilled beers; it was late afternoon. This was the first time I felt scared because of a hangover.

Since my mum's death, flying had become an issue for me. I had broken down at the gate on a BA flight from London to JFK to do some promotion before another tour and was led gently to one side by the airline staff. The pilot in his crisp white short-sleeved shirt came to see me, reassuring me that the flight would be safe and not too bumpy. He even supplied me with the weather maps. I drank my way across the ocean and back home again.

In 1990 I was flown to Cupertino, California to work on some musical ideas with Apple Computers, a sort of brain-storming event. Sadly my brain was not behaving itself. Each day a group of us would sit around talking about the future, and if Apple could help music expand via the internet. It did, and sadly I missed the boat due to a hefty hangover. I really enjoyed my time there and wished I'd stayed around the table with the other people I met, who later went on to be part of Facebook, Twitter and Apple Music. One morning, while staying at a hotel in San Jose, I got up to watch David Frost interview Elton John about his drinking and new-found sobriety. I sat on the bed in my bathrobe in tears as I saw myself reflected in his every word. I knew I had to change, but I just didn't have the courage to. Back home, I met up with my good friend Barnaby; he'd been into rehab and was a new man. To see him like this was an inspiration, but sadly I still didn't want to stop. He had been in Farm Place, a rehab down in Surrey. I visited him there but thought it was full of Mars-bar chomping alcoholics, which they were. Barnaby and I used to be in each other's pockets when I lived on Crooms Hill. We smoked and drank and stumbled together. I've still got a broken scaphoid bone in my wrist from a drunken fight we had in my flat one night. All harmless fun. The landlady had a cellar full of sherry and we managed to clear a few cases out one weekend and for some reason stuffed the empty bottles up the chimney breast. When I moved out some months later they were all discovered. We went to any lengths to quench our thirst in those days. In the bad old good old days when we were naughty boys we used to visit Will Palin in Devon and be all *Withnail and I* on the moors and in the villages of the north Devon coast. Barny and I enjoyed our dizzy friendship.

A few months later I went down to PROMIS, a rehab centre in Kent. I drove by in my car then drove home again. I went back a week later for an interview, and the counsellor tried to check me in there and then. But I drove home again in denial, hiding behind the fact that Squeeze were about to go on tour. Another few months passed, and this time I went to see a Dr Robert Lefever in London. He recognised my anxiety and the state I was in, and how it needed to be cared for. He said I could benefit from a few weeks in treatment. I sat in my car and wept. Soon afterwards, I had lunch with our former manager David Enthoven, who had sobered up after years on drink and drugs. I sat there with him, talking rubbish and gradually making myself feel worse, until he put his hand on my shoulder and said, 'Come back, Diffy, when you sort yourself out, and we can talk again.' David held his lantern up for me to see the light, but I refused the offer, even though I could feel the penny dropping at an alarming rate.

Squeeze were sliding into a never-ending date sheet of venues that were getting smaller all the time, the songs weren't as engaging as they once were, and lyrically I was drilling down into the deep underbelly of my self-centredness. Being away from home and in a place that made me nervous and scared did me no favours. The drugs gave me panic attacks, I couldn't ride in lifts, and my flying phobia took off. I was thin then fat; up then down. I was drunk then drunker. Nothing had changed in five or six years and I'd pushed Glenn away, possibly the closest person to me. I knew Glenn wasn't happy and I often felt rejected and I felt the rejection had worked both ways. We were like two clouds that came together to create thunder. We'd managed to use our songwriting as a bridge between our often complicated personalities, but there was precious little other communication. At least, that's how it seems to me.

In 1992, a tour came up that began at a Fourth of July fireworks event in Chicago. I scanned the dates with fear. I was in no fit state to go on the road but I knew I had to. I couldn't let everyone down. At home, things were tense. Grace was growing fast and Heidi had banished me to the spare room as my drinking had become too secretive. I must have been a heavy weight to have around the house with my intensive mood swings. A usual evening for me would be to put Grace to bed, sit and watch TV with Heidi till 11 p.m. or so, then wait for her to go upstairs. Once she did, I'd get out a bottle of red wine and start tipping that back, then go to my desk with some cocaine under the pretence of writing. Heidi's father had been an alcoholic, so she knew exactly what she was living with, and once I'd been sent to sleep at the other end of the house, the loneliness and fear collided and I was scared. I felt so depressed but had no idea what to do with it, or what it was. It came and held me with its black sheet, cradled in the breath of stale wine and fags. Her cold shoulder definitely gave me food for thought, which of course now I'm very grateful for.

I packed my suitcase, said goodbye to Heidi and my beautiful daughter Grace, who looked so sweet in her little crib, and left Sussex for London. En route I'd planned to see Riley and Natalie at their mum's house in Greenwich. I had to stop the car on the A21 to be sick at the side of the road. It was as if I had a Norman helmet on my head, it was so painful. I knocked on their door in Greenwich and waited. The door opened and there was Cindy. I walked in and cried in her arms. I was overwhelmed with sadness; I was leaving home again and abandoning my children for the shelter of a few more beers and some American fans.

In my pocket was the number of another good friend, Chris

Briggs. I called him and he called Barnaby. This was how it worked; the sober army were out to get me. In Barnaby's car, going around the roundabout on Blackheath, he called Squeeze's manager John Lay and told him I wouldn't be going to the States with the band, who were at Heathrow, waiting for me. Then he called PROMIS. Two days later and I was in a very different group, with tears rolling down my face – sweet and salty tears of hope and regret. Over the years my drinking had got slowly worse and my inability to communicate was choking all my relationships, including with Heidi. It was growing on me like a beard, and by the time I fell into PROMIS, it was way down to my knees. I could not feel the emptiness because that was all I knew; I could not feel the loneliness because that was exactly how I wanted to be. The darkness was like treacle, I could not move for its attraction and sweet taste; I wanted nothing more than more of the same each day. Chasing the hangover around the room was never much fun, but once I caught up with it I was back on target in the frame for another bullseye of red wine, cocaine and beer.

Every drunk's story is different. There are a few obvious similarities, but each of us builds slowly to our fall. Mine started when I was eighteen years old, and without a day off for good behaviour it slowly ploughed on until I was thirty-eight and on the ropes. My first drink was harmless enough: a few pints at The Sun in the Sands in Blackheath with my brother Les. The taste and the way it made me feel lifted me from my teenage angst and propelled me into being a young man. Within a few years I had to drink, I thought, to get to sleep, and along with the smoke and the crafty drugs I was building into a nice long progressive overture of darkness. On tour I drank at first with everyone else as part of the crowd, the payoff to a good gig, which we always had. Then it took on more of a central role. My whole day would be geared around the brew; it was pivotal that nothing got in its way. Hangover followed sound check followed show followed drink, and then back in my room the secret bottles of booze, wine and sometimes vodka. The cocaine drifted like snow on the mountains of in security that it conjured up on a daily basis, again some of it secretive. It changed my mood, made me even more devious than normal, and destructive.

It was fun at the time, or so I thought. Staying up late on my own was dangerous. I found myself falling into bad habits and making perfectly easy relationships very complicated, especially with people I loved, like Glenn and Cindy, and in the end Heidi too. I stacked up dark clouds above my head that were fed by hours of dedicated drug-taking and wine-glugging. I was not that nice and I'm so sorry that for so long I caused people such deep hurt. Having been there and done that it was now time to understand who I was, and why I had let myself down in such a way. It was not so much the amount of drink and drugs I took, it was more the way they made me feel and how I reacted to them, given that I have always been prone to the darker feelings of the soul. My imagination can lock me in, it can drug me and fold me over. It was time to put my cards on the table, the few I had left. I had become stuffed with sadness, but at last I was being unpacked.

I wasn't allowed a phone call for a week. I couldn't see Heidi for a week. I just stewed. Squeeze toured on until the end of August, and every now and then I would get reports of what was happening: the usual madness, but this time augmented by the addition of Steve Nieve and Pete Thomas, who were devils with good intentions. This is from a local paper that reviewed a show: 'Guitarist-vocalist Glenn Tilbrook popped out onstage first for a solo rendition of "Pulling Mussels (from the Shell)" and then was joined by regular bassist Keith Wilkinson, keyboardist Steve Nieve and drummer Pete Thomas. Notably missing was guitarist and lyricist Chris Difford – the Lennon to Tilbrook's McCartney. Who, in Tilbrook's words, "ate a piece of bad fish".' Not only had I eaten some bad fish, but I was breaking bread with a bunch of people who would change my life for ever – a day at a time. I was sharing a room – with a Japanese diplomat addicted to sleeping tablets and the drummer from a world-famous 1970s rock band – and sharing my feelings. Feelings I'd no idea I had. I was surrounded by like-minded people, and for the first time, I felt loved and understood as an addict. I was safe.

The only communication you could have was from a phone box under the stairs; it would only accept calls in. The first call I got was from David Enthoven; he simply said, 'Got ya!' and laughed loudly down the phone. I fell into his laughter. I'd done the right thing – I knew I had. I'd been feeling guilty about missing the tour, but it soon passed. My career could be put on hold while I sorted myself out, and luckily the band were hugely sympathetic. They wrote to me almost every day from the tour. I was so grateful. They were having fun without me, but I knew I was in the right place. Miles was slipping into the background again, but I was fond of John Lay and happy for him to take a larger role. John handled the whole thing with dignity and understanding.

Rehab was a strict regime. Up at 6.30 a.m. for prayers and readings, breakfast and group therapy. There was a break, then another group before lunch. Afternoons were spent in small groups, then in workshops or psychodramas, which I felt nervous about at first, but which ended up making me inquisitive about myself. Family day was on Sunday. Heidi would come with Grace, or my dad would arrive with my brothers. It was awkward (my dad thought I was in a nuthouse and kept making jokes about straitjackets) and I was pleased when they left so I could get back into the pain and anger groups.

The head counsellor was called Beechy. He was a softly spoken man from Belfast, and was so clever with his workshops. He got people to gently let their feelings be realised, and he cunningly used music and visualisation to open us up. 'I Can't Make You Love Me' by Bonnie Raitt did it for me – it cracked me in two. I was in pieces the day he played it to me while asking how I felt about my family. Psychodrama work is extremely skilled; some people are opened up but can't be put back together again. It scars them. There's a rhythm to it. You go around the room and find someone who's feeling emotional and ready to open up. It's like a Mike Leigh play; there's no script, but you know that in the last twenty minutes you've got to bring the person back and give them affirmation. Often sessions would end with someone lying on the floor with everyone laying hands on them to leave them stronger.

As well as the psychodramas, we had groups that dealt with our various other personal issues. One of the things I had to deal with as an addict was my secrecy. My secret life was incredible, a dizzy out-of-kilter balance of reality intertwined with a furtive imagination. I was ducking and diving between the two. It was put to me that I should let go of my secret life in favour of a more honest relationship with myself. I revealed to the group one afternoon that I had been keeping in contact with a girl I had once met in Boston. We communicated by way of letter-writing and the odd meeting here, there and on various tours. I really liked her; she was calm and wrote to me with such love in dark moments. It was time to let her go. When I next flew to LA, we arranged to meet for lunch. I had made up my mind to say goodbye to her. She beat me to it; she revealed she was getting married. It was over, and we were both free. We have never been back in contact and she remains very firmly in the fairy tale of my past.

One secret down, many more to go. The addict loves a secret, but they can be the death of good friendships and often marriages. It was a tough lesson to learn so early on in sobriety. A secret world provides many things; it fuels the imagination and has me walking a tightrope above the gasping, frustrated people below me. It takes me back to my childhood, where it all began, where the imagination first leapt into action. There is nowhere to hide when you are in rehab and all of your emotions and behaviours are being observed by eagle-eyed counsellors. One morning everyone seems in good spirits in the group, smiles are exchanged and a general hum of friendships vibrates from chair to chair. Then in walk two of the counsellors, who put two chairs in the middle of the room and ask us one by one to take a seat. We take it in turns to sit back to back. For five minutes you have to sit and listen while the person behind you tells you exactly what they think of you, followed by a brief affirmation. And then it's your turn. It's so hard to say what you feel about someone, but they can't respond: they have to sit in silence as you speak your mind. It seemed like the whole group hated each other; it was just like being in a band but without the honesty. By the end of the day everyone seemed closer and on a more even level of emotional captivity. I tried to imagine this happening on a tour bus in the middle of a tour. It would be murder, but then touring is not recovery. I was up to my ears in treatment, recovery, psychodramas and meetings. Then there was a phone call from the box under the stairs. It was John Lay, calling from the States to tell me that Maxine had passed away. I walked into the front room of the house and cried like a baby. My roommate, Simon, gave me a cup of tea, and to this day I can still taste it on my lips. The next day we did a workshop on 'the passing of Maxine'. One of the counsellors, Philip Bacon, put a red velvet cushion in the middle of the room, telling us that it was Maxine and this was my chance to say goodbye and to tell her how I felt about her. At the end, a jug of water was passed around and everyone's glass was filled. They all lifted the glasses up to their heads, said a prayer and put the water back in the jug. I then poured a full glass containing everyone's affirmations, which I drank down. It was so moving; so perfect. My counsellor let me go to the funeral at the church in Benenden, and there were all her friends and family. It was a service full of love, as befitted her. Jools played the piano. Sadly Glenn was still on tour in America – the tour I was meant to be on – and couldn't be there. The fact that I wasn't with him and the band made me feel awkward and guilty, but in Maxine's passing I found the strength to know I'd done the right thing.

At the wake, her mother hobbled about on her crutches and took hugs from everyone, which she embraced with a whisky kiss and a sob of great control and gesture. She'd lost her husband Felix just before Maxine died and was now grieving the loss of her two most beloved people. 'Darling,' she said. 'Give me a kiss. She always loved you so very much.' Anthea never gave up the fags, the afternoon nap or the whisky. I went to visit her several times after Maxine died. She always managed to greet me with a big hairy kiss and a 'Darling, how nice to see you!' Behind her baggy red eyes was the love of youth and days gone by. Radio 3 was always on in the background. She gave me some pictures and press cuttings she'd kept of the early Squeeze days. I was so grateful. Her head tilted to one side as we sat and talked about Maxine and how wonderful life had been; about Felix and Benenden. She died shortly afterwards. It was so sad. The family were moving on, and their world was passed down to their son Kent, who looks after it all now with such great care. After a walk to Maxine's grave, I got in the car and was driven back to PROMIS, where I dedicated my sobriety to her – and still do. Because without her in my life, there'd have been no songs about people who live in Clapham. Of course I placed the ad in the shop window, which was how we found each other, but she made the connection – no one else did. And nobody else held it in their hands like she did. That ad in the sweet shop window cost me 50p, and from that I have my whole life, my children and my future. A 50p I had stolen from my mother's purse. It stuns me when I think about the path I might have taken had we not come together. So I thank Maxine, as the keeper of the keys that unlocked my small and complicated world.

Beechy had me in his office one day and told me I might need a sponsor. The phone in his hand was given to me, and on the other end was Elton John. I couldn't believe it. Just the evening before I'd been listening to him on the radio, and 'Someone Saved My Life Tonight' and 'Don't Let the Sun Go Down on Me' had reduced me to tears in the back of the minibus that took us to meetings in

Dover and Canterbury. It was he who'd first pulled the trigger on my addiction back in that hotel in San Jose. Elton said he would look after me and that I was to call him every day without fail or he'd rip my head off. I was beside myself. We were in daily contact for the whole of that first year.

Immediately after coming out of PROMIS, I was on a pink cloud. I went to AA meetings three times a week. Rehab is like a bandage – you can put it over the wound, but you still have to heal the wound afterwards. The hard work comes later. Luckily, I lived near a fantastic meeting at St Mary's Church in Rye. It was such a great, strong group of men and women, and we all supported each other. Sometime later, in 1993, Elton played at Earl's Court for two nights to raise money for his AIDS foundation. I went along to meet him for the first time. We'd talked daily on the phone since he first called me at PROMIS, but we'd never come face to face before – though I had seen him play back in 1974. I arrived backstage two hours before the show. A square of Portakabins served as dressing rooms and Astroturf had been laid down in front of them. A few tables were set up on the fake grass and generally the atmosphere was homely – or as homely as backstage at a gig can ever be. Elton was dressed in blue shorts. He was no taller than me, and for the first thirty seconds of our meeting, I tried to stop myself from gawping at him like some star-struck fan. We got along very well. We talked in a backstage kind of way – very short paragraphs about how things were, what was going on.

Elton and his friends tried to make me feel at home, but I felt very out of place most of the time. There were all these very wealthy people milling about, and here was I, insolvent and wearing a worn-out suit as best as I could. The backstage zoo consisted of some very exotic creatures, from Joan Collins to Stephen Fry. Paul Young was there too – it was good to see him again. His youthful face had dropped since the last time I'd seen him, six years ago; the grey hair had found a home on his head, as it had, no doubt, on mine. Elton's close friend John was a lovely chap who ushered me around and never let me stand alone in a crowd. His brother James was just as polite. They came from Chapel Hill in North Carolina, where Squeeze had played in the past, so we talked about their love for the band, about Chapel Hill and about Joan Collins.

It was a long night; the show was two and a half hours. It was a re-education in the talents of Elton. His piano-playing was much better than I remembered it to be, and his voice was powerful. 'Don't Let the Sun Go Down on Me' sent a shiver through the 16,000 people in the crowd and the chill bolted down my spine, bringing a welling of tears to my eyes. It is such a fantastic song. In my car on the way home, Radio 1 broadcast the concert. I turned it up loud and cruised back to Rye on a high of satisfaction. After that, I went to Elton's house, we went to meetings together, I went to his shows. He inspired me so much to keep coming back, because it does happen if you work it. Being sober isn't easy when the world around you mostly drinks, but in time it becomes a way of life. Elton had meetings each Sunday at his home in Windsor. It was a large, warm and friendly house with a well-stocked garden and grounds; indoors, rose candles burned in every room and flowers lit up every corner. The meetings were strong and afterwards there was Sunday lunch.

One night Elton called me and asked if I could send him some words – he told me what the brief was and gave me his fax number. I went to my office and looked out of the window toward the sky. I was in my happy place; the place where words are gifted to me. I sent the lyric over to him, and the next day he called and invited me to his home. He placed the fax on a piano and the song, 'Duets for One', was written in about three minutes flat. I stood behind him wondering if this was really happening to me. It was. We drove over to a studio he had close by, where a band that included Chris Rea was waiting, and the song was played through and recorded in about half an hour. I was in heaven. The song can be found on Elton's *Duets* album; it's the only one he sings on his own. I felt blessed.

The one-day-at-a-time mantra suits me – I like taking it slow, seeing what each day can reveal. I open my arms and life walks in. When I feel weak, I return to the meetings and to the places where I got well. I'm never far from either. Today I like to work with sober or like-minded people, and I find drinking as a culture ugly and unfriendly. If I'm in a room with someone who has been drinking, I have to make my excuses. But it seems that the music industry has changed over the past fifteen years, and more and more people shy away from the drinking culture, the drug abuse and the darker corners of stardom.

Younger people naturally have a need to push their boundaries, and alcohol can help break down the walls of communication. And for a time, it worked for me. So I understand the good-time person who hasn't got the same issues as I have – he can dance and drink, he can be in a happy place. It's just not my happy place. As a drinker, I never had a day off; it was a constant dedication and commitment. I was always thinking about the next drink or planning the next secretive meeting with someone who could feed my addiction. I really enjoyed my time in the headlights. I regret not a single day. Though the happiness has been tinged with darkness, it's got me to where I am today.

The order of sobriety is a simple one: it's keeping it in the day, making sure you come back and sticking with the winners – those who are sober and in a good place. And I feel so grateful to have discovered this way of life, for without it I would be a very different person. One drink was never enough for me, and the energy I put into being a drinker was enormous – more than I'd put into anything else in my life. Everything took second place: the band, being a father, being me. Slowly I listened to the advice I was being given and in time the order fell into place. I was one of the lucky ones. To be in rehab is a very privileged place to be; most people have to find the light from AA meetings alone, which must be a struggle. I can't describe the feelings I'd found; they were open and full of life and colour. One-day-at-a-time is a mantra that most people now have heard of, but you don't hear it so clearly when you are blinded and deafened by the drinking that rules your life and emotions. Drinking can be fun and most normal people have healthy drinking habits. Sadly I can't be one of those. Nonington was a wonderful place to get sober, and in the Kent countryside I felt the cushion of love soften my fall, providing me with the simple steps that would guide me for the rest of my life.

ROYAL PARADE MEWS

The first thing that struck me about being sober was that I could read my watch – when I was drinking, my hand would shake so much I had to guess the time. I was enjoying life again, and when the band came back from the 1992 tour, Glenn called me at PROMIS to see how I was doing. He sounded happy for me. We had a meeting in London, so I picked him up in my car en route from Rye and he quizzed me all the way into town. He was inquisitive in an understanding way. I was hopeful the heavy penny might drop for him, but then I wanted to convert everyone to this new way of life – over the years I've learnt that it works through attraction rather than promotion. Glenn was supportive of my recovery and was very kind. He kept his drinking to himself and the parties he loved out of my earshot, which was very respectful.

By the end of the year we were in the studio – the one that Glenn had built on Royal Parade Mews in Blackheath. It was small, compact and homespun; it was Glenn in every way. At first I was uncomfortable there, but soon I was feeling relaxed and at home myself. It was situated above an alleyway in which rats would run between the bins at the back doors of the local restaurants. There was a long mixing desk and boxes of leads everywhere. This was

Glenn's shed. Glenn would be busy with gaffer tape and T-shirts, as he and Pete Thomas tried to deaden the sound in the room in which the drums were set up. From the outside, looking in through the window, the studio must have looked like a shop on Carnaby Street. Old tour T-shirts hung in rows, like a museum to the years of Squeeze that lay behind us. I could look at them and see my life stretched out in cotton. It was touches like these that made this very much Glenn's studio – a nest of tidy bits and bobs, hundreds of LPs and old copies of *NME* and *Melody Maker*.

He was happy in his new home and I was more than happy in mine. I was going to AA meetings and aftercare, and generally managing myself well. But once in the studio, I was sprung back into a place of mismanagement, a place of shared misunderstandings. When you get six-year-old boys together in a playground, you often find a leader, a scapegoat, a bully, a joker and a pleaser. Add thirty-five years and you find those same boys at a recording session in Blackheath. As well as Glenn and me, there was Keith Wilkinson on bass and Paul Carrack back on keyboards which was a nice surprise. Pete Thomas, who'd played drums for Elvis Costello when we toured with The Attractions, was now in the band – he was the only drummer I've ever worked with to call me before an album and ask to see the lyrics. We had the greatest line-up and Pete was a brilliant addition to the band; a very safe pair of hands.

The album was co-produced by Pete Smith, a cockney sparrow who'd worked with Sting on his *Dream of the Blue Turtles* album. He was fun to be around – as was his drumming namesake – so the atmosphere was generally buoyant, but he was also forthright and incredibly driven; his ear was well tuned and he took no prisoners, particularly when he thought he was right about something. Sadly Glenn was exactly the same, and the two of them often clashed. The songs were hard to arrange, as we all had strong opinions about how they should sound, and we spent hours working out feel and pace, often chasing our tails. It was Glenn's studio, so he stayed back and fiddled after we'd all gone home.

My drive back to Rye took more than an hour, so I was in the car for upwards of two hours each day with just my friend the radio for company. I was really enjoying writing again, and ideas seemed to flow when I was behind the wheel. I wrote 'Loving You Tonight' on the A268 on my way home one evening, and 'Cold Shoulder' was also written in the car. It was raining so hard that I pulled over and went into a church to scribble down the lyrics I had in my head. My notebooks were brimming with words, colours and ideas. Sobriety offered so much creativity and hope.

Sunlight streamed through the windows of the studio where five went mad about recording, and mad about getting it right. The heat was turned up as we pulled arrangements around like a pack of wolves over a skinny carcass. We tugged verse and chorus to and fro. Long faces melted into smiles, though happiness could quickly turn into furrowed brows. Strangely, though, there seemed to be little tension. That could be because we all had the same goal in mind. Success. A hit. *Top of the Pops*, the glory of which was fading at this point but still worth a punt. Big stages that stretched around the world, and food and water for our families.

'Third Rail' became the first single and we all had fun recording a video for it on the Tenterden steam railway down in Kent. The song shivers in the shadows of 'Is That Love' but still packs a punch. The big song on the record, though, was 'Some Fantastic

Place', inspired by Maxine's death. The first few lines were written at my desk in PROMIS, the rest on my kids' school desk in the playroom at my house in Rye. I cried when Glenn first played me the song; it was beautiful. Cunningly, he'd lifted the guitar solo from a tune we'd written together when we lived in Max's house in 1973. Another gift. The song has to be one of my proudest moments. It was as if Maxine had come into my soul to write the words. It was a truly spiritual experience. Delicately we sculpted our way around this song, as it meant so very much to us. We both loved Maxine and we wanted to do 'Some Fantastic Place' justice. Glenn and I often come from very different corners of the spectrum, but for this song we met in the middle and came up with something that would evoke the love that she – our closest friend – gave to us.

At home the weekends would fly by. Being there with the kids around meant that time never had a chance to stand still – Monday would come even though Friday wasn't quite finished with. Riley and I played a lot of football. He loved to come to the house. He would play with Grace, and with Sybil, our bull mastiff, as though he lived there all the time – and I wished he did. Natalie also loved to come and see Grace, and she loved the house and all the freedom she had to roam there. I was never happier than when all three of them were in the garden running around with each other.

Miles Copeland was somehow still lurking around the perimeter fence of Squeeze trying to manage the band. He'd signed Keith our bass player to a publishing deal and then persuaded us to have one of his songs on our record, a song that did nothing for me. Glenn was more understanding than me and helped him work through its recording. I was still really happy with the album. Bob Clearmountain, who'd worked on Bruce Springsteen's *Born in the USA*, flew over from LA to mix it all at Real World Studios near Bath, where we'd recorded *Play* a few years earlier. It was such an idyllic location, nestled down in a lovely little village called Box. The food was amazing, the river ran beneath the studio floor and there were ducks on the pond. You could see them from the mixing desk. It cost a fortune, but it was worth it.

Glenn had co-produced with Pete Smith, and all of his hard work was rewarded in the sound and arrangements of the record. I will never forget the thrill I got listening to the album on the A21, driving back home after the last day of mixing. My car has always been the best place to listen to music, it's my stereo on wheels and I bathed in the album's glory on that sunny drive. Glenn has always been closer to the songs and the production than I have, that's not my skill. It takes a tidy mind to listen and balance the nuances of each song. I don't think I've ever wanted to produce records, but Glenn has always been there at the sharp end of the ship, painting with his musical palette of many colours.

That summer Glenn and I were invited to play at part of the Phonogram Records convention by our loving A&M MD Howard Burman. The *Devon Belle* river boat cast off and headed upstream for a night of handshakes and cold salmon along the River Dart in Devon. The firmest handshake belonged to the head of Our Price Records; my hand was squashed like a melted KitKat in his grip. I was warned that it might be hell, but that it would be a good thing for us to do. Out on the upper deck tales of the riverbank were exchanged, and we slowly mingled with the mainly male population of executives. Only a handful of women were spotted on board. Then after the buffet and chat it was time for us to play.

'A&M without Squeeze would be like A&M without its trumpet,' Howard proudly announced. Howard was a nice enough chap but really never filled me with any confidence as an MD. Unplugged and in front of the heads of this, that and the other, we blew our very own trumpet: our songs. We played six numbers to a warm, respectful crowd who encouraged us back for an encore, not that it takes much to do that. We had just arrived back alongside the dock as we strummed the final chords of 'Tempted'. What a relief. It was a miracle that I got through the set – I had zero confidence. Being back in the promotional saddle reminded me of how much I hated it, playing largely to people who are too busy thinking about themselves and what's in it for them. If it were a board game I would always try and miss this square out.

Maurice Oberstein, the head of Sony, made the evening for me by reflecting on the days when he once came to see Squeeze play circa 1977, and remembering smugly that he didn't sign us then as he knew that we would never make it. The skin on Howard's face visibly dropped into his beer. I was newly sober and to me this really felt like hell, record company hell. Squeeze was, and still is, a business like the corner shop, and we needed to bear that in mind as we weaved our way from album to album, and from tour to tour. So evenings like this could only do us good, as even in our matured years we still needed to convince the people upstairs in the record company that we are worth our salt. Back on dry land I ran for my car.

The following night we were on stage at The Inn On The Park in St Helier, Jersey, to a sell-out audience who were crammed up against the stage. 'Smashy' the DJ, with all the nauseating presence of a chihuahua, introduced us, and on we bounced into the lions' den to play our first date of the Some Fantastic Tour. It was loud and fun; our set consisted of seven new songs and a random selection of old chestnuts. The first encore was packed full of them, glowing and pulsating for the eager sweating crowd. Paul Carrack sang and played with great soul and confidence, it was so great to have him back in the band. Behind me on drums, Pete Thomas kept the whole thing pegged to the floor, the finest of song drummers. Keith Wilkinson and Glenn smiled a lot, grooving on the club atmosphere, it was good to be playing again. Technical problems can often throw all best intentions out of the window, and I had a few that night. There we were playing what our fans like best, the ones they know. However, the new songs found comfortable ground within the set and went down equally well. We had attracted some people with their baseball caps on the wrong way, they gave us the old swinging arm treatment, even on the slow songs like 'Cold Shoulder', a valiant show of appreciation, but then this was the Channel Islands.

All the greats had played there before us. Gerry and the Pacemakers, Stan Boardman and Lindisfarne, to mention a few. Was the scampi-in-the-basket circuit just around the corner, I wondered. Back at the hotel I got on my knees and prayed. On the way home I took the catamaran across the Channel, plain sailing all except for the piped music, 'Tubular Bells'. It created a soundtrack for my tiny but imaginative mind; I found myself in a movie along with people of all shapes and sizes who lived in little worlds all apart from one another.

When the time came to disembark and collect luggage, they all came together to fight for their places next to the six-foot stretch of carousel. Four hundred people all in one or another stage of being animal and all I dislike about crowds. I waded in elbows out and retrieved my bags as they passed by. The hairs on my face grew by the minute until I was safely in my car, another place of refuge. I turned on the radio and there we were, our new single 'Some Fantastic Place' in all four speakers, sounding wonderful. We were back.

Touring and promoting the album felt like a new lease of life with me being sober; I started to really enjoy the ebb and flow of our show from a new angle, a new head space. Playing live was always fun, the circus life we led was very comfortable. We were fed and watered at each show after the sound check, our washing was taken care of, all we had to do was prance about, try to look good and keep time. It's a doddle being in a band when things are going well.

On stage one night in Bristol the band were on top form, with my funny legs bending back and forth across the stage; Glenn sang like he was in heaven and we hit the audience between the eyes. In the second encore after 'How Long' I introduced the ace up our sleeve. 'We have had many keyboard players in our time, Jools Holland, Don Snow, Paul Carrack . . . Please welcome Elton John!' The crowd looked at me as if I were joking and near silence fell on the hall, followed rapidly by a huge roar as Elton sat at the piano and started playing the opening riff to 'I Heard it Through the Grapevine'. I too was in heaven. We then launched into 'I Saw Her Standing There' and the place went nuts. When I looked around the stage the ecstasy on people's faces was so pleasing to see, not a grumpy jowl in sight. After the show it was hard to contain my excitement, hugs all round in the dreary dressing room. Elton really enjoyed it too, praising Glenn up and down the hall and shaking Paul's hand with true admiration. Outside in his car I heard tracks from his new album, which practically blew me away – with sixteen speakers blasting out it was hard to remain in my soft leather seat. I felt like a little boy who had just climbed into a car for the very first time with my legs dangling down. What I heard was very special, my emotions were tickled to the roots. Elton sings with such great power and confidence; he was on full throttle with this new album. I felt very privileged.

The next day in the local paper we were front-page news, with a huge picture of his nibs at the piano. The new album *Some Fantastic Place* was soon sold out in the Our Price down the road from the Colston Hall. Bristol was suddenly our kind of town. The same day Elton had been out to his local record shop to buy up all stocks of the album to give to his friends, so we might get a chart position yet. Touring was special again for me, I really loved it: the atmosphere seemed new and exciting. The sobriety I had been working on definitely helped open the valves of appreciation, and with a good sponsor and regular meetings I was doing well. I lost weight and looked trim in a nice stage suit. All I had to do was keep the emotional ball in the air.

We then took the album to Japan for the first time on a short but very successful tour. Sadly, Paul Carrack couldn't come with us so we took Andy Metcalf instead, a man who liked to party and play well for his supper. Japan was so interesting, and the first thing I wanted to do was find an AA meeting. My old roommate from PROMIS met me in Tokyo and took me to an English-speaking meeting, it was hard to concentrate as the savage jetlag was hounding me to sleep. I flew with my friend Chris Topham who was captain of my Virgin flight. I first met Chris in Norfolk, Virginia many years before when he flew as an RAF pilot on an F16 with his mate stumbling Lou. They were top gun in every sense of the word. Chris is such a big music fan and these days he still flies for Virgin but he also finds time to run a vinyl record label.

On the flight to Tokyo I sat up the front with him as we flew across Russia for hours on end. The turbulence scared me but he had his feet up reading the newspaper. I found it all reassuring but terrifying at the same time. These days being in the cockpit is of course impossible.

The tour around Japan lasted about ten days, it was an eye opener and very calming as we visited the temples and sushi bars of each city we visited. The audiences were passionate and loved to involve themselves in our songs, it was orderly and brilliant. The flight home, without Chris to cuddle up to, was not so brilliant. The turbulence still vibrates in my consciousness today. I loved the gadget shops in Reppongi but wrestled with the constant promotion schedule that was timed to the minute, each day all day. I managed to find some lovely gifts for Grace in a department store one afternoon when the building started to shake: it was an earthquake. I'm not sure how big it was, but it was enough for me to stand and shiver while shoes in racks moved about and comedy music was piped through the intercom to calm the nervous shoppers. We were well looked after in Japan, it was a great experience, I just wish it wasn't so far away or I would visit more often.

It was a busy year for us promoting the album and we gave it everything we could but there were things to deal with in our own lives; it was tricky to balance home and work. *Some Fantastic Place* was a huge hit for us. Elton bought twenty copies for his various homes and cars, and we had rave reviews in Q magazine and *Mojo*; musically we were back in the saddle. Paul Carrack then left for more solo work, and Pete Thomas went back to Elvis's commitments on tour and in the studio. I was sad to see them both leave. The next year Glenn got divorced from Pam – there were some tiny hats in the air around Blackheath in celebration – and the following year married a lovely woman called Jane, who was a schoolteacher. Their wedding was down at Huntsham Court in Devon. Huntsham was a place that had become a drinking hole for me over the years, a dark Gothic hotel set in the red Devon soil. The sun shone for them on that lovely day, which was nice to see, and the air was thick with old faces. Glenn settled into a new life in a different tempo from the one before, and seemed happier for it. He then became a father for the first time, a wonderful thing for any young man. We both seemed to be in a good place.

In 1994, I went on my first writers' retreat, as a guest of Miles Copeland at Chateau Marouatte in France, a grand purchase he had made mainly from Police royalties. I drove down in my Saab, of which I had a total of fifteen over time, and was very nervous. But once inside the castle walls I was relieved to find friendly faces. Twenty writers from all over the world gathered in one place to write songs; it seemed magical.

Miles made each group work with one of his writers – of course he did. I had a nice room in the main tower with a sloping floor and a grand four-poster bed. I wrote with Alannah Myles on the first day. She insisted on lighting frankincense and the room filled with a mystical fog, so much so that I couldn't see her across the table. A crap song ensued.

Cher was joining us the following day, and when she arrived, Miles showed her the rooms around the castle. She chose mine to move into, so I moved out, but not without first taking with me the peg of wood that kept the bed steady on the sloping floor. Cher ruled the roost and chose who she wanted to work with. I got on really well with Patty Smyth, a lovely person with a great voice, who spoke the same new language as me, both of us being sober. She was dating John McEnroe and they were going to get married. I kept in touch and later that year I met up with her in New York.

Driving back through France after the retreat I thought, 'I could do that – I could run my own workshop.' So I called my publisher EMI and organised a week down at Huntsham Court in Devon. It was filled with talent – Suggs, Kirsty MacColl, Lamont Dozier, Graham Gouldman, Cathy Dennis and Gary Clark to mention just a few. Some great songs came out of that week. I have been running songwriters' retreats for twenty-five years now, sometimes twice a year. We moved location from Devon to Kent, to Italy and back to Devon and then Wales, mostly in old houses, or hotels. I love the writers' weeks. I've never made a bean from them, but it's a worthwhile thing to do. Recently I have been running them in Glastonbury, a stone's throw from the festival site, at Pennard House, an eccentric and wonderfully run place. The Buddy Holly Foundation now fund the event, and it has established itself as one of the leading writing camps in the UK. Peter Bradley helps me put the show on the road, along with the ever-so-whispering Bob Harris and his lovely wife Trudie. We had forty-two writers caress our retreat with some amazing songs in 2017. I felt so moved and proud to have reached the milestone of the 25th year. Pennard House is a very special location and the event seems to grow and grow with each year, like the roses in its beautiful garden. I'm so proud of all the songs that have been written at the retreats down the years. It's more about the friendships made than the songs. The songs are merely stepping-stones, hopefully to lasting relationships between the writers who attend.

One of the most interesting writers' weeks I have worked on was on Cunard's *Queen Mary* 2. I have crossed to New York four times teaching people to write songs. I take with me close friends and fellow writers and together we instil confidence in would-be writers of all ages, but mainly the over-sixties. On the first ever morning at sea I was greeted by 150 punters all keen to learn how to write a song. Thank God I had with me Squeeze drummer Simon Hanson and writers Chris Sheehan and Matt Deighton, among others.

Over the course of the five-day journey to New York we gradually mould songs from blank faces and perform them in the theatre on the last night. It's so much fun. On one crossing we had Roger Daltrey on board. He insisted on having my cabin as it was the largest, which I had no problem with; after all, he is one of my idols. We played a secret show for the crew below decks, which resulted in chaos. Some great songs come from those crossings and it can be very moving. Coming into Manhattan on the deck of the *Queen Mary* is something else, well worth the crossing in whatever the weather. Mostly fog.

GALSWORTHY LODGE

My memories of Miles Copeland are of a man whose first record was 'Wake Up Little Susie' by The Everly Brothers. I can remember him playing it to me in his house in St John's Wood when we first met. We listened to the song together and I watched him being taken to a different place by the harmonies, then he turned and wrote down the expenses for the meal we'd just eaten on a piece of paper. That kind of summed him up. Miles was sacked for the last time just after the touring had finished for *Some Fantastic Place*. He had pushed us too far with his handling of certain issues. He and John Lay went around the same time.

The Police came closest to the success he had imagined for us, but when they broke up, Miles then sold their family silver, and his share of their publishing deals went roughly the same way as ours. I'm still in touch with Sting, who I admire for the way he sees his past as being as important to him as the present. He just acknowledges how Miles played a vital role in his success, but times move on. I'd like our songs back please, but that's just not going to happen. The masters are owned by Universal for the rest of my life. The publishing is with BMG and they won't even talk about readjusting our share more evenly. It's sad really, my kids will never own my songs or benefit from all the hard work, they can never be handed down. All because we signed away our future for £15 a week to a man who doesn't even get a mention on our Wikipedia page.

I think Glenn despises Miles for what he did, but I can't harbour resentments in that way; it's done, we move on. Yes, he groomed us expertly. He was a devious manager, unlike Shep, unlike Jake and certainly unlike David. Miles now manages a troop of belly dancers. I think that says everything we need to know about karma.

So with Miles out of the picture it was time to think again. Step this way, new manager Paul Toogood. Paul took the role on for a year and made a hash of the VAT payments, so he went too. He would drink tea with me and beer with Glenn. It's a shame it never worked out.

We ploughed on with another album, another new band. Keith Wilkinson was still on bass, but we now had Kevin Wilkinson (no relation) on drums, with the keyboards open to session. Kevin's drinking was even slyer than mine used to be – he knocked them back in secret but always delivered a great show. Pete Smith was still on board as a producer. It was a small miracle. *Ridiculous* felt like an extension of the previous album, though the songs were harder to come by. Again we spent days pulling teeth over the arrangements. The album was rich with layers of sound, but the hits had to be torn from our hands. 'Electric Trains' was a powerful song we were proud of, while 'This Summer' was a dead ringer for 'Sunday Street' on our *Play* album. Danny Baker championed the song on London Radio but that was the extent of the album's radio appearances. Another Keith Wilkinson song and the album was complete – a complete extension of where we'd already been.

Were we repeating ourselves? Who cared? A&M cared enough to keep fussing with the mixes and treating us like possible new wave pop stars, which we were not. Some of the songs were mixed in Sweden – the obvious place to mix a Difford and Tilbrook song – and Glenn and I weren't even consulted. It cost us a fortune. A poor show all round. Things were in decline; the music industry was hanging on to anything it could find to keep its apparent greed alive. Britpop was one such animal, and we were soon to be hailed as its ambassadors. Oasis were huge, Blur were at the fun end of the stick but we seemed to be hanging around like confetti left on the church floor after a wedding. We even tried to write in that Britpop style; we were clearly clutching at straws.

Touring was amazing fun, though. It was all starting to feel very grown-up – especially with the likes of Kevin Wilkinson and former Sly and the Family Stone member Andy Newmark on the revolving drum stool. We had already done a tour of full acoustic shows during this period with Aimee Mann and Paul Carrack, which threw up some lovely moments in faraway places. Aimee was so much fun to work with; she carried an air of intelligence about her that was mixed with deep and clever humour. We recorded with her in London at Konk Studios, owned by The Kinks. I sang on a couple of songs, as did Glenn. Aimee was easy to love as a friend and we got on really well.

For the first time in my life on that tour I felt as though I could play the guitar properly. For many years I'd had a default setting, which was 'bluff'. I managed to get through the songs with just enough accuracy to not upset Glenn – though he often held me up to the light for not paying enough attention. Glenn's always been a very good teacher, but I'm not a very good student. And perhaps I couldn't hear what he was trying to say because it was him saying it. He has always been so patient with me. Over the years my playing had been at best muddy. Gilson used to call me pork-chop fingers and in the studio most of my guitar parts would be replaced as Glenn always felt he could play them better. I'm not even sure if I feature on any of our albums up to *Some Fantastic Place*. There are some background parts on *Frank*, but most of what you hear on there is Glenn.

Early in 1995 Elton called me and asked if I would like to come over to listen to his new album called *Made in England*. I drove over the next morning very excited to hear the new record. En route I was bursting for a wee, however there were no services at that time on the M25 in Surrey. I thought I would hold it until I got to his house. As soon as I arrived I was whisked into his Bentley and sat in the front seat. All 200 speakers blasted the new songs at me at high volume and I was suitably impressed. Gradually though my bladder was warning me of imminent danger. I did not have the heart to ask to step out of the car for a toilet break, so I held on. The album rolled on and I found myself distracted in a big way. As the last track skipped by, a song called 'Blessed' which was five minutes long, I felt trouble brewing. At the end of the song he looked at me as if to say, what do you think then? All I could say was could I use the loo – naturally he had no idea that I was in so much pain, almost fainting from the strain of holding in my requirements. Doors slammed and I leapt out. I was red-faced and totally embarrassed. Relief and a cup of tea followed in the kitchen moments later and, to top it all off, there was Elton wearing Marigolds washing up a few cups. Thank God these days we have the Cobham services on the M25.

A few months later and Squeeze were dropped by our label; A&M passed on us. This was final. Glenn suddenly separated from Jane, which was very sad. He soon found happiness again when he met Suzanne Hunt at one of our rehearsals. She was one of our road crew. Suzanne was a lovely person, easy to talk to, easy to like, and she did a great job on the road for us; she worked hard. I remember well when Glenn met her. We were in New Orleans, and I saw them come into the hotel very early one morning looking happy and embracing. They were like soulmates on two different tour buses that became one. After a few tours Suzanne became the band's manager, which was a natural promotion and as a team they worked well. So much seemed to happen at once. They formed a record label together and had ambitions to take Squeeze and go it alone without the safety net and all the trimmings of a major label. I, on the other hand, wanted to hold on to the umbilical cord that was attached to the major labels and felt we might lose everything.

I was confused and slightly worn out by all the sudden changes. I was also missing the valuable AA meetings which had become the backbone of my sobriety.

At the beginning of 1995 my third daughter Cissy had been born (in a birthing pool in Hastings) and I now wanted more than anything to be at home with my family. I was so happy with that part of my life. Cissy was my pride and joy; she would come everywhere with me, walking the dogs in the woods or into Rye for shopping. Grace was always by our side too; she was a good sister and they seemed to get on well together. Nat and Riley enjoyed the extended family and gave both the girls plenty of cuddles and time to play.

There was an empty barn in my garden at Old House and I decided to build a recording studio, which would be for everyone to use – a chapel of music in the most idyllic spot. Despite Heidi not wanting it there, she eventually became studio manager and helped run it, which she did really well. At the same time, for my sins, I was producing a record for Eddy Grundy from *The Archers* as a favour to my brother Lew who was an avid fan. One afternoon the owner of the studio marched in and said that everything was for sale, as her husband Alvin Lee had deserted her for a younger model. I said I would have the desk, but first I called Alvin who seemed not to care at all. It was meant to be. It was great having such a fine creative space across the lawn with its newly plumbed-in Helios mixing desk from 1971, and lots of old classic equipment besides. It took a few months to build but it was worth it. The studio became a great place for me to co-write, which I did, having been inspired to do so by Maxine. At first it seemed like infidelity and I kept it from Glenn. I was shy; I felt awkward sleeping outside of our marriage. Once I became more comfortable with the idea, though, I was off like a balloon that had been let go.

The recording of the next Squeeze album, *Domino*, was much harder work than the previous two. I sat in Glenn's studio for weeks while he tried to separate oil from water. It must have been so hard for him to read the empty words I had presented to him for the album, I could hardly believe it myself. I think I was well and truly drifting at this point, the passion was waning and the last gasps of a band were being shuffled about on the studio floor. I wanted to be at home, and I wanted to spread my wings above my own nest. Some of the backing tracks from the album were put down at my studio in Sussex and I enjoyed having everyone down to the house. I think it gave us all clear heads after the small confines of Glenn's studio up in London. Once the record was done it came out as *Domino*, as was the plan. There was no money to promote the record and no vision for its release other than touring with yet another new band, which comprised Ash Soan on drums, Hilaire Penda replaced Keith on bass, and on keyboards Jools's little brother Christopher Holland. In retrospect, I'd given up the ghost inside. Ash was a great drummer to work with, but Hilaire – though brilliant – was a complicated jazz player trying to bend his way around simple pop songs.

I didn't enjoy the experience very much, though there are two songs on that record I really love – 'To Be a Dad' is a fine piece of work and 'Without You Here' is a beautiful song that I wrote for Glenn, mindful of the fact that Jane was taking his two sons to live with her in Australia. It was unkind and he was in a great deal of pain.

The rest of the songs were tossed off like pancakes on a less-than-emotional grill. The band had become just Glenn and me, really, and it didn't feel like the full shilling. I had drifted from the dream of being in a band to being almost an employee of a band that was going around in circles. Glenn had these wonderful ideas about change and how the record industry was the enemy. I was holding on to the castle walls as people were being tossed out into the moat. He was right in a way, but it was all going too quickly for me. I was scared to lose what I could not keep. People I knew in the industry were being put out to graze; perhaps he was right.

Glenn always says at that point I left the building, but it was up to him to turn the lights off. We were both heaving the elephant in the room further and further up the hill. I had clearly left the band in my head but just not told anyone about my feelings, mainly because I had lost control of them. If only we had talked things through and been more responsive with each other. Or maybe it was just me. I was prepared to accept that. Glenn had been playing solo shows, and had already put out a solo album that I'd not heard – and at that point I wasn't in a rush to hear it either. I was envious of his new career path but sadly I had no way of communicating how I felt to him. He was in another space and time from me. During the same period, Squeeze had gone through three drummers, two producers, three managers, two bass players, a dozen tour buses and crew. At our peak we had written 'Some Fantastic Place' and at our lowest ebb we'd written a song called 'Bonkers'. Which summed it all up. Being at home with Heidi, Grace and Cissy was now more attractive to me than work, and with the building of my studio I knew I could bring work home with me. The wheels had come off the bus.

The early Nineties were years of lost hope and feelings of unmanageability. I was skating on thin ice all the time and not thinking things through very well. Not even my brother Lew could fathom out the darkness I had found myself in. When music became my life, Lew had supported me – as Les did too. He always came to see Squeeze play and was full of encouragement. I wrote my first poems when I went to stay at his house in Hampshire, where he lived with his wife Christine and their two children Sarah and Simon. I sat by the River Test and scribbled words in my A4 pad; words that became covered in dust before being reborn as song lyrics.

When Squeeze were being managed by David Enthoven, Lew became our accountant. He very cleverly tipped money into a pension for me; he sorted out my tax and helped me invest. He remained my accountant – and Glenn's – until the 1990s. Lew knows more about Squeeze than I do, I think; his constant mining for royalties and who is owed what seems to be a dedication no other accountant could match. He has always been fair and hugely generous with his time. I love my brother. It was hard for him to say no to me though. From my perspective, he was the ideal person to be controlling the chequebook. Cars were the bane of his life and he had to be incredibly patient with me. I almost bought a Bristol one afternoon, but he intervened. He called the garage to tell them I was on day release from prison and wasn't to be trusted. He missed the Maserati, though; it ended up on my driveway at the farm in Rye. Heidi wanted to kill me for buying it as we had no money to pay for food, or the taxman, but Lew cleared up the mess and the car was returned. I managed to sneak another car in the following week.

In the morning, ta-dah, the curtains opened to reveal the gleaming new Maserati. A car I could not even get down our lane or get the kids in! It did not go down well and the addiction went on until I went completely skint. I had no money, but I had a nice car. Heidi was not impressed with my behaviour. I was spending to feel better; it had got out of control. From cars to simple things like DAT players or shortwave radios, which I had many of. Sometimes I would hide things in the boot of the car, and when Heidi went to bed I would sneak them in, hide the boxes they came in, and make them look like I had had them for ages. I flew on Concorde and stayed in all the best hotels; I was out of touch with reality. Heidi and I were at rock bottom and I was lost in a secret world with Squeeze, where my confidence had been kicked into the long grass. My addictive behaviour had begun to creep back in the form of shopping, poor relationships and not standing up for myself. I was reduced to a weak and empty complicated shell – one I couldn't break out of. Again the anxiety grew. I saw yet another tour schedule I couldn't face. Home was a house with many cracks forming in its foundations.

I had stopped going to AA meetings altogether – this was my downfall. That's the lesson we learn in AA and one I always manage to brush aside: the further you drift from it, the more you start falling apart. It's meant to be a bridge to normal living. Some people think they've already reached this, but it's not possible for addicts to do that. After years of sobriety, people assume you're all right, but you need to regularly reconnect to the goodness. I had found the old black dog again, sleeping just underneath my bed. Depression was not visible from the outside, but I felt it from within and in my relationship with Heidi. Things began to drift. I was conning counsellors into thinking I was doing OK in a fifty-five-minute session of hoodwinking, and then leaving with a bombshell. Squeeze were off on tour again, this time on the back of an album I had lost faith in and with a band that was not really Squeeze, although it was full of great people. Steve Maidment, who helped run the studio with me, came to see me off at a hotel close to Heathrow airport. I broke down in tears and kicked the room to pieces as I looked out at the runway in front of me. Steve helped me calm down but could not get me onto the plane. I could not take the pain of separation and the onslaught of what I knew would be a long and possibly difficult tour. I did not get on the plane: I watched it take off and then drove by myself to the gates of The Priory, where I collapsed in a heap on the steps. I was done.

Once at The Priory, my counsellor told me I needed to get back on the programme and work hard on myself. They poured me into their Galsworthy Lodge treatment centre which was on the same grounds as the Priory Hospital. I also needed to find another accountant – my counsellor felt Lew might have been complicit in my actions and I needed someone in charge of my finances who I couldn't manipulate, but I didn't completely agree with him. However, Lew was replaced, but by this time he'd gone to work for Elvis Costello, whose affairs he ran successfully for many years. It was good for our relationship and he was brilliant with Elvis.

In all honesty, Lew had nothing to do with my bad behaviour. I was the guilty party, the one who shopped and stole and lied and cheated his way around. Addiction is a very patient disease; the darkness is right there on my shoulder, waiting for me to creep into a weak and empty place. I was soon on antidepressants. I stayed on them for many years. My time in The Priory was in effect to get me through the depression I had been suffering, and suffering in silence. I was not sharing my concerns or speaking my mind to Glenn or to Heidi about the way I thought things could be; I was just going with the flow. Sometimes the easiest option, but not always the best. I was not speaking my mind; I was not man enough for that. I was on the ropes with myself, and with Glenn I was losing the focus on my creativity. It was so sad. I was all over the place and needed to find my feet again. I had let everybody down, again. Depression came to me in many different disguises. I didn't want to look out and check for the reality around me because I felt safe in its darkness. I felt I had let my children down who were young and at home wondering why, and where I had gone. Riley and Natalie seemed understanding, maybe because they were a little older. They supported me with equal amounts of love when Heidi and I were at each other's throats. It was often tough for them being in the middle and I felt for them. Riley followed in my footsteps a few years later with his own trip into treatment. We ended up supporting each other. Maybe it is a family disease after all.

To go back into rehab meant I had reached a new rock bottom and to prove how mad I was I had dark windows put in on my new car; it was taken away for tinting while I was in The Priory, picked up from the car park and replaced the very next day. I think that sums it all up pretty well, as did my peer group at the time, who raked me over the coals in a Wednesday-afternoon anger group. I was in group therapy all day long, and going in the minibus to meetings in Chelsea and Richmond; four weeks of step work in which I wrote down how bad I felt and where I'd been, then shared it with the group. As at PROMIS, there were good people to hold my hand and there were complicated relationships to unravel – the ones with my brothers, Heidi and Glenn all needed a good seeing-to. One afternoon Pete T came in to visit me. He came in twice more to help me understand what being in a band can do to you; how the relationships born out of youth and a shared vision can, over time, give way to anger, resentment and fear. It was so kind of him to spend those hours with me and I felt very lucky to sit with him – he had been a lifetime idol, and now he was a personal mentor. It was his job I had been after all those years ago when at school, and here he was in front of me: larger than life but softer than I could ever imagine.

The group at Galsworthy did some empty chair work one afternoon. Chairs seem to play a big part in any rehab routine. In this exercise, you place someone you need to speak to in the chair, but they of course are not present. Heidi would not come to therapy so she was in the hot seat. It took some doing to verbalise how I felt. It was painful and, egged on by counsellors and the group, I screamed and shouted, something I never do – I normally prefer the quite life. It was an incredible experience. I repeated the process a few years later at Cottonwood, a workshop in a hotel in London. I went into a long weekend with a fantastic counsellor, Rockelle Lerner: her workshop on letting go of fear really helped me out of a tight emotional spot. The empty chair work she is so skilled in had me reaching deep inside. She broke me down and then built me back up again and it really worked for me. It was similar to the feelings I had during psychodramas back in PROMIS. It hurt but I knew it would do me good.

My time at the Galsworthy was just a sticking plaster over a deep wound. Rehab and weekend retreats can only be this. The real work is achieved in the everyday world. A high wire above the emotional streets below walking between the mother, the sea and the father, the forest, it's a bloody nightmare some days. With the help of anti-depressants, I kept a level head and the word Cipralex became as visible in my bathroom as Colgate.

OLYMPIA

In 1997 when I first went to meet Bryan Ferry, I was nervous and shaking with fear – which was just how he liked me, as it turned out. I was introduced to him by Squeeze's ex-manager and mentor, David Enthoven, and at first I was employed to help him write songs. 'Lyric doctor' was my full title. His offices were pristine and ran with a quiet hum, everything in its place. There were cupboards full of notepads and Berocca; drawers full of files and files full of photographs. Tour posters leant against the walls. Books were piled neatly on tables – tables that were covered in white blotting paper. Jars full of pencils; cups and saucers, tea-pots and silverware in the kitchen, to one side. Beyond the office, there was his bedroom, bathroom and drawing room, with its grand piano covered in books. Downstairs there was the studio with its antique Trident recording desk; guitars and keyboards – all vintage.

Most of the time Bryan marched around the office finding things for people to do, including me. His style was that of an old school-master, and I liked that about him. His tea was always poured to perfection. And why not? I'd adored his music as a twenty-year-old, obsessing over Roxy Music records. I even took his first solo album, *These Foolish Things*, to a hairdresser in Kensington one day and said I wanted my hair like his, lagoon blue!

It was intelligent pop music and the whole sound of it was so well-crafted and unique. The glam side of me desperately wanted to be part of it all. Every nuance of Bryan's recordings over the years had been thoroughly thought through and I'd been totally in awe of his lyrics and vocal style – which I found so touching. The journey that Bryan took us all on was incredible. It's a style I've tried to emulate many times without success.

In his recording studio was Phil, who ran the mixing desk and chewed pencils. He had the patience of a saint, as did we all. Robin Trower, his guitarist and co-producer, bit his tongue most of the time and clapped loudly in time to the things he liked, like a dad trying to be hip. Alice was nineteen, French and beautiful – she made the tea and filed the photographs. She stayed in a hotel as she hadn't yet got a place to live. Mr F had discovered her in Spain, babysitting a friend's children. She talked on the tracks we recorded in a young, polite and sexy way. Alice was being watched at all times and she knew it. She was no fool. Auntie – Miss Mann – sat by the phone and ordered olives. She was an all-round wonderful woman who'd known Bryan and Roxy all her life; she was part of him in every sense. Without her, the day would crumble. Nigel Puxley, otherwise known as The Doctor, hunched over his Mac, his hair hanging down over his eyes to cover his age and historical drug habit. I wasn't sure what his role was at first, but gradually I understood that he and Bryan went back to the very beginning, and like Auntie he knew where all the bodies were buried.

One of my first days with Bryan involved going to the Dorchester

Hotel, where Sasha, a Russian pop promoter, was waiting with his Orthodox priest. Yes, really. First things first, he asked me to join him for an early-evening Chinese meal. We sat together and ate our food, which he chose, getting to know each other while holding chopsticks. Our first date went well. I was in a black suit with a white-spotted black tie; he was also in a black suit with a white-spotted black tie – we were a strange couple. I drove a Jaguar XK at the time and he loved sitting beside me as we raced around town in the darkness. After the meal, we drove over to Park Lane. The eighth-richest man in Russia, with gold teeth and a whole floor of rooms, was waiting for us. At the hotel door we met his bodyguard, who spoke into his arm and took us into the lift. My car was parked for me. On the fourth floor, the door opened and we were met by another dark-suited man with an earpiece. We were seated in a suite down the hall and told to wait. In came Sasha with another bodyguard and his interpreter, and we shook hands and sat down. Sasha was a big man with a mysterious beaming smile. We watched a DVD of Bryan playing live; he looked awkward. A tray of cold vodka appeared and, being teetotal, I refused. The guard said it would be bad form for me to refuse. I said that if I drank the vodka it might be bad form all round. I took a glass and feigned sipping. Mr F tipped his back with a face like a child taking his medicine. We talked about future shows in Moscow, then in marched two chefs with a chariot of Chinese food. Apparently we were to eat with the Tsar. This was not on my memo. Gingerly tossing rice and giant prawns around our plates, we both tried to look surprised and hungry – which of course we weren't. After a few long hours, we managed to leave with firm handshakes all round. Back in the Jaguar, Mr F said nothing. I dropped him off at his place and he still said nothing. I then drove on to my new lodgings at The Gore Hotel in Kensington, where I stayed during the week.

We had many slow days in the studio working through lyrics – pulling teeth springs to mind. But soon I could add something new to my CV: chauffeur. I drove Bryan around town all the time; to Sotheby's and Christie's, where he'd dive out to look at the paintings. I would sit in the car by the kerbside with the radio on. All I needed was the chauffeur's hat. I mentioned this in passing to Bryan, and he went to Jermyn Street and bought me one. The gesture would have been funny if it weren't so loaded. After this, we drove up to Alastair Little's restaurant in Notting Hill for lunch. For a chauffeur, I was extremely spoilt. The food was beautiful.

Most afternoons were like this. Bryan always liked to have a dinner date. If it wasn't me, it was Lord Somerset. Two or three times a week we'd go out for lunch – usually to Cibo, an Italian in Kensington. We always had the same seat. To regularly have dinner with someone I'd grown up dreaming of getting to know was wonderful. My feet didn't touch the ground. I felt like a little boy in the company of his favourite teacher. The icing on the cake was a trip into the West End for dinner at the Groucho Club with Mrs F, David Enthoven, Brian Eno and Michael Stipe of REM. Eno had toothache and made good with a salad and some painkillers. He balanced the conversation very carefully and seemed charming. Moving to Russia was his main topic; he was going there for six weeks to get away from it all. He could have saved himself a trip and come to my hotel – it was full of Russians.

Mr F sat at the head of the table, Mrs F at the other end, smoking delightfully and looking debonair. They were like bookends that glared at each other through cigarette smoke, words drifting like clouds from one end of the table to the other, nothing much being said. I'd have been so happy to be in Bryan's shoes, let alone in his jacket. I'd never met a fifty-one-year-old who looked so cool. Michael Stipe sat like a leprechaun hunched over his small plate of food. I looked at him and saw no signs of the 80 million dollars he was meant to be worth. His head kept folding into his body as his eyes fixed like headlights into the distance. Jet lag. We talked about the past and how REM had once opened for Squeeze; it was some years ago and I was in a very different place now. I was a huge fan of the band and loved the way they stuck together as a team. Squeeze were never normally team players, and the grass always did look greener on the other side. We exchanged admiration for each other's work, and the butter was passed. The apple crumble was cooked to perfection and was the envy of all present, which made me feel very fat as I delicately spooned in each mouthful. Stipe had the yoghurt.

Life in the camp was often farcical. If Bryan fell ill with a cold, everything came to a standstill while we all figured out what was for the best – though nothing ever was. He would sing a couple of high notes, which would then snap, and we'd be diving into the vitamin cupboard, putting ginger in hot water and generally hopping about. My job one morning was to listen to what had been going on musically over the previous few weeks and make notes on what I thought. Then Bryan came in, read the notes and walked away without comment. I listened again to all the songs on the CD and made more notes; this time he agreed with me but wanted another opinion. The Doctor came down from his busy desk upstairs and shuffled about on his heels. He looked earnestly at the boom box and shrugged, then I tried to write down what his thoughts were. Mr F walked back in and asked me if I'd brought my video camera, but I hadn't, so he tried to send John, the other driver, down to my house in Rye to collect it – a round trip of nearly 200 miles.

I was also asked to watch a rare French film and note down each time the woman screamed. Halfway through, I thought to myself, 'Didn't I used to be in Squeeze?' One day at The Gore, I looked into the mirror and saw this fat face there. I was a pink balloon in tartan underwear. The great white chin of pride ducked down onto my shirt, and everywhere I looked, impressions were confirmed. I had put on weight that year, eating up my teenage dreams at delicate lunches and dinner tables for two.

One day Alice, who worked in the office as studio gofer, asked me if she could come to the studio in Barnes where we had been working. I asked Bryan and he said of course. As I walked in with her, a very famous guitarist turned up to work in another studio just at the same time. He saw her and set about finding out more. He came to me and asked me to pass on a message to her: perhaps she'd like to meet him for dinner one night? She thought this was very funny, but I saw more than humour in her smile. Her red lipstick painted a very different picture. That night, he made a pass at her and the next morning invited her to hear his new album.

When Bryan got wind of it, I was banished from the studio. I was left so confused. I slithered about in the garden at Old House Farm and waited for something to happen. The phone didn't ring, so I picked it up and made some calls to the office, but Bryan wouldn't speak to me. So I faxed him. The next morning, he called me and we made it up – sort of – then it was back into the Jag and up to London, where the frost was thick on the ground. We shook hands and the week ended with a cordial smile.

Life returned to normal for a few months. I enjoyed my car and my hotel room. I loved my life with Mr F. Dave Stewart was producing his new album – I found Dave so interesting to work with; he was a buzzing bee who was always here, there and everywhere pollinating his wares. He filmed everything, he stored all he saw, he was mad as a hatter. What to make of it all? I could not. I dared not. Mr F took me to the Royal Albert Hall one night to see a band I'd never heard of called Blackstreet. The place was buzzing with atmosphere, and the bodies in the crowd swayed and shook as the music lifted everyone to another place – not bad for a Tuesday. The band were great, the drummer was an amazing player. It was nice to wake up in the morning not knowing about something as great as this then going to bed exhausted, having been fully educated. We were two middle-aged white men in tweeds trying to look cool. We stuck out like sore thumbs. But he always managed to carry off the look wherever he happened to be.

Back at the studio, the mood was altogether different. I picked Mr F up from his house in Kensington and he was in a very happy mood, with a teenage smile. Funny things happened, though. The lyrics to the new album were on my PowerBook, but they didn't match those on the Mac shared by The Doctor upstairs. We were both summoned to the table and commas were moved and hyphens created; spellings were changed. The Doctor was barked at – the whole thing got very heated indeed. 'Let's see now, does martini have a capital M or a baby m in this case?' Such things were very important in Bryan's world. It was all about spacing, timing, interpretation of the master vocal and what Bryan wanted. His attention to detail in everything we did was inspiring and exhausting all at the same time. I loved to try and keep up with him, but of course I never could.

Meanwhile in the studio, a tribe of people worked on bringing new beats to old songs. The studio would always employ at least one programmer to try new things out. Long, boring hours in front of a screen with the latest plug-ins. It was like Grand Central Station and all trains were running late. But we all knew that when they eventually left the platform, Mr F would be in the signal box sending them in different directions, having first checked that The Doctor and I agreed with Robin Trower. Then Robin would agree with Bryan and, in turn, he with us.

Auntie would then arrive to agree as well. We all agreed that Bryan was, of course, right after all. I sharpened pencils until they were all the same height in the jar. I made tea with just the right amount of milk. I kept quiet when I was not spoken to. It was a dream job helping Bryan to find lyrics from his notepads and transform them into verses and choruses for new songs for an album that didn't come out for another four years. But I was tired of that room and I was tired of that coffee, those sandwiches and the crisp white shirts. My chin rested on my collar and my tummy created a schoolteacher's paunch in my ever-blue jumper – I was tired of that too. I was tired, but not really of my job or Bryan – just of me. Suddenly I was let go, my term had come to an end, so I packed my school bag and I raced back to the country to the family and the studio that had just been built. I was missing my girls, the dogs and simple walks in the woods at weekends. One did pay for the other, but it was hard work.

Three years later, I walked back into his office. Nothing had changed. Although my life did have its own changes, as I was now living back in London in a flat in Wapping overlooking the Thames. I was a single man again. Bryan grilled me to within an inch of my life. Did I really want to be his personal manager? David Enthoven had once again put me forward and I drank the poison from the vial. Bryan's recent divorce from Mrs F had turned his world upside down and he wanted to work.

My role was to find him shows, and the corporate gigs came thick and fast once I put the word about. This was all new ground for me and I had to learn on the hoof, which made my heart race with every call I had to make. It was testing but rewarding. The first of these was at the Natural History Museum, just a mile or so from the office, at which Bryan was supported by James Brown. He was paid a fortune, but still demanded a hotel room close by, even though he could have walked back to his own bed in less than ten minutes. He delivered a short but stylish set of hits, then went home and left the hotel room empty. My sub-role that evening was to get his son to video the female dancers, who were sexy and outrageously good. He would use this footage to teach his dancers how to move. Dancing underneath the dinosaurs of the museum was a sight I will never forget: I was as transfixed as he was.

At around the same time, I was asked to help arrange a photo shoot for an advertising campaign featuring Bryan that would run in glossy magazines all over the world. The photographer was Lord Lichfield. The plan was to meet in Hyde Park and the shoot would take place in the orange glow of fallen leaves in the autumn morning light. Again, Bryan insisted on a hotel room, at the Four Seasons on Park Lane – though this time he did actually stay there, with me in the next room. On the shoot, I stood by and watched, throwing in words of encouragement every now and again as Lichfield snapped away. I was trying to be in the right place at the right time with the right comments, but it was hopeless. Bryan hated the cold and the park, and although I could tell he admired Lichfield he found it hard to work for him, and things seemed to become frosty. And when, a few weeks later, the pictures arrived, he was not keen on them. He asked Lichfield to airbrush out a gap between his legs as he felt it made him look as though he was wearing an ill-fitting suit. This didn't go down well and I was caught in the middle. It was almost pistols at dawn. But things moved on quickly; other pressing matters arose. We'd run out of Fortnum & Mason Earl Grey. Bryan was recording again, but the output wasn't enough to excite EMI so I was summoned to an office to discuss another hits collection to fill the gap. The sleeve design for this took longer than the making of most albums, and each picture suggested was pored over for days, leaving grown men weeping over cold coffee. I was inspired by Bryan's keen eye and attention to detail but it was something I was not very good at. We eventually released the album and went on tour to promote it. It was a very strange time. In Australia, Bryan's guitarist Mick Green had a heart attack on stage – he was saved by two doctors who were at the show. Bryan didn't seem to notice it happen behind him and carried on singing.

Since my last stretch, poor Mr Puxley had passed away, and Bryan had replaced him with a Glaswegian fan who knew more about Bryan than Bryan did. It seemed ridiculous to me that you'd not only employ a fan to work in your office, but you'd also fly him down from Scotland on a Monday, put him up in a hotel all week, then fly him home again on a Friday night. There was a strangeness about the man that meant I didn't trust him, and his snooping around the building bothered me. When he took some time off sick, the studio engineer and I noticed that some boxes had been moved and that tapes were missing from the collection. Later in the day, I saw that some posters from old Roxy shows were also missing.

I was summoned to Bryan's room and ordered to fly to Glasgow to watch the man's every move – stalk him if needs be. I'd gone from chauffeur to spy in a few short years. I couldn't track the man down: he wasn't at home and his phone had been cut off. Months later, we found him in a hospital, suffering from serious depression and being constantly watched by the nurses. We never recovered the tapes or posters. Bryan was understandably shocked by the betrayal and it felt as if everyone in the office suddenly became guilty by default. I think it took him a while before he trusted any of us fully again.

During this second stint, I had a call from a wealthy fan who wanted a private show from Roxy Music – and was prepared to pay whatever it took. Bryan asked me to call around and I managed to persuade all the old band members that this was a good idea. I even got them in the same room at the same time to discuss things – a huge feat in itself – but it felt like the first day of primary school. Everyone was ridiculously shy and there was lots of standing around, much twiddling of thumbs. Phil Manzanera was the one who knew how to open Bryan up the most.

The show was magical. There were only about a hundred people there, which was a shame – a lot of very rich people, it seems, have plenty of money but not many friends. And afterwards, Phil asked Bryan and me to his studio to hear the bones of some new songs, which Bryan very reluctantly agreed to. We stood and listened, and I was absolutely thrilled at what I heard. Bryan didn't seem too impressed, but the next day he was back in Phil's studio pushing some of his own ideas around, some of them involving lyrics I'd turned up in old notepads I'd found in a cupboard. The fire was lit, but it soon went out.

The tension of being on call all the time slowly got to me. There were no gaps in the week. I managed to see my kids from time to time, but with Bryan in my life too it was becoming too much. He couldn't make up his mind about another show I was organising for him – even though things like private jets were being thrown into the deal – and it all came to a head. I drove back to Wapping and called in sick for a few days, then spent hours each day asking myself whether I needed this in my life. When I returned to work, I was let go. Bryan wrote me a letter, which remains unopened to this day.

I felt a massive sense of regret. Though I was relieved to be free of Avonmore Place, I felt as though I'd failed. There was no new album, no reunion with Roxy, no more dinners at Cibo. And for all Bryan's faults, I missed him. He was a man with whom I was besotted as a teenager, and whose records I'd constantly played and studied. He was mysterious and generous, he was angry and he was gifted. The week I left, we were in the studio and he sat at the piano and sang Traffic's 'No Face, No Name, No Number' while I stood behind him and felt the tears come to my eyes. His voice, though fragile, reduced me to rubble.

It was a tough job and each week I bailed water out of the sinking boat with nothing more than a china cup. But a very expensive china cup, as you can imagine. David Enthoven always told me that I should stand up to Bryan and shout back at him if he barked at me. Man up, he would say. It was good advice. But I was just a boy, a fan in very expensive sheep's clothing.

THE STRAND

In 1999 I was invited to the Ivor Novello Awards in London. It's without doubt the best music-award ceremony you can go to; it's well-run and each year I know more and more people there. I have two Ivor Novello awards on my desk and I'm very proud of them both. On this occasion, I was a guest of my then-publishers EMI. The manager John Reid was there too, and on his table was Marti Pellow, lead singer with Wet Wet Wet. In the papers recently there'd been pictures of Marti being wheeled away from a hotel looking gaunt and wasted during his much-publicised heroin addiction. But tonight he looked fresh-faced, suited and booted.

We had met once before when I wrote some lyrics for Marti's band. I remember going to a studio in Berkshire where they seemed to be living at the time and working with Graham Clarke, who was their main writer. Sometimes they used the studio to do their laundry; so decadent. At the height of their fame they'd fly in curries from Glasgow to studios in Norway on private planes. Marti was sitting in a dark room eating chicken on the bone. He asked me how I managed to keep myself sober; I could only just see him as the light was so bad. He was on drugs then without doubt. He was like Marlon Brando, sitting in the darkness whispering in his Glaswegian accent. I was scared for him and felt his pain.

At the Ivor Novello Awards, though, he was very much sober – but nervously so. I gave him my number in case he wanted to chat about recovery or go to a meeting with me; that's what AA people do. He called a few weeks later and I arranged for him to come to Old House Farm. He arrived in his car and we sat on the lawn. It was a hot summer's day and we talked about writing songs, about recovery and about him leaving his band. After a few cups of tea and some cake, we looked around my studio and he met the girls, Grace and Cissy. Later on we had a takeaway curry from Rye and he moved in.

Marti stayed at my house for almost two years. Slippers and pipe, Ferrari and a sense of humour; he was a funny and delicate soul. He asked me to hook him up with songwriters I trusted, so each week became filled with people coming and going to the studio in my garden. He had swapped one addiction for another. We were up all night and all day chasing songs with bemused writers down from London. It was good fun.

After a few months, Marti asked me if I fancied managing him. I accepted, as I was already organising his diary with his PA Rowan, who was lovely but lived way up in Scotland. I walked into Universal to discuss a possible solo album but they wanted me to work with someone more skilled as a manager, and that person was Clive Banks.

Clive and I met, and I agreed he was much more suited to the job than I was – his track record was impressive, and he had an enviable reputation in the music industry. His wife looked after

Madonna's press at the time. Clive was a creative and loving person who I really liked hanging out with; it seemed to work and we formed a company to look after the boy. Marti and I had a friendship and some good people to work with; we had 110 songs, but still we had no album. I'd write the words, plucking them out of thin air as Marti sang, and another musician would provide the vamps and chords. A three-way split. We had everyone down to try and co-write, Andy Caine, Gary Clark, Gary Kemp and Graham Lyle. Graham Gouldman, the postman, the baker, the farmer and anyone else who would be passing by, it was exhausting. Then we had a programmer who would stay up late and make the songs sound great. This was mostly the job of Paul Inder, a tender man with eyes the size of computer screens, who was the son of Lemmy from Motörhead. He was fast and he was patient too, but he did have very smelly feet. He lived in a converted ambulance in the garden, which Heidi found intolerable. They fell out constantly. Especially one night when the handbrake on his ambulance stopped working and it ended up in a field; it had to be pulled out by the local farmer. Heidi was not impressed. She sent him packing and it took me a few days of negotiating with her to allow him back. He was priceless in many ways.

One night when I was in bed, I opened my eyes to see Marti bending over me, whispering for me to come and hear a new song. It was 3 a.m. I got dressed and crossed the garden to the studio. I could smell something; it was too much aftershave mixed with something else. He was slurring and bullying me to stay awake and write more words for him. He wasn't well and the next day he drove himself to The Priory, where he stayed for the obligatory twenty-eight days. I visited him each week. My driveway, I later discovered, was strewn with empty vodka bottles hidden in bushes and ditches.

When Marti returned to Old House Farm, he threw himself into work. He was on a mission and we all had to ride with whatever it was – often I would try and creep away, but he was on full burn most of the time, writing as much as he could. It tired me out. I'd pick out lyrics, order food and cars, plan tours and book musicians, then write more lyrics. He was a funny sod and really good company. He got on with my kids and became like an uncle to them, buying them sweets and picking them up from school. And I enjoyed going to Glasgow with him, meeting his folks, who were much like mine.

Marti paid rent and mucked in – sometimes. He was generous and kind. The first solo album gathered mixed reviews, but he wanted to push on; the next one was being written and in his head the one after that too. He had his sights on being the next Robbie Williams, and talked to us constantly about getting film work or appearing on stage. He wanted nothing less than James Bond as his first role. Clive and I knew, what with his strong Glaswegian accent, that this would be hard work and at the very least he'd need some help. But in Marti's mind he was a superstar.

He wanted badly to be a great solo success but Marti, unlike Robbie Williams, didn't have the likes of the very talented Guy Chambers to help mould his songs into hits. He had me. This infuriated him and we ended up nose to nose, with him yelling and swearing into my face as Grace and Cissy looked on from the trampoline. To say sorry, he bought a curry from the Indian in Rye for everyone that night – and picked it up in his Ferrari. He would often shoot from the hip, but he would make it up soon after. He felt embarrassed by such outbursts; he was really a softie and full of love. I understood his concerns and tried hard to shelter him.

Clive and I managed to get him an audition for Billy Flynn in the West End show *Chicago*, and I drove him up to London. I pushed him into a small room with two young men from the theatre; one in red braces, the other in a running suit.

I stood outside on tenterhooks and listened to him singing. When he came out, we walked through Covent Garden together with him cursing about being stuck in a room for an hour. He got the role. Marti had to work hard to speak and sing in an American accent, and his teacher was consistent and patient – much more patient than I was. He was practising at the Pineapple Dance Studios in Covent Garden, so I'd wander next door to watch girls warming up in leotards. As a manager, I was on the lookout for talent. That was my excuse anyway. It was the highlight of my day. I went to see *Chicago* with Marti, in a checked shirt and dark suit. I was welcomed as the guy who supported the star, who showed up on time and got the coffees from Starbucks. Clive very kindly pointed out to the producer that I'd done my own show only the other night and that it had been fantastic, but they couldn't have cared less. Marti had his picture taken and hung out with the cast members, who surrounded him like mist around a mountain. They swam behind him in the room, smiling and trying to understand what he was saying.

Rehearsals were a success. Sitting in the stalls watching Marti go through his paces, I imagined how great it would be to write a musical and have it staged like this. Choreography and story are so important; there is so much to learn, but where do you start? Maybe having that passion is enough. Being backstage at the

Adelphi Theatre on the Strand watching Marti was a lot of fun;
and the cast laughed and joked and generally made the new boy
feel very welcome. The Royal Room – in which the Queen hung
out whenever she came to the theatre – became my office, and
between its red-and-gold walls and its framed posters for West
End hits of the past, I started to breathe again. Marti's life was
now cushioned by daily rehearsals; I was needed less and less.
Marti nailed it – he was brilliant at being Billy Flynn – and I felt
very proud.

One evening, on my way home from the theatre, I walked into
the NCP car park and saw a young man beneath a makeshift
shelter in a dark corner of the exit ramp. He was sitting cross-
legged on a sheet of card fixing heroin by himself. I passed him
slowly, and though I was in a pinstripe suit and carrying a brief-
case, I felt closer to him than I did my own shadow. I said the
serenity prayer and left him there to enjoy his evening, to sail
the night fantastic. In my Jaguar, I calmly pulled out into Drury
Lane and set off towards the calm of the country with Radio 3
playing and a nice empty road in front of me. Worlds apart,
maybe. The following week, I receive a call from young Marti: he
has jammed his Ferrari in the pinch points of the ticket barrier in
the same NCP and he can't move the car. I'm asked to come and
help, which I refuse to do. Some things are just out of a manager's
remit.

I watched the show about twenty times. I really loved it. Marti
did us all proud, but he was soon on to the next task: Broadway.
Clive and I delivered his request, but sadly, when he arrived in
New York, there was an actors' strike and he ended up sitting in
his hotel room for a few weeks. He was fuming – which he was

an expert at doing – but there was nothing I could do but wait for the strike to end. So he came back to the West End, then toured *Chicago* around the UK.

Meanwhile, he recorded two more solo albums in Memphis with producer Willie Mitchell. We took Phil Brown to engineer, who we totally trusted; he had worked on Marti's previous solo albums and on my solo album a few years before. A steady pair of hands. The recordings were incredible; I had never heard Marti sing like that, with so much soul and tenderness. We also recorded a fantastic album of country songs with John Wood; not sure what happened to them. We were never lazy and I was on full spin all the time.

One day I took Marti to see Deke Arlon, an old-school manager with a big desk with inkwells and a house in Spain, who had looked after Ray Davies. I left him there with his new career. It was like dropping him off at boarding school.

When Marti lost his mother, I went to Glasgow to hold his hand at the funeral. It was a bright day, but cold. I stood to one side as his family took centre stage; the other members of Wet Wet Wet turned up to pay their respects. I was the only Englishman there and I felt it. After leaving the graveside, we moved down the hill to a small hotel where some sandwiches had been laid on. I walked in and the band's keyboard player came up to me and said, 'You've stolen our singer.' His look scared me. The atmosphere was sudden and cut from glass; I was on the edge of another band's empty stage.

Sadly Marti and I have not kept in touch. He called me a few times for directions to various theatres, and then nothing. Our backgrounds were similar; his parents had the same three-bar fire as mine, the same furniture, the same sons who'd gone off to do what they wanted and followed a dream. We had different needs, but we'd both had to grow up in a world of minibars, fast cars and Top 10 records. And, in Marti's case, tons of cash too. Working with him was great fun. I enjoyed the tours and the fun we had up and down the country. I was his manager-cum-chauffeur-cum-writer-cum-takeaway-orderer-cum-backstage-guide-and-confidant. Hotels were always of a high standard and his car became my home.

Who would have thought it just four years before, when he was on heroin and every bit the fallen pop idol? He was lucky to be in such a great place. And I was lucky to have been there with him, for better or for worse. He is one of the hardest-working singers I know, on both stages: the theatrical and with his band the Wets.

HELIOCENTRIC

Francis Dunnery came to my house in Rye to change my life forever. We had first met at a writers' retreat at Huntsham Court in Devon, which had become something of a bolthole for me during the last few years of my marriage to Cindy. I'd go there to write and relax, drink, eat and walk in the beautiful countryside. Francis had been in a band called It Bites; he was a larger-than-life human being and a great guitarist – he was from that prog-rock school of musicians that had really learned to play their instruments properly. We wrote together on that trip. One evening he knocked on my door yelling, 'I need a meeting, let me in!' I knew what he meant, and we went to his room and sat around a copy of the *Big Book* – the AA bible. We soon got to know each other well. His presence was immense and it was almost as if he could read my mind. It was he who led me to the microphone to make my first solo album. I was terrified as I stepped up to the plate.

I'm not sure how it all fell into place, but one day I was at home doing nothing much and the next minute he turned up and set me writing and recording. It was an intense session that ran for about a month, with people coming and going – notably Dorie Jackson on vocals, who magically managed to lift my voice on invisible strings, tuning it and keeping it warm. Dorie was a very gentle person who was so lovely to work with. Ash Soan, who'd played on Squeeze's *Domino* album and was someone I loved being with also, came in to play the drums. He was so creative. We had Matt Pegg on bass, who I knew little about, and the rest was down to Francis. He played guitar, he played the upright piano we based most of the songs around and he cradled everything in his way.

We listened to his words and fell to his views, rightly or wrongly. I loved working from home. My studio – called Heliocentric after its unique Helios desk that I'd got from the famous Basing Street Studios in London – was in the garden and I could look out of the window and see my girls, Grace and Cissy, riding horses. Heidi kept house, and fed and watered us all through the recording. The sound we evoked was that of childhood, and the deeper we went, the harder it was to keep from crying. Phil Brown, who'd engineered Jimi Hendrix, The Small Faces and Robert Plant, brought his tender touch to the album.

The studio – my studio – was a nest of chords, words and feelings, and felt unlike any place I'd ever worked in before. Francis had to wrestle vocal performances from me – and with some patience, too. He knew it would be difficult. I tried so hard to sing in tune for him, and spent hours working on each line to get it right. I was not a natural singer. I never have been. He was well versed in astrology and drew on my curiosity from time to time; he even read my chart one afternoon. He was spot on. We sat, he talked and he described my life back to me. He could feel my present self and where my journey had taken me. It was very emotional when he revealed my life, shallow and painful as it had been. Before this reading the closest I got to astrology was reading my chart in the

Sunday papers for fun. This was the real deal and very deep, just like Francis.

During the recording we talked all the time and had a good laugh. It was open and fun, like no other album I'd ever made before. 'Parents', a song about my mum and dad, was emotional and so haunting to record – its lines prised every feeling I had about them out of me. I was in therapy, but on a couch of guitar, bass and drums. Francis wanted me to get deep down into family – about what it was like for me growing up.

We used a school piano as that link to childhood. He'd studied psychology and believed that by dredging down, you reveal treasures that have been deeply buried. In doing so, he opened me up to being a better writer in many ways.

'One Day', a wonderful, dark song, had me flying into the unknown, exploring the anxiety of fear. Francis knew exactly where that came from and how to lance its boil. He really knew how to reflect me. He made me look at my feminine side with 'Cowboys Are My Weakness', and even managed to rake me over the hot coals of Glenn with a song called 'No Show Jones'. 'Get it off your chest,' he said, so I wrote the song about me not turning up for the tour when I went into The Priory, and tried to address the differences between Glenn and me. I don't think Glenn paid much attention to 'No Show Jones'. He had also written a song about me, on one of his solo albums. We were both hissing like snakes in the undergrowth of our separate lives. Silly really.

I was so proud of the studio as a creative place to work and enjoy. Thanks to my brother Lew and his close management of the situation, we were able to balance the books. Elvis Costello part-funded the build, yet he never came to record there, which

I always found odd, but very generous of him. Other than during the sessions for that album, the only other time I recorded at my home studio was with the jazz musician Guy Barker. We wrote an album together. I was the Chet Baker of Rye. This is a record I'd love to revive at some point, as I really enjoyed singing in the jazz style. Guy was imaginative and fun to record with, but his band were way above me in terms of musicality. I was merely mucking out to their intelligent brass lines. They were way too smart for me.

Bands came down all the time to record on my treasured Helios desk, the studio's homely atmosphere being one of its selling points. Heidi grabbed hold of the situation and began to manage it on a daily basis, supplying lunches and dinners for our musical guests. Bryan Ferry came to record there once; The Pet Shop Boys came and ate scones while programming tracks. Paul Weller spent a month there and named his album after the studio. Supergrass recorded there and named a song after Grace, which thrilled her to bits. We had musicians from all over the world: India and America, Canada and west London. Trilok Gurtu came with his drums for some recording and we wrote together. It was a very uplifting event, even though I felt out of my depth. Once we had Wayne Shorter fly in for a session with the incredible Portuguese singer Dulce Pontes. He stayed at the Oast House B&B up the road from the studio. Bob, who ran the B&B, found it all too much dealing with such people; all he knew how to do was full English with fag ash as a topping. But the comings and goings of such famous people never fazed him. Paul McCartney would slip into his bar for a pint every now and again; it was that simple.

On my own album with Francis, we couldn't get the vocals right at my studio in Rye. Francis rightly thought I was too distracted by the house, Heidi and the kids, so he took me back down to Hunt-sham Court. It was torture as he lashed me line by line, stretched me on my metre, tied me to the depth of each word. He beat me up so I'd deliver the goods. Driving back from Devon, he revealed his plan to release the album, I Didn't Get Where I Am, on his own record label in early 2001. Without a major label there was no money for promotion or PR, it was not going to come out of thin air. It reminded me of when Domino was released a few years earlier; yes there was ownership but there was no clear benefit from its value if there was no money to let people know it was out there and in the shops. It was clearly just my take on things, and possibly one a dinosaur would own in these modern times of indie home-spun records that nobody would hear. The right people heard it in the end and I'm very proud of each and every song, and I thank Francis for his determination to get it right and make it sound wonderful.

My album was a success as far as I was concerned. Good friends were constantly in touch to tell me how much they liked it: Elton bought ten copies, which was lovely of him and very supportive; Elvis Costello wrote a glowing review. I Didn't Get Where I Am was never going to rock the charts, but that was a thing of the past for me. Like skateboards.

BRUNSWICK SQUARE

The day my dad passed away in May 2001, the sun was shining on the hospital and on the cemetery in which my mum lay waiting just a few streets away. Ha Ha Lane, Charlton – a funny name for a street with a graveyard. I'll never forget the day. Dad waited for me to come into the room before he drew his last breath; he wanted all three of his sons by his side. There he lay, head propped up on green pillows. I'd been downstairs on my mobile talking to Heidi, who was at home with our daughters in Sussex. The nurse called for me and I came up from the car park. Dad looked at us all, and then he went. In the yellow room where he lay, we stood and cried and held each other. The family tree had lost its major branch.

Hours later, I sat outside in my car with the sun beating down on me, looking out at the Technicolor world my dad was no longer part of. At eighty-three years, he had had a long and good life. The next day, in the car park outside the hospital canteen, I bumped into my very first girlfriend, Sharon. She was still thin and tall; her features still much the same as when we first kissed on Westcombe Hill in 1970, and when we used to go dancing in Catford all those years ago. It was a complete shock to see her there. She hugged me and I cried. I cried most of that week following Dad's

Glenn in midair outside The Bell in Greenwich on Jubilee day. (*Jill Furmanovsky*)

The centerfold from Squeeze's Madison Square Garden tour programme.

Me with a fag down The Albany, before it burnt down.

Squeeze with JB, backstage at the Marquee Club in London.

Oh no it's the Nineties – and I'm in a nice suit!

The three amigos looking happy and ready for business.

Brighton Pier,
a little worse for wear
after a long night.

Looking into the future.

Playing live in the early days, when we could both get off the ground without needing surgery! (*Jill Furmanovsky*)

An *NME* front cover taken at Crooms Hill in thinner days.
(Jill Furmanovsky)

Chewing the cud with Glenn in his studio during the recording of *Cradle*.

Mrs Difford and me, on the most important of all stages.

death. It was odd to find someone that removed from my life yet somehow connected. All the wonderful weaves of this great tapestry seemed to come together.

Later that day, I went walking in the woods near my home, and reflected on my life with my dad. The dogs I'd been walking looked tired and lay down in the fallen leaves. And in that moment, I could taste the rhubarb he always stewed for me to have on my Weetabix before bed. I could smell the chicken boiled in a bag on Saturday nights. I could taste the sweets – milk bottles, blackjacks and the fruit salads I liked the most – bought for me when we went down to the allotment, where he was among his friends. This was our hideaway from the rest of the family. Dad did what he did all afternoon and I played with my cars in the heaps of earth and bits of mud and stone. The smell of his shed was a cross between wood, lime, old cans, nails, creosote, brushes, oil, damp and heat, earth and clay. Smells that are with me today. They pin my memories to the past almost as much as records do.

The gasworks on Tunnel Avenue had been my dad's life outside the home, a grown-up world of big trains and big lorries. Right up to his death he would go back there and enjoy the company of other retirees he knew; the last of the summer wine. They all came to say goodbye at his funeral. It was moving and very funny. The gasworks folk were our second family, who would come and go through our lives. It was nice to know my dad was being looked after when he left the house in the morning.

From the hospital in Charlton, they took Dad's empty body to a funeral home on Blackwall Lane, across the road from Greenwich Hospital, where my mum had died a few years earlier and where

I had been born. Across the road from where I saw my first racy film at the Granada Picture House and from the gasworks where he spent most of his life. Lew picked out a suit for him to wear; around his neck was the old Gas Board tie. I didn't want to see him there made up like he was leaving for work. He was on his final journey and this time he wasn't coming back; and though he looked great, I remember his hands were like fallen autumn leaves in texture, lined and faded with life.

Outside, in the busy traffic, I sat in my car and thought about all the times we'd ridden past this corner of Greenwich on his green bike. Then I drove up to Combe Avenue, where time stood still. The fish still swam in the tank above where he used to sit, the kitchen was cold and still smelt of leaking gas. I looked around and decided not to take anything but memories from the house in which I learnt to listen to music, where I learnt to kiss, where I enjoyed colour TV for the first time and where I learnt to play the guitar and write my first songs.

The wake was held in a hotel on Blackheath; Lew organised everything. Sandwiches and cake; beer, and sherry for the ladies. Pictures of Dad hung on the walls, and books of remembrance were laid out neatly on the tables. He was loved so much – I was proud to be his son. Everyone said nice things about my old man. Elvis Costello came in support, as did Glenn. We hadn't seen each other for some time, but this was not the moment to mend bridges. I felt his love and was grateful to him for joining me on this moving and very sad day. My dad was respected by all of my friends. Jools would often say he'd seen him at the shops and that he'd made him laugh. Funny old sod that he was. Mrs Jones from next door was there to say her goodbyes, with a fag on the go and

a large glass of sweet white wine in her hand. She was so generous to my dad; it was so nice to see her again.

I sat outside the hotel and looked out across the Heath towards
our old home at Combe Avenue. A perfect, simple vision. There I
was: schoolboy, skinhead and hippy. There I found love, football
and drugs. There I found music. The Who live at Leeds, David
Bowie, Frank Zappa, King Crimson, Prince Buster, The Small Faces
and the rest. I thanked my dad for giving me my home and my
roots. I thanked him for giving me my first pushbike, which in
turn gave me my first taste of freedom.

I write about my dad in my songs. 'Sidney Street' on my *Cashmere If You Can* album is about his journey to war. I was always
asking him about the war, but he never wanted to talk about that
part of his life. Unlike a lot of men of his generation, he never
glorified those days and I admire that. War isn't pretty, unlike
rock 'n' roll. I can talk about that all day long. I'm that bloke in
Squeeze; the one who sang 'Cool for Cats'; the one who wears
his inside on his sleeve, etc. My dad's formative years were much
more meaningful. What an easy life I've had in comparison to his.
Out of bed into my socks and jeans, on to the stage, wreak havoc
with some songs and walk away happy with some cash – no dead
bodies.

Dad was never sure about the music I was playing, but he grew
to love it, and it eventually made him proud. The support he gave
me at first was non-existent, but then my piano-playing did only
consist of three notes and some very basic thumping, mostly inspired by The Velvet Underground. From there, I moved on to a
bass guitar, then a guitar with four strings, and then a band. From
pub gigs in south London to touring shows in America. After my

mum died, I flew my dad to New York – him, Lew and Les out in a limo all night long. Squeeze were playing Madison Square Garden. A second sell-out show. It was his first journey on a plane, his first trip outside the UK since the war. He loved the city, but he couldn't understand why all the lights were left on at the World Trade Center at night. It was money being wasted, he moaned. A constant refrain.

After Dad died, his three boys went in different directions. Perhaps I could have seen that one coming. Les and Lew fell out over money, and I was piggy in the middle, but refused to be drawn into the fray. I prefer to think back to the hospital room in which we stood and hugged each other, and held on to our past, trying never to let it go. But that's what we've had to do. Each day flicks past, one after the other, and here you are one minute and gone the next. The man in the doorway no more; the funny man with the jumper and the slippers. Tall and handsome, hair to one side like Bobby Charlton, a cross between Eric Morecambe and Gregory Peck. Priceless humour, dry and pointed sometimes. Lovable from a glance. A hard worker and a keen gardener. A drinker in moderation, a smoker in the evening also in moderation. A soldier with medals. Ruddy-faced and hunched over, distant and tired, shaky and fragile.

Sidney Lewis Difford spent the last years of his life watching football and snooker on the TV, and reruns of *The Two Ronnies*. He enjoyed his own space more than most. I often felt uneasy when I went to see him, but now I understand the comfort provided by being alone – that space created, carved in precious time. If there is another world, I will see Dad there and we can sit together and not say very much; we were so good at that after all. But we will know, just by being father and son, that what we're saying is all we need to say. We never did play football together, or board games, we never built train sets or climbed mountains, but we did love each other. He rooted me in a garden where I flowered into the person I am today, complicated but calm, a chip off the old block maybe. How could I look back and say anything other than thank you, for giving me the best years of my life.

After my dad passed away, I went back home, but my time at Old House Farm was coming to an end. My relationship with Heidi had run out of steam; it was flat and both of us were to blame. Therapy was not going to glue us back together; she thought there would be nothing to gain from it. She had been told that I would always be an addict and therefore always be the way I was. It's here where I think she threw in the towel. Telling the children was the worst thing. We sat them down and told them I was moving out, as Mummy and Daddy weren't getting on. We still liked each other, but we couldn't be together any more. They went to their rooms to smash things up and slam doors. I walked through the fields and cried as I felt the curtains coming down on my family. Heidi and I had put so much work into our thirteen years together, but now we were just too tired and were hopeless around each other. We weren't talking and it seemed that every corner we turned, we had issues there. I do think that underneath it all there was love, but our communication had emptied and the relationship just slipped away.

I moved into a cottage in the garden, which worked for a while, but I realised it was totally over when I got back from a gig at Glastonbury. I booked a van and packed up all my stuff the next day. Leaving was quick and very sad. I remember so well seeing the house in my rear-view mirror as I drove away. The girls were standing waving in the garden, and I felt my heart breaking in two. I cried all the way to London and felt very depressed about the way things had ended up.

I left Rye with my writing desk, which was hand-built in the style of a pile of neat books, a design I stole from the original *Queen Mary*'s Art Deco library. I also took many of my books and clothes; a few pictures and gold discs followed along later. It still felt like I had lost everything in a separation that, like the divorce, seemed brutal and cruel. It was agreed that sometime in the future I could take more of what was mine including my original writing desk which was bought with my first PRS cheque. Sadly its roll-top beauty remains at Heidi's house and not at mine. I moved to Wapping: a view of the Thames in a very nice flat above the cobbled streets. I knew Wapping well and managed slowly to rebuild my life. The kids liked coming to visit me, we had great times walking up and down the river. It felt like another stepping stone. The studio carried on and Keane recorded their two big albums there. Heidi seemed happier and life moved on for us all.

After my years in London working with Bryan Ferry, I then moved to Brighton. I found the sky and the sea intriguing; I loved being able to walk everywhere and soak up the youthfulness of the city. On a sunny day it's the best place in the world. It was such a creative place to be and it was important for me to be close to Grace and Cissy, who were now at school just up the road at Brighton College.

I lived in Brighton for six years, and did some teaching at the local college of music, which was really enjoyable. In that time I moved flats six times, so I got to know the area very well. I also met some lovely people along the way. It was different from London and more like a village, but by the sea. I needed to find a home but that wasn't possible. I was packing and unpacking, chasing mixed emotions and a relationship up and down the flats and mews of Brighton and Kemptown. It's a long story best left to another time. Thankfully I had the safe care of Martin Freeman, a local councillor who I trusted. Emotionally I was not always a happy bunny in my relationship there, and at the end of the six years I snapped. I ended up back in rehab for a few weeks, this time for relationship issues. It was very painful, but not made any easier by the neglect, in my view, of the counsellors who allowed mobile phones in the rooms. People were constantly on them and losing their focus, including me. My friend Gordon helped me more than rehab could with his pearls of wisdom and love, as did my manager Matt. I vowed never to return to those helpless feelings again, but it would take some doing. I was grateful that my girls Grace and Cissy were at school just up the street. It was always so good to see them, but it must have been hard for them to see me often in such a fragile space.

While living in Brighton, I decided I needed to get off my arse and learn more about myself, so I signed up for a diploma of counselling at the CCPE in London. Each Thursday and on some weekends I would join a group and work through the various basic challenges of being a counsellor. By the end of the year I was working in triads learning my skills, but my head was side-tracked by work and I could not always concentrate, and so many books and essays tested my patience. I was not very focused, but I was enjoying the group therapy, which was at times intense. Tears were often shed over sandwiches at break time with the other members of the group, most of whom went on to work in social services or have clients of their own. Which is what I would have liked.

I took some of my skills into treatment centres, where I would lead a group with music and therapy. I found this really reward-ing. Some people fell asleep – which was fine; I would have too – but others joined in with the songs and the story I had to share with them. At one centre in Bournemouth we collected enough songs for an album, which we printed up for friends and family. I also had time to take the workshop into Wandsworth Prison, where I had a captive audience. They loved to muck in with the songwriting.

My next solo album – *The Last Temptation of Chris* – was recorded in Brighton, in my small flat in Brunswick Square, and at a studio not far away in Eastbourne. Singer-songwriter and close friend Boo Hewerdine and I wrote most of the songs, and Boo co-produced the record with me. It was a very different experience from work-ing with Francis, but Boo still had to work hard to tease out the vocals from me. John Wood, who'd worked on the early Squeeze albums, came to share engineering duties with him. But sadly, he wasn't keen on the computer technology Boo was using, and I felt him slip into a mist. I'd pulled John from retirement to record the album, and it wasn't long before he went back to Scotland to concentrate on running his B&B.

I enjoyed the writing process with Boo. He was easy to work with and we had loads of fun. When I wrote for him I felt inspired in a different way than I did with other people. I was very pleased with 'Reverso', a song about vasectomy changes. I'd had my knackers bricked so I knew a bit about the subject. After Cissy was born,

Heidi had decided she didn't want any more children, so I did the manly thing and agreed to have the snip. I remember lying on the bed just before the anaesthetic kicked in and a beautiful Australian nurse came in and whispered kind words then said, 'Did I see you on *Top of the Pops* a couple of years ago?' If I think very deeply about it, it does feel like being put out in a field on your own to graze. Heidi made me feel hollowed out like an old tree, and with not much left inside I buckled with loneliness and dreamt of someone to hold.

'On My Own I'm Never Bored' summed up my time in Brighton; its lyrics reveal what I saw from my front-room window. 'Battersea Boys' was a story told to me by a man called Jim who was in a hospice close to where I lived. I wrote his story into a song and gifted it to him. He sadly passed away, but his brother, who the song is about, turned up at one of my solo shows. It was surreal, and wonderful to meet him. It was a very special moment.

Eastbourne was an odd place to record, but the results were really great. It's a fantastic second album and I'm very proud of it. Boo and I had forged a relationship that I knew would last a long time, as it has. It felt odd to tour on my own – though this was helped by the fact that I was never actually on my own. Dorie Jackson and Francis came with me on my first tours supporting Elvis Costello and Chris Rea, and Boo was by my side the rest of the time. Dorie helped me to tune myself when I first stepped back out on the road, her voice being so correct and powerful. These days I tour with Melvin Duffy on guitar and Arcelia, a vocal group from Kent, who are magnificent and need no rehearsing.

At first, walking on stage without Glenn and the backdrop of Squeeze frightened me. I'd quiver in the dressing room, waiting for the call to stage, worrying about what to say to the crowd. But soon I was in conversation with an audience who mostly hadn't come to see me, the support act. Francis helped me warm up, and made me think about what to say. He also helped me rearrange Squeeze songs to sound like they were mine, which they were – despite me assuming for years they were Glenn's. Francis was a hard taskmaster, making me grumpy before I went on, but it worked. Supporting Elvis was the perfect introduction to being a solo artist, and – good friend that he is – he looked after me from the top of the bill. The Chris Rea tour was more difficult – his audience seemed uninterested, even when he was on stage – but Boo made the experience fun with his dry sense of humour and his harmonies. Dorie was a good person to have on the road, too; she was fun and often balanced out the workload, selling merchandise and so on. I was a very happy boy.

Touring became a new place for me to be; driving around with an acoustic guitar in the boot of the car was easy work. We played all over the UK, but sadly we couldn't sell out the venues. It was a bit embarrassing and I had to pay the band's wages whatever happened – mainly by selling CDs after each show, which also helped to pay for the endless curries in the dressing room. To change the mood, I made some home movies and bought a big screen to show them at my shows. It was a pain getting it in the car, but the audience seemed to love my editing skills; it gave them something to watch instead of a fat bloke and another bloke with a beard. Matt Deighton joined us on guitar at some of the shows, and as I got to know him more, I wanted to write with him. The chemistry between us was calm. We wrote his album *Part of Your Life* – one of my favourite records – together at my house in Rye and, just as Francis had done with me, I listened to his story and reflected what I'd heard back at him as lyrics. I was the rhyming psychotherapist. Matt at the time seemed confused and depressed, but I'm pleased to say that's behind him now. He was a diamond to work with; he had a fantastic imagination and a pure gift for melody and darkness.

Cashmere If You Can, my third solo record, was an album of deep darkness. I was in the wrong place at the right time in my head to record it, but one thing led to another and soon I was in the thick of it all without ever thinking it through. I worked on the record with Leo Abrahams, a fine guitarist and producer, and – at great expense – a band of top players he'd put together. I felt a little out of my depth. Leo co-wrote some of the songs with me, but I don't think I did them justice – I let him down by metaphorically nodding off on the job. The ones I'd written with Boo in earlier sessions fared slightly better. 'Goldfish', with guest vocalist Kathryn Williams, and 'Wrecked' are the two tracks that stand out to me now. On reflection, we did well to come out with an album at all. Leo had the patience of a saint. *Cashmere If You Can* was expensive, and my manager, Matt Thomas, and I coughed up a heavy price to put it out on the internet. An app was built; it was all going off-piste. And I finally realised there was no money for me in making records any more. But even though solo touring and recording is largely vanity-driven, it's so enjoyable and fulfilling for me to play alone on stage to a house of happy faces that I continue.

During the recording of *Cashmere*, I was playing a solo show in Blackheath. The usual appreciative crowd appeared at the venue as I sat in the dressing room warming up with my customary take-away curry and tea. There was a knock on the door and in walked

Bob from Combe Avenue, who I had not seen for so many years. In his hand was a Tesco bag. After we'd said hello, he handed me the bag with its contents of quarter-inch tapes on reel-to-reel of me as a seventeen-year-old singing and playing my songs. I had completely forgotten about them. I was so moved to have them in my hands. In the studio we found a tape recorder and I heard this young voice singing songs in Bob's bedroom. It was the voice of a passionate young person slightly influenced by Bowie and Reed, the songs deep and dark, the playing gentle, simple and oddly in tune. I was blown away as I was transported back to the young me, at the beginning of the journey that was always going to lead me to this moment.

Being a solo artist is like wearing different hats; sometimes it makes me look like Elvis and at other times it makes me look like a pantomime horse. It's a role I've found difficult to cultivate, but I'm finding that the more I do it, the more I like it. Being on stage is good fun. I talk more and try to engage the outside world with what's going on inside. My history with Squeeze carries weight, and people want to know all about this part of me.

It's an honour to share my journey, which I do in between solo strummings and gentle versions of classic Squeeze hits.

I continue to enjoy a writing partnership with Boo Hewerdine as he delivers something very different to Glenn. We have an unreleased album in the wings. When we come to release it, I think people will like what they hear. The new songs are funny and charming, very me-and-him in some ways. I also love to write with Paul Carrack; I send him words, he sends me melodies and somehow it all fits. Hearing his voice wrapped around my lyrics often finds me crying in the car; the soul is enormous. I also enjoy working with Jools, who comes from another place musically, though it doesn't happen as often as it used to.

We do tour together from time to time and it's a wonderful experience to sing with his Orchestra and play alongside Gilson, who I love and admire for being a wonderfully poetic drummer and good friend. Who would have thought that back in 1973? As I cast my eye over each of my solo albums, I can see a different me to the one in Squeeze. Working with other people engages another part of my soul and I like it that way. It's the writing that I enjoy – it opens me up and hopefully reveals something new every time I put finger to keyboard. It's what I do. If I were a plumber I would be fixing sinks; if I were a pilot I would be flying planes. But I find it's writing that connects me to my higher power. I feel plugged in, sparked up and nourished if I manage to hook something great. It's a hobby more than anything. And today, my solo career simmers in the background feeding my new-found hunger to be heard as an individual, not just that bloke who sang 'Cool For Cats' in Squeeze, lovely though he is.

ANCHOR AND HOPE LANE

Les was the troublesome brother; the tall, skinny one who drank and smoked and swore at my dad and never came home when he was meant to. My mum would be up all night with worry. My parents struggled with him when he was a teenager; he once knocked my dad out on the stairs after a drunken night, and he pushed my mum to her limits as he borrowed more and more money from her. Money she never really had. He fought with my other brother Lew over most things, too. Lew was the academic one and this was to be a lifelong bone of contention for Les, who thought our parents loved Lew more because he was brighter than him – or indeed me. You had to love Les, though; he was such a warm person. He played football really well and enjoyed riding his scooter with girls on the back down around Combe Avenue. If ever I were in trouble at school or on the estate I would go to Les for help. He looked after me, and when I started out in a band, he would always come to the shows and support me. His musical tastes were Bo Diddley and The Rolling Stones, Eric Burdon and – in the end – Squeeze. He tipped my scales musically when I was younger; all that R&B he played in the house drove Mum nuts, but it showed me that nice wasn't always right or good.

The first time I vomited from drinking too much was when I went to visit him up at the Sun in the Sands pub in Blackheath when I was about eighteen. It was lunchtime. He was at the bar on his stool with all his mates around him, and they all gave me their time and support even though they thought I was a dippy hippy. I had a pint and a pie then I had another pint. I was trying to be the man Les was – the bloke who played darts, followed the football and drove home drunk. An hour later, I was outside the pub being sick against the wall; inside my brother and his mates just ploughed on as if nothing had happened. Les got me work, too. I helped him scree walls with plaster in a new housing estate down by the river, then we'd go and get plastered ourselves in the pub. I worked down the docks with him, and at Ready Mix concrete in Catford. He looked out for me and showed me the basics of ducking and diving. Les was my 'fence' once when I was working at Biba in London. I was in the stockroom and found myself moving some gold lighters around. The next day I came to work with an empty guitar case, filled it with the lighters, struggled home on the train with it and took it to Les. He sold them around the pub and gave me a cut of the profit. I managed to keep my job, everyone was at it. My prize steal was a folder covered with a fine leopard-skin print. I still have it, still with nothing in it.

When Squeeze went on tour in 1986, we took Les with us as a minder. He was a big chap and looked tough, and he brought along his mate Terry Kibble from the pub. Terry had been in the army and had served in the Falklands War, and was very scary. Having the two of them on a tour bus was delightful: cards and beer, women and song. Terry managed to get us out of bed some mornings for a bit of training, running around the hotels so we could keep fit. Running on a hangover is not a good idea, and I bailed out very quickly. Those two and our manager David Enthoven were a team, big drinkers all and very funny with it. A good mixture of private school and secondary modern.

Les had a good heart – even if it did have a hole in it. He managed to maintain many friends and was always there when I needed him. But I could see he needed help – his drinking had become an issue and his wife wasn't happy with his anger and temperament. He watched me like a hawk as I got sober in 1991, and one afternoon he came to my house in Rye and asked for help. He moved in for a few days while I sobered him up, then I arranged for him to go into PROMIS, where I had been. They kindly took him in even though we couldn't afford the fees. He got sober and remained sober. It was great for his health and for his family; he has two lovely daughters, Kim and Claire, by his first marriage, and a son, Josh, by his second.

Without Les in my life, I'd have had nobody to call when I felt lost and in need of family support. He gave it in a way that was non-judgemental, and with so much love and understanding. He hadn't got a pot to piss in, but it never mattered to him as he lived a day at a time. He always knew the hole in his heart might kill him, so he was carefree and never worried about tomorrow. When he got sober, it all fell into place for him. He enjoyed the community of AA meetings and gained many new and dependable friends. It was a joy to see.

Then in 2007 he died in hospital from *Clostridium difficile*. He was Squeeze's biggest fan. He used to drive me to the airport and held my hand, and collected me again when I returned from wherever I'd been. He gave me all the love I needed to get on that plane and beat the anxiety that had lit its fire in my soul. He was a lovely man and a wonderful brother, and I miss him every day. He lived the champagne lifestyle on lemonade money; he really did live a day at a time. Some days I'm in the car and I think, 'I know, I'll call Les,' and then I remember he's not here. It's like losing an arm but still feeling it.

By 2007, Glenn and I hadn't seen each other – or even spoken very much – in eight or nine years, since I'd recoiled into rehab. But after we buried Les in Benenden, a few plots away from where Maxine lay, I flew to New York to honour his passing and to be with him in the sky as he left for the heavens above. When I woke up the next day in my room at the Soho Grand, the phone rang, and it was Glenn congratulating me on flying after such a long time. He knew what I was going through; his own brother had died as Squeeze were just beginning to take off, when he and I were living in the house on Crooms Hill. His brother was a haemophiliac and sadly died through complications. When I see footage of us playing outside The Bell in Greenwich on Jubilee Day, I can see him in the crowd, but I don't ever remember there being any more than a passing hello – but when he passed away, Glenn was knocked for six. I remember seeing him crying and distraught, but we just didn't share our feelings in those days in a way we might do today.

My good friend and US touring agent Steve Martin boldly found me some solo dates to play while in America. On our date sheet were Nashville, Birmingham in Alabama, Chicago, Minneapolis and New York. I flew out Dorie Jackson to keep me in tune and Melvin Duffy to add sparkle. Glenn had already toured in the US a number of times but this was my first adventure, and sadly it was not well populated. We played well and travelled well, and in doing so I suppose I showed a new-found commitment to touring and, more importantly, flying. It was a start. Glenn takes to the road much better than I do, he is a dab hand at the old soft shoe on stage with his masterful fretboard work and his voice which never grows old. Mine however at that time was in need of some work, and on that tour I felt the scaffolding rising into place.

While I was in New York, I went to see Nicky Perry, my girlfriend from all those golden years ago. She had a tea shop called Tea and Sympathy, and that was what I needed. We talked for hours about Squeeze and our journey; she was hoping we might get the band back together. I was still grieving the loss of Les.

A month after touring in America, Glenn and I met for a nice lunch in Blackheath. My then manager, Peter Conway, and Suzanne, Glenn's manager, were there too. Glenn looked much the same as ever. He sat uncomfortably opposite me and we may have mirrored each other. It was good to see him again and I was excited about the possibility of being back together. Suzanne and Peter played hosts to our delicate conversations and our tiptoeing closer and closer to each other. Trust was hard to find, for both of us, I guess. It was potentially a big moment in our lives. I was struck by how serious Glenn was about us working together again, and how he carried himself; there was little room for light or laughter in that meeting.

He was considering re-recording our hits so we had some ownership of our masters, and we talked about touring with the band again. At first I wanted a fresh sweep of the broom, but Glenn would benefit from his band, The Fluffers, who already knew the songs from playing them at his shows, which made sense, although a brand-new band would have been exciting. The Fluffers were made up of former Death in Vegas drummer Simon Hanson, Stephen Large on keyboards and Stephen's wife Lucy Shaw on bass. It was a job lot. John Bentley's name came up and it was decided he'd be better on bass and would give the new-look Squeeze wider appeal. I hadn't seen John in hundreds of years, but when we did meet again he was just the same: small in stature, but large in love and musicianship. The most perfect person for the job. The band was formed and we quickly made hay in Glenn's studio down by the river on a trading estate in Charlton, on Anchor and Hope Lane.

This studio was a larger version of the one he had in Blackheath, ample amounts of chaos gathered together around the creativity of love. And a collection of Hoovers, a Steptoe and Son front room of stuff. Word got out and we were soon back on the road – first in the States and then in the UK for one of our legendary Christmas tours.

2008 was a very busy year. My album *The Last Temptation of Chris* came out on Stiff records no less, to great reviews, but sadly it was dwarfed by the touring of Squeeze. Glenn and I were giddy with awards: we got a lifetime achievement award at the Ivors, which I cherished, and the same at the Nordoff Robbins. At the Ivors we were given our award by Mark Ronson, whose mother I had just had tea with in New York. He was very humble and I was beaming with pride. Glenn and I hugged on stage in front of the music business' great and good. It was a fabulous day. This was my second Ivor, the first being for the lyrics for a film I had worked on called *Still Crazy* featuring Bill Nighy and Jimmy Nail, another proud moment.

Lily Allen gave us the Nordoff Robbins award a few months later.

It was all making sense to me, we had re-engaged with ourselves and our history and the respect around us fired our ambitions to get things right this time and make it last. We were back on the map and people wanted to reward us for our dedication and ambition down the years. However, the old behaviour quickly set in. Peter Conway was my voice and he very softly expressed my words and feelings to Suzanne, who'd then speak with Glenn. He in turn would bat the verbal ball back the other way. We communicated through emails and managers. It was exhausting for us all, and heavy work for Peter. Squeeze went on tour to America and it was agreed that Peter would oversee the first half and Suzanne the second, which seemed fair enough to me. Then one day Peter called me from LAX airport to tell me he was quitting the tour. He wasn't happy and found the whole Squeeze banquet hard to stomach. I had to let him go. He was such a nice man, but I had to agree with him that it was sadly just not working. I started to feel the claustrophobia of the past creeping back in. But playing live again on the bigger stages made me feel happy.

Glenn had this mad but wonderful idea to re-record all of our hits on the *Spot the Difference* album, and it was pure genius on his part. Simon Hanson was Glenn's anchorman; he worked hard at playing exactly what Glenn wanted him to play. He was replicating the brilliant drum parts laid down by Gilson over the years, a tough job that he did well. Glenn played all the rest of the instruments, even sometimes on the original guitars and keyboards. The end result was an almost perfect replica of the originals. Thanks to the co-production of Andy Jones, the record was well received by our fans, who wondered why we would ever cover our own songs. It took some explaining.

My new manager Matt Thomas tried hard to find a small label to help promote it and cover some of the recording costs. He felt this would give it the best chance of being heard and for the songs to be used in films and on television commercials. The album was a great idea, masterfully achieved. We would finally own the rights to our songs. Sadly nothing happened with the recordings, it was expensive too and the tour profits seemed to soak away into the black hole of recording the album. Hopefully in the future they will turn a coin.

In 2010 our Christmas tour took old fans by the horns. By this time Matt, who I'd met at a therapy workshop in London a year before, had his feet under the virtual management desk; he handled the strange and delicate set-up carefully and diplomatically. He was a master of balancing emotions. Matt was my voice and he very softly expressed my words and feelings to Suzanne, who'd then share them with Glenn. What we really needed to do was talk to each other a little more. Matt did instigate various meetings and for the most part they were fruitful.

In rehearsals for the tour, Glenn told me we were going to learn a dance routine to perform on stage. I handled it badly and walked out. I was not in the mood for dancing.

Steve Nieve was in the band for this tour, and the two of us remained at the back of the stage each night while Glenn and Simon led the routine from the front. It was Chuckle Brothers time; we looked like five minicab drivers. It was uncomfortable for me and I hated it. My head wasn't in the right place. I was distracted by a relationship that was turning me inside out. I had lost all grip on reality. I was tending the emotions of my adolescent self, who in turn was chasing the same in the other person. I dipped in and out of depression once again, only to be held by my good friend Gordon. He had been security for Sting, Robert Plant and others. He was a kind and very serious person who lived off Portman Square, where I spent a lot of my time at a club called Home House. Matt Thomas was wonderful on that tour, as was Gordon, who drove me from show to show and kept the dressing room jolly and me partly sane. I wore dark glasses on stage to hide my puffy eyes and the emptiness beyond. I was feeling deeply depressed and in no-man's-land emotionally.

Squeeze ploughed on with more tours across the States, which were fun. My cloud lifted. We made money, we lost money. And the last UK tour we set out on was amazing – we sold out all the shows and made CDs of the performance available to fans in our Pop Up Shop, as soon as it finished. One of Glenn's inspired ideas. It was hard work selling them at the merchandise stand. It kind of breaks the magic, or any slight magic a band might have. Up close our fans are lovely people, but after two hours on stage I'm knackered and want a warm bed to lie down in. But it was worth the effort. It was a Christmas tour to be proud of. Our royalties were once large cheques that came in the post twice a year; these days it's embarrassing. Thank God for PRS. This keeps the pie in the oven, as Squeeze manage to get good historic radio play across the country. We are something of a national treasure, a heritage act, which makes me feel as though we should be behind a twisted red rope in a museum.

Matt was a brilliant manager and close friend; he held my hand during some fragile relationships that came my way. He was in the room with me, so to speak; he was bright and focused on my chaotic, complicated world. I felt for him. I could take my darkest fears to Matt and share them with him, and that's what a good manager should be, a person who listens and loves and enjoys your music too. In 2012, the band went into the studio and recorded some new songs – our first new material in fifteen years. The BBC made a documentary about us, which was revealing and wonderfully put together. Our story was out there. With all the tension and lack of communication between Glenn and me laid bare, it was sad to watch, but overall I was proud of our journey, warts and all.

Beard or not, Glenn was on a mission, and I wanted to be there by his side. In the grand scheme of life, the beard meant nothing to me. But the new songs did. And I initially felt excluded during the writing and recording of them. I had sent more than twenty-five lyrics to Glenn since we'd been back together, which he had largely ignored, and I was beginning to wonder how bad they must have been. Inside, I knew that my stories of heartfelt sadness inspired by the recent break-up were not filling him with fire. Looking back at them I can see why.

One survived from the wad of tears in my notepad, a song called 'Tommy', a lyric inspired by a real-life incident, when my then girlfriend, now wife went into a post office and saw a timid black man and his son being attacked by a drunken racist idiot. I'd heard nothing from Glenn in the six weeks since I'd sent the song to him, and then one night the demo arrived via email. I was blown off my chair; it was incredible. He'd recorded it with beautiful strings laced over his lovely melody and my tragic words. The song took on another beautiful life of its own as 'Sonny' on our most recent album, *Cradle to the Grave*. His musical genius had returned and I could see and feel the future about to change around me.

'Cradle to the Grave' was a typically great Squeeze song too; its chord structure turned its wheel precisely over the verses and we rolled along. It came about when, one afternoon in Glenn's studio, he asked me to write something that would capture life's journey, from the cradle to the grave. I found the idea appealing and went home and worked on a lyric.

The new songs went into the set; then, before I could catch my breath, they were mixed and out on an EP. I argued to slow things down, but Glenn was driven as he always was by another imminent tour. Suzanne had an idea for a 'Cradle to the Grave' video and soon we were in The Pelton Arms, a Greenwich pub in which Glenn loved to play, making a cheap but fun promo with our children playing us as younger Squeeze members. My son Riley looks so much like me on the screen it's scary, and the older cast were locals and friends of Glenn's. 'Tommy' also had a short video made for it, and we used both as backdrops on the Christmas tour. Our tours were beginning to look properly produced, and to good effect. We could not afford just to swagger on stage and play our songs; these days people wanted more, and with videos and lights we managed to shape a really good show around our songs. I felt part of this new creativity as gradually we shared our ideas. We added some of our solo songs to the live shows; we played 'Still' and 'Black Sheep' from Glenn's albums, and 'Cowboys Are My Weakness' and 'On My Own I'm Never Bored' from mine. It was lovely to play all of these songs together, and the band made them sound like Squeeze songs. My two were rearranged by Glenn, which gave them a slight left turn that the audience seemed to like.

More recently I discovered what Glenn thought of my solo

albums. He liked *I Didn't Get Where I Am* but seemed ambivalent about the other two. His solo records mostly passed me by, though the most recent, *Happy Endings*, is really great. Lyrically it's very strong, and I can see now why he pays more attention to the lyrical side of things in Squeeze these days. He really digs in and magnifies his thoughts in an open and honest way with me. Sometimes it's frustrating, but often inspiring. His album melds family with a happy spirit, which is Glenn. He likes a night in the pub, friends around the house, good food and song, and it's all there in this honest and open recording. I have never been to his house – I don't even know where he lives!

Summer festivals were great for the band to play. WOMAD, where we played a proper set, was amazing in the July heat; we played full tilt and went down a storm. Latitude was exciting, as were some of the smaller festivals. We had come a long way from the playing on the wooden pallets of 1973. At V Festival in Essex we had a short and sweet set to play, and the best thing for me was meeting the brilliant comedian Peter Kay backstage after we played. We got on like a small house on fire. He was a huge fan of ours and I was a big admirer of his. Peter knows where all the B-sides are buried. He told me about the time, years ago, when he'd been waiting to get his record signed by the band outside the Manchester Apollo. Apparently he'd offered me an extra-strong mint, which I turned down; then I signed his album and knobbed off in my car. Now look where he is, and who's laughing now!

At the Coachella festival in 2012, I got to feel what it was like to play a US festival. This one was neat and tidy and it ran like clockwork. No beer cans in the grass, and no feeling of claustrophobia because of the crowds. Radiohead inspired and lit up the hot night sky with a mystical coming together of collective minds, a band all singing from the same hymn sheet. As a band I thought we were not as cohesive as I imagined Radiohead to be, but we could be just as serious with our music.

At this point I was feeling like I was drifting again. I was over-thinking everything and everyone. The short festival sets didn't appeal to me, and there was an internal yearning for new songs. I was seeing things through those old rose-tinted glasses you find in the dressing room after a good show. I found it harder and harder to put pen to paper.

When Glenn and I first met in our teens, we shared a place in our minds where we could have ambition, with shared ideals. Compromise was always going to be painful; after all we are two very different people bound in a powerful creative partnership, both struggling to be heard and respected. Both of our lives have changed so much since the early days – and for the better. When we first started writing together, the sun seemed to shine every day. I would write pages of words and Glenn would beaver away at the piano or guitar, coming up with the most amazing melo-dies. He was patient and gentle as I got my head around his often complicated chord structures, and as a result, I'd try my hardest to learn from him. We spent that summer of 1973 up to our ears in music, as his record collection and mine came together in the giant listening booth that was Maxine's house. Our journey slowly gathered pace, and between then and now we have writ-ten hundreds of songs, played hundreds of shows and recorded thirteen-plus albums. I have been in awe of Glenn's musicianship all this time – even when we weren't talking to each other. And I've always wondered what it would be like to be him, up on stage sweating like a goose but being able to pluck any song out of thin air and deliver it perfectly. It's a gift he has. Being in Squeeze in this third act of our lives has had its moments, but walking out to face an audience with Simon on drums, John on bass and Stephen on keyboards made me feel confident and very happy. Having the band back together was a learning curve. Our songs drilled deeply into the history book of my life.

We are lucky: younger people are coming to our shows, as fans bring their children – and even grandchildren – to see us play, and I love that so much. As I get older, I understand that we have a contract with those who buy tickets to see us. The songs they want to hear must be in our set and we must play them no matter what.

It's a tall order to keep all of the people happy all of the time, but we have a good crack at it.

CAVAN

There I was minding my own business when I was asked by a friend to record a young band from Cavan in Ireland. It was September 2012 and I was fresh back from a fantastic Squeeze tour of the US. The only spare time I had was before our biannual knock about Britain that December, so I went up to London to see this band – The Strypes. I met them and the drummer's dad Niall Walsh in a coffee shop and it was obvious to me they were going places. They were all fifteen and sixteen years old, smartly dressed and very friendly. Their broad Irish features made them look like jockeys ready for the rock 'n' roll hurdles ahead.

I booked a studio, Yellow Fish, close to where I lived in East Sussex, on the advice of Boo Hewerdine, who was keen to co-produce the sessions with me. Boo was the perfect person to have on board; he's a really good producer and has a keen ear when it comes to building songs. The band came down and set up shop, and within the day we had twelve great songs – mostly covers, but full of excitement, youth and passion. It reminded me of early Squeeze recordings. The circle had been joined in my head in a unique way. I was observing myself back at the starting gate. We were all stunned by what was taking place. Ross, the singer, was bunking off school to be in the studio; he was very shy and had to wear dark glasses when he sang to summon up enough confidence. Josh, the guitarist, blew me away; his playing and his writing were way beyond his years, and he was such a nice guy too. Pete was just sixteen but his bass-playing was so informed, inventive and right on the button. Evan was amazing on the drums, especially for someone so young – he kept great time while knowing so much about the music he and the band were covering. He was the historian, just as Glenn and Jools had been in Squeeze, and he was the most opinionated, but in a very inspiring way. He had the future all planned out, though this as I know can be fateful.

Niall, Evan's dad, was doing all the running around for the band, playing the role of dad on the one hand and manager on the other, and he'd mentioned to me a few times how he felt a little out of his depth. There were actually two other managers in tow, who had organised a few shows for the band and had paid for the studio and my small fee. But I felt the band needed more experienced management. To me, it was obvious they were going to be something special, and I knew I wouldn't be on their journey for long. They needed a record company and a producer who could hone their future for them. I couldn't do that.

So they went off and we kept in touch. Niall called for help here and there as contracts appeared and the two managers took more of a role. It gathered speed very quickly. The penny really dropped when I went to see them at the 229 club on London's Great Portland Street. I was so excited that night – watching them live was an exhilarating experience. Niall came up to me afterwards and asked my advice. The contract they'd been offered was too heavy

and far too restrictive for a fresh-faced outfit at the very beginning of their career. My own experience of rum deals lit up a few
red lights on the internal dashboard.

I was rehearsing with Squeeze that December when I got a call
out of the blue from Elton. He said he'd heard about The Strypes
and that I'd been working with them, and he asked me if they'd be
interested in meeting with him and possibly signing to his company, Rocket Music Management. I called Niall, and before I knew
what was going on, Elton had called him at home in Cavan. Niall
was blown away. Cavan is a small town, about an hour's drive
from Dublin, and not much happens there. Then suddenly Elton
John calls and puts Lily Allen on the phone to say how much she
loves the band too. They had a simple choice to make. They came
to London to meet the team at Elton's office, and the next thing I
knew they'd signed a contract and Elton was back on the phone
asking me if I'd consider working with them again as a mentor.
I was thrilled. Within a month, I was there in the Rocket offices,
finding my feet at the beginning of an entirely new journey. It was
magical to see the excitement in the band's faces.

The Squeeze Christmas tour came to an end and I pondered the
changes to my life. I was back in co-manager suits and ties in west
London, just two roads away from Bryan Ferry's office. In fact, Mr
F and I had an Audi-off in the street one day, when I parked mine
next to his – the same one I'd ordered for him a couple of years
before. All his windows were darkened glass, but he had them half
rolled down. I could see him in his dark glasses, peering out at me.

The Strypes' two previous managers sued the band, they settled
the case, and in my view the move to Rocket was the right one. Not
that it was any of my business. Record companies offered up all

the toys they could muster – iPads, CDs, box sets, bags and other swag – to court the boys, and every day was like Christmas. It was exhausting, but it was amazing to watch and be on the edge of it all. After a bidding war, Rocket signed them to Mercury Records. It was the right home. Plans were hatched for the first album and Elton was keen for the band to record with his old friend Chris Thomas, who'd produced part of The Beatles' *White Album* and had worked with some amazing artists – The Pretenders, The Sex Pistols, Pink Floyd and Pulp among them. I had lunch with Chris and Julian Wright, The Strypes' manager at Rocket, to discuss this, but Chris wasn't keen. He had retired and was resentful of the industry he'd left behind. Elton pushed him, though, and eventually he gave in. Before recording the band set up in a house near to where I lived in Sussex called Tilton House, and there the boys rehearsed some of the new songs. One afternoon I invited Jeff Beck over to surprise them, and to his credit he jammed along with them for an hour, faces beaming with the genius in the room, a complete legend and a very magical afternoon for us all. He wanted them to play The Yardbirds in a film he was making, but sadly nothing came of it.

We booked Yellow Fish studios as the band had liked their time there with Boo and me, but as Chris would only work short weeks, the band had to fly in and out from Dublin all the time. The momentum was stuttering. They were cool with it all, though, and in between sessions we booked London shows to keep the pulses racing. My diary had become very full all of a sudden and I wasn't at home very often. But important seeds were being sown. I desperately wanted the band to have the success that had eluded me at their age. I'd watch them from the side of stages, feeling the rush and excitement I'd had back in the days when Squeeze would play pubs and tiny clubs, before our lives changed forever.

Elton had the boys over for Sunday lunch one afternoon; I picked them up from Heathrow and we drove up to his house at Windsor. The gates opened and in we went to be greeted by His Nibs, his hubby David Furnish and creative consultant Tony King. Julian Wright and the lovely Charlie Dunnett, who'd first spotted the band, were there too. Sunday lunch was to die for, though the band seemed timid – I think they were a little intimidated by the surroundings and the banter. As I drove them back to the airport, I asked them what they'd thought of the day. Ross said the roast potatoes were the best he'd ever had. That was it. We were off and running.

The shows that followed were amazing, and Elton even turned up to a few – once arriving in a helicopter on his way back from Thailand to see them in Brighton. The crowd packed into a small pub was amazed to see him there as large as life. The set got tighter and tighter, and I managed to pull together a great team of people to work with them. It was going well as far as I could tell; everyone seemed happy and taken care of, which is all you can ask for on the long and winding road to fame.

Chris Thomas worked hard to get his head around the limitations of Yellow Fish, and he did well to record the band in the way he wanted. Chris was such a nice man to be around, although sometimes difficult to read. He'd tell the boys stories about The Beatles and the session would stop while all ears leaned towards his words. I enjoyed the recording, too; the songs developed well, with lots of venom and youthful verve. I even enjoyed the sandwiches that Niall and I had to go into nearby Lewes for every day. The band stayed at Mount Harry – a wonderful old pile on the other side of the town. Its owner, Chelsea Renton, was so welcoming. She looked after them and provided them with fry-ups and chips all night long. She was happy to entertain and support them away from the studio heat. She created a home away from home for them.

Short days and short weeks meant it took three months to record the album, and it was during the final stages that the band really started to take shape as young people. They were growing like triffids. Either that, or I was shrinking. An idea you think is great is tossed aside for someone else's better idea, and it hurts but you won't concede and you sulk. It's your band, then it's not; you divide and rule with subgroups; you're not the lead singer, but you want to be. You think you look cool, but you know someone else in the band thinks you look like a wanker. I've been there and I've survived.

In a short space of time, The Strypes had the album mixed in LA, were offered a tour with The Arctic Monkeys and had a sleeve shoot with the photographer Jill Furmanovsky. Jill took pictures of Squeeze early on; it was like going back in time for us both. One thing just led to another and there were always a million balls in the air. The album mixes proved to be the last straw for Chris Thomas; even though he didn't want to do them himself, I think he felt hurt when others took his place, and he left the building. He refused to have his name anywhere near the record – which was a shame as his production was so incredible.

As the album promotion rolled on, it was clear the band had lots to say; almost all of them wanted to talk, but in the end they had to learn how to share the spotlight. Interview slots were dealt around. It worked well. The Strypes are so knowledgeable about themselves and music, the old iPad being their history book. They are always digging deep into the YouTube vaults to find new old things to listen to, and there's not much you can teach them. Not that I ever attempt to try. Japan licked the band up like fresh cream; they were adored and were waited on hand and foot during two sell-out tours in 2013. Europe started to come to the party, and though gigs in the UK were selling out too, the audiences were mostly men of a certain age.

The band thrive on the mosh pit and I can see them raise their game when people toss themselves about like lemmings. Bodies fly around; it's as if a school of salmon has suddenly reached a row of rocks – they leap into the air and land on each other with tails wagging. Watching the band reminds me of being on tour in the early 1980s, and sometimes it's as though I'm seeing myself in an earlier life – with my mouth wide open, breathing in the heavy fumes of excitement from the crowd as they hear my songs for the first time, watching girls looking longingly at the lead singer. The energy you provide in that situation is massive and it comes from deep inside; it's a need to impress and be the leaders of the pack, wolves on heat, sweating under lights, running around on small stages, using the monitors as springboards for height. It's so great, but now I'm in my sixties all I can do is watch like a parent, hoping they don't break a leg or faint from the heat.

At the end of the show, I hand out the water and hug the band one by one as they come off stage. In the dressing room, Niall really justifies his role as the fifth member of The Strypes;

he translates how they feel and deals with any niggles or cross words. He also doesn't mind picking up their pants. I've heard a few healthy rows in their dressing room, but nothing nasty. It's all very understandable and typical of a young band. Again, it takes me right back to the early days of Squeeze: a small, hot room with sweaty clothes thrown on chairs, boots on the floor and a rider of crisps, Skittles and soft drinks – though in my case it was always crates of brown ale or lager. Now I'm the one who makes it all possible – I'm not the Wizard of Oz, pulling levers behind a velvet curtain though; they are.

When Squeeze were first signed, we knew that if we didn't make it with our first record, we could hold on for a few more. The music industry just isn't like that today, but at Mercury Records with Mike Smith in charge, it's as close as you can get to that situation. Mike is a generous person, and gives his acts plenty of guidance and ideas about co-writers and producers – essential in an industry that has changed beyond recognition from the one I first entered in the late 1970s. Music is now listened to in a totally different way. The internet has created so much freedom for artists and it has taken away the power of the major labels. Squeeze sold 30,000 singles a day at our peak. If you sold 30,000 records now, you'd be at number 1 all year round. The Strypes sold 129,000 copies of their debut album – mostly in Japan and the UK, with Ireland a close third – but they make a much better living on the road than we ever did, thanks to record company support. Mike is aware of all of these parameters. His job, along with the effervescent Ted Cockle who runs the label, is to sell records and advance the band's talents, and all sides have to listen to one another for this to work. It doesn't always happen, though. How could it, when we all know what's right?

Elton gives so much to the boys; he calls to see how they are doing, he comes to see them play and he always invites them to the Rocket Christmas party – which, for all the glitz, is a work do just like the ones back in those black-and-white days when I used to go with my dad to the parties at the Greenwich gasworks. Elton feeds everyone well, then makes a speech about each and every artist he has on the books. He thanks the assembled staff, he makes jokes and I'm deeply touched by his care and attention. David stands by his side and is just as impressive with his encouragement to one and all.

The boys were not naturals at all this swanning and schmoozing, though; Josh seemed the only one who would mingle and make small talk. The rest of them looked slightly out of place – like they wanted to go home now, please. I know that feeling well. I however enjoy the mince pies with Ed Sheeran and Elton, and discuss the comings and goings of people way more famous than me or The Strypes. We are all a little out of our depth. But the band is held in high esteem by the great and the good. There's Jeff Beck, who jammed with them when they were staying at Mount Harry; Jimmy Page, who was at the side of the stage at Earl's Court; Wilko Johnson, who joined them on stage at Canvey Island; Paul Weller, who gives them studio time. Their music and attitude seems to touch performers from a certain time and place; it moves creaking limbs. It's always been my dream, though, to turn younger people on to live music and the excitement it brings. And though it's mostly mods at their shows, the front row is expanding slowly with younger wannabes. In Derby, I saw a front row that was completely young and female. How the band raised their game that night! It was magical to see.

The Strypes went back into the studio at the end of 2014. Album number two was recorded in the Dean Street Studios where Glenn and I had made the *Difford & Tilbrook* album in 1984. It was great to be back in Soho, but this time I took more of a back seat, and watched and listened as the band got stuck into twenty new songs. Josh was now nineteen and had discovered girls and vodka, and he'd also got heavily into hip-hop music. I don't think the rest of the band were impressed. I sensed Evan and Josh – the band's two leading factions – pulling in different directions. Josh was spreading his wings, hanging out in London and jamming with a new set of friends in Chiswick, while Evan was steadfastly devoted to the bluesy garage sound that had become the band's trademark. One day, when things took a mellow route with loops and backing tracks, Evan got so upset that he kicked a sofa and stormed out of the studio into the busy Soho night.

I knew exactly how he felt and it was hard for me not to take sides. Change is so hard, so difficult to embrace when you're clear in your mind how your world should be. You genuinely feel your band will be wrecked by one strange turn of events. All I ever wanted in Squeeze was the simplicity of bass, drums, keyboards and guitars, and when change came into the room it rattled me. The irony is that it's been Glenn and all the change he's brought in over the years that has kept Squeeze going. Staying in the past would only have hindered our progress.

With The Strypes, Josh was only trying to open up the way for the new. Being radio-friendly does require compromise, and there are decisions to be made about credibility versus success.

For me, it's obvious. Success pays your pension. But try telling an eighteen-year-old that they should be thinking that way, and all you'll get is blank looks. When you're that age, you're on the front line – nose against the mud as you climb out of the trenches with your drumsticks and guitars. You're on a crusade to change the world with your music and your know-all attitude.

Being involved with The Strypes has connected me with a younger part of myself and that's an amazing feeling. So what is my role? I'm a mate and sideboard for them to put their drinks on; I'm personal management, and a mirror for them to wash their faces in; I'm observer and hod-carrier while they tuck into bowls of chips and takeaway food in the dressing room. Whatever my role, it's doing me the world of good. Because of them, music excites me again. They are now on album number three called *Spitting Image*, and Pete the bass player along with Evan the drummer have knocked up some fine songs with some very inspired lyrics. Josh has had to raise his game, which is no bad thing as the band have grouped together more closely thanks in part to the wonderful production of Ethan Johns. Ross is singing better than ever and with miles more confidence, and Evan is still the best young drummer I have heard. Josh is a big talent and a very special player. Paul Weller was only too eager to pluck him away for a few days to play on his new album.

The band recorded the new album at the legendary Rockfield studios in Monmouth, where Squeeze had recorded in 1976. I went to visit them while they were recording and nothing much had changed over all of that time. In a cupboard were the very tapes on which we had recorded. I had no idea we had recorded so much. Golden days – ones I find hard to recall. Like The Strypes I'm curious about the past and find it hard to live in the present, but that's where we all are, for now at least.

NUMBER 18

Ziggy Stardust, Obscured by Clouds, Talking Book, Eat a Peach, Honky Château, Exile on Main Street, Something Anything, Transformer and *Clear Spot*; all these albums appeared in 1972. I was on a musical journey that has brought me to where I am today. During that fruitful and inspirational year, I was mostly stoned and living on the dole. I had nothing to complain about. I celebrated my seventeenth birthday, and the same year, Louise Fielder was born.

In 2011, Squeeze were asked to play on a Radio 4 comedy show. It was something I really didn't think we should be doing, but my manager Matt Thomas thought I was wrong, so we did it. I turned up at comedian Arthur Smith's house and sat on my amp in a crowded kitchen filled with radio people and invited guests. That day I was feeling very positive as I'd just come from seeing Maureen, my therapist. She was straight with me; she made it abundantly clear that I should know what I wanted from a relationship and have all the boxes ticked. At that moment, I had no boxes to tick. All my relationships had chosen me. I was feeling delicate and extremely lost. As Squeeze played another version of 'Pulling Mussels (from the Shell)', I looked out across the busy room and saw the most attractive smile I had ever seen. For a moment I was lost. 'I could spend the rest of my life with that woman,' I thought to myself, and inside I was pulling loads of impressive shapes, like James Brown.

On the way out we said a brief hello, and I walked to my car and dragged out my departure from my parking space as long as I could, in the hope that she might leave at the same time. She was standing at the door with Peter Curran, one of my favourite radio voices and lovely all-round chap; they looked like they were in fits of laughter together. Later that night we searched for each other on social media and words were exchanged. We had bitten the bait on the hook and the discovery began. I sat in my flat watching the screen for words, a mint tea to one side, tantalised and smitten with her humour and wit. She seemed exciting to me.

A week later, we had dinner at Home House, a club in London's Portman Square that I've been a member of for many years. We sat at a table by the fireplace and glanced at the menu; Louise looked nervous and incredibly beautiful. We talked things over, forking small pieces of our meal, then I drove her home. Home – that was a place I'd not yet found in that period of my life. I was living in Bentinck Mews in Marylebone; very expensive and smart, but it wasn't really home. It was a place of cold nights and long afternoons on the sofa thinking about the mess I had got myself into. The boxes needed ticking. And packing, again. I drove Louise home in my Audi, which might as well have been my home in those days, as I was driving around so much, and when we got to her house, where her family were sleeping – three kids and a husband she was in the process of separating from – I carefully leant over the gearstick and armrest to kiss her goodnight. She turned, and our lips met just below the rear-view mirror. That short kiss lit a fuse inside of me and the fireworks went off all at once.

I drove back to my mews house and started emailing her again; each day we were engulfed in chapters of humour and openness. We were finding out about ourselves. A few days later she dropped the kids off at school and came over to see me. I was waiting on the corner of the street; we hugged and went inside my bachelor pad. The discovery continued for some hours. In the few, very fast months that followed, the boxes were ticked one by one; we were in each other's lives as though we had been there forever. Maureen was gently prodding me to take care and slow down, but how could I? I had fallen in love with a wonderful person, there was clearly no doubt about that.

Some months later, after Louise's husband had moved out, he was on holiday with their children at their house in France when he was taken ill and very suddenly died. It was all so unimaginable and sad. He was a talented TV producer with many friends. Louise and her children were shattered. I stepped away; it was not my place to do anything other than support Louise from a distance, who proceeded to manage the passing of her husband with such courage and love for her young children, who had been there at the very end. It was heartbreaking. I retreated to Marylebone for my daily AA meetings and coffee with Gordon. He was so close to me at this point and like Maureen gave great advice. Louise wanted me nearby, so far from being in the shadows and giving her the space to grieve, I was there alongside her to give her love and comfort.

A few months later David Enthoven very kindly invited us all to see Take That at Wembley Stadium. The children were excited, and so was I. Robbie was the highlight of the show and came on stage via a long rope high above the rest of the band, bursting into 'Let Me Entertain You' right on cue. It was a night on which I could really see how wonderful Louise was with her children, and how close a unit they were. I felt privileged to be part of the outing. I think it was tough for everyone, but David made it as smooth as only he could.

Louise is warm-hearted, a loving and patient mother, a very trustworthy friend and a person who supports me in ways I'd not thought possible. I'm so lucky to have met her and to have her at my side. I have found her humour to be a constant flame that keeps all of our friends warm. She listens without prejudice and gives without expecting to receive. The fact that she has so many good friends tells me everything I need to know – she loves all of them and is loved by them in return.

My time in Marylebone had come to an end; I was running out of money again and needed to move somewhere more realistic. I had just read a book by the clergyman and writer Peter Owen Jones and it inspired me to go and see him read from the book at The Old Market theatre in Hove. We met after the reading and I asked him if I could come and visit him at his house in Firle, a small village near Lewes in East Sussex. When I went to see him, he sat in his small office and let me talk about my life and how low I was feeling before I met Louise. I cried and he listened with love. He said that what I needed was home and community. Then he led me down the street to a house and said, 'You should live here.' Number 18, The Street. It was a biblical moment. I met the person who was living there, Chelsea, and Peter told her I might rent her spare room. It almost happened, but fate took that moment away from me. A few months later, though, not only the spare room but the entire house was available to rent. I was in heaven. Louise thought I was mad to move to a small village; at that time, she was not a country person. But I was.

Firle is the most beautiful place on earth. In time, Louise and her children, Linus, Pebbles and Mitzi, moved in too. She sold the London house and committed to a life in the countryside with me. A year later, I walked her up to the beacon on the Sussex Downs just above Firle and asked her to marry me. She said yes. Her face lit up as we walked and hugged the sky around us. We had the most romantic wedding, with curry, music and all our friends, on a cold and very wet day in April 2013. It was perfect – even with the horizontal rain. Peter married us in St Peter's Church in Firle; the circle was being joined together. I had found home for the first time in years. Gordon Hough was my best man, and what a great best man he continues to be. Gordon is a wonderful friend who has saved my life many times; he is funny, he is love. His stories are incredible. Lou's father gave her away.

Glenn and Suzanne were there too, and Glenn was in tears when we walked down the aisle. I was in tears as well, and we hugged as we left the church. It was a very significant cuddle; it felt deep. People from all corners of our lives were in the congregation; family on both sides. From school there was Danny Baker and his wife Wendy; from the big stage, Peter Kay, who had been so kind to me during my darker times, and his wife Susan. Lou's dad made a very funny speech and my brother Lew gave us his well-rehearsed look back at my life. He was very funny too and had everyone in stitches. Gordon's speech was poetic and honest;

he gave me a cheese sandwich in a bag as a closing gesture – it was what he often gave me in the car after a show when he was driving me around the country. He made a perfect chauffeur, when I let him drive, which was not very often. The Strypes flew over from Ireland to play for us. Niall and his wife Anne came over too. Tony King and Julian Wright represented Elton. Outside the riding school, where our reception was held, the rain lashed down and the wind gusted in from the beacon and the Downs above. We were all cosy inside, though, with our massive heaters and bellies full of curry. After the reception we drove to Lucknam Park in Wiltshire for a brief honeymoon and a very long sleep.

Apart from me, Lew is the only Difford left from our branch of the family tree – a tree that goes back through the foggy 1960s and down the ages to Somerset and France, where the Diffords struggled up from originally. In September 1993, Squeeze had been playing at Bristol's Colston Hall. After the show, as I hung out with the band and our friends in the cavernous space downstairs from the depressing dressing rooms, Lew came in and introduced me to a woman – a Difford by birth – who'd spent the past few years researching the family tree. The first traces of the name now synonymous with a songwriting partnership that stretches back some forty years appeared, aptly enough, in and around Glastonbury – home now, of course, to the legendary music festival. Many of my forefathers were buried there and documents dating back to the 1700s show we weren't a wealthy lot. The odd sheep was passed down from generation to generation, but that was about it. When the railways came, my great-grandparents took work on the track, following it all the way from the West Country to

London, where they settled in Charlton, which is where Lew, Les and I came in.

The woman had our genealogy all mapped out on a long white roll of paper. I could clearly see where Les ended and his family preceded him. I could see Lew there with a million grandchildren and I could see family members I've either never met or who appeared once or twice when I was a young boy. There I was too, with my twig growing from the tree: four children, and now the new Mrs Difford and her brood. And as our wedding climaxed, I could feel the family tree growing.

My children were all there and embraced our marriage – they have always supported me with open hearts. Natalie and Riley, Grace and Cissy are the cornerstones of my life. When Natalie was born, I walked with her strapped to my chest through the woods on Toys Hill, near where we lived in Edenbridge. She was loved and educated in London and at Sussex University. Now in her mid-thirties, she lives in New York, where she has been since 2006. She loves the New York city life, and she loves to travel. Her work in film is finding her awards and mentions in Oscar-winning films. I'm very proud of that. Recently she has produced two great films, *Gimme The Loot* and *Tramps*. When I was her age, I was on tour – no surprise there. It was 1987 and I was in New York with Squeeze at Madison Square Garden.

Riley was the second best man at my wedding – he read the serenity prayer for me, which was lovely. Riley is sober like his dad. I loved taking him on long drives when he was a child; he would sit in the passenger seat as we raced around London and the Kentish countryside.

He is one of the nicest people in my life; a wonderful, big-hearted son, dreamy and full of dizzy ideas like me. He also lives in New York, married to the lovely Natasha, who is related to Florence Nightingale, which will come in handy for young Riley.

Grace is a talented photographer and is working all of God's hours to make a name for herself and to afford to live in East London which is so expensive. She enjoyed horse-riding, shooting and swimming as a child. Her journey from Brighton College to St Martin's in London was colourful, as is her way. She is fun to work with and she has been on many Squeeze tours as a production assistant. She always seems to be happy and is fiercely independent, which is a good thing. She is a sweetheart and loves a curry just like her dad. She has been to India several times, and I'm green with envy.

Cissy came along in the early days of my sobriety, and to me is a sobriety gift of love. She is like me in many ways, and I remember long walks with her as a child, taking the dogs up through the woods and back in all weathers. She excelled at Brighton College and she went to London to study English literature. Not an easy transition for someone as tender as she is. With her English degree under her arm from Goldsmiths college I'm sure she will light up many an empty page with her imagination and words. Cissy works hard, also loving living in East London not far from Grace.

Linus, Mitzi and Pebbles, Louise's children, are very special young people. Bravely they have accepted me into their mother's life and into theirs. They are all growing rapidly and bringing with them the focus of early-teenage life; the house is a cauldron of social demands and domestic issues, some of which I have not had to deal with for many years so that I am retraining myself to control my expectations. Family is a beautiful thing and Louise is so good at being mother and wife, controlling all our needs one at a time with grace and good temper. It can't be easy. Binding the new family with the old has been a steady and gradual journey. At the wedding, all seven of the children – mine and Louise's – danced and joined in with the happiness of the evening.

All those years ago, when my palm was read in a small, colourful caravan at the Lammas Fair, I never thought the reading would come true. But I've had a big family and a life in music – though the prediction of the long life remains to be seen. Maureen, my therapist, asked me to open my hands each morning and let whatever was out there into my life. I did just that, and Louise walked in. I'm not afraid of what might happen in the future now. I'm grateful for everything I have. I have nothing to complain about, no real regrets. Life, I've realised, is about belonging and having dreams you'd still like to realise. I do. I'm just not sure what they are yet.

WORTHY FARM

Glenn and I are a very odd couple, but that's what makes us special. So in 2014, after we'd rehearsed being together in the guise of Squeeze, we began rehearsals for our next tour – one involving just the two of us, which would begin with us getting out of bed Eric-and-Ernie style and end in rapturous applause and a few giggles. The 'At Odds Couple Tour', a title my wife Louise came up with, was one I'd been looking forward to for a long time, and unlike previous acoustic jaunts, I found myself feeling more at home on stage with Glenn and with myself. The nakedness of acoustic music brings honesty and fear in equal amounts to the table, but after just a couple of gigs I felt my confidence return to the point where I actually enjoyed being under the bright lights. Alongside all the old favourites – 'Tempted', 'Up the Junction', 'Black Coffee in Bed' – we each played a solo section, which made our combined musical journey join up. The show was glued together with a Q&A led by Miles, Glenn's driver. He was the man in a golden cape running down the aisles with a roving microphone. He wore it well and it seemed to work.

I have known Glenn for forty-six years, and though we're not always close, we know each other well. We have travelled so far together and risked many things musically and sometimes emotionally. In this third period of Squeeze we find ourselves getting closer than before, but it took time to find our feet with each other. It was a slow but fruitful build.

At first the tour was hard work – I felt the old feeling creeping back in, the weak confidence within me and the yearning to slow down. I called David for advice and we went for lunch. He was so understanding and told me how I might handle the new world I had entered into.

I let go of all of my fear around my relationship with Glenn and the way I played on stage and freed up the emotions that had been locked inside. And by the end of the tour I was wanting more and more of the same. We went to America for five weeks, which was very tough on us both, but it brought us closer than we had ever been. Hugging each other in the dressing room and both missing home and, more importantly, missing our families. Walking on stage was hard, but I adopted the mantra 'Tits and teeth, darling, tits and teeth.' Tonight, Matthew, I will be Chris Difford of Squeeze. It was another of David's simple tips. Speaking of Matthew, sadly myself and Matt Thomas went our separate ways. It seemed to make sense for Rocket to look after me as I had managed to get to know them all so well and I trusted the process of change. As a company they are locked into the music industry in a way that perhaps Suzanne and Matt would not have been. I was sad to lose Matt, but it was very amicable and we still work with each other closely together on charity work. He runs Music Support, a haven for people in the industry who seek help with their addictions and depression. Matt has done a fantastic job bringing this out into the open, and I help where I can.

After all the duo touring, we turned our minds to the new album. In the second week of January 2015, I got a call from Glenn to wish me a happy New Year and ask whether I'd like mackerel soup for lunch in the studio. Suzanne sat us down to talk about plans. There were many. Most pressing was the new album to accompany my old school friend Danny Baker and Jeff Pope's new TV sitcom *Cradle to the Grave*, based on Danny's memoirs. The show was so funny and I felt so lucky to have been given this massive opportunity. Our task was to produce one song for each episode of the show – eight in all – plus the title track, which was already in the can. But though the TV people were over the moon with the songs, things had changed a lot from the early scripts, and they found it hard to place them in the show, which was really disappointing, though we did manage to get a few on screen. I watched each episode as it came off the machine in the editing suite and was blown away by them. They were funny and brilliantly scripted, and Peter Kay was totally believable as Danny's dad Spud. It's a hilarious show from start to finish and I was so proud to hear our songs coming out of the TV. It was hats-in-the-air time all round.

Glenn and I were drafted in by Jeff Pope to play cameos. I was the grumpy drummer, which suited me well, and Glenn the pub organist. We spent the day together in Manchester, mostly in the good company of Peter Kay in his trailer. I love this man; he is so gentle and funny, a real one of a kind who has helped me through many a tough moment with a shoulder to lean on. Laughter filled the day, and with Danny there too it was a belly buster of a visit.

The album was a coming-together of minds; we really worked hard to be in each other's company, and it paid off. It's as good as

East Side Story, filled with precious moments and well-produced songs. 'Open' was about my wedding to Louise, and 'Nirvana' was a story that Glenn and I worked on together from my idea about a couple reaching old age and the kids having left home. It was a struggle to wrestle some of the songs from within, but it made the recording interesting. Glenn would challenge me from time to time on what I was writing – I was finding it hard to focus on the metre of some of the songs, mainly because they fell over older melodies. It was not writer's block as such; more writer's haze.

I was blown to the side of the road by the weight of our new relationship. He would pore over each line almost word by word like a member of the musical forensic branch. The dynamic had changed; we were writing songs as one. I think that his time apart from me, having to write his own lyrics, had made him a more detailed and mature writer. The balance of our separate views on life would change the words sometimes for the better, and my share of the partnership began to alter. At times we almost wrote in the same room, but we settled for the next room with the door open. It seemed to work. Glenn's words would be more factual than mine and mine perhaps more emotional and dreamy, a good combination for this album.

Laurie Latham co-produced the *Cradle* album with Glenn, and we used Jools's studio to mix. John Bentley was replaced by Lucy Shaw on bass. John did at least play on half of the album. I was sad to see him go, but I agreed with Glenn that we needed the change and to his credit he said if we ever needed him back he would be at the end of a phone. A true gentleman. My voice, alongside Glenn's, is the sound of Squeeze. For the first time in years we were joined at the vocal hip, and I believe that was one of the secrets of the success of the record. However, I had no leads on this album; it has been seventeen years since I sang a song on a Squeeze record, and that was 'Bonkers'.

We got great reviews for the new album and were back on form. 'Happy Days' was a radio hit and we were being playlisted for the first time in years on Radio 2: a great feeling. The *Cradle* album sold 50,000 copies and was well received in the press and by our loyal fans. Since our first album all those years ago, times have moved on. Spotify is now the parental record company to one and all: it pays pocket money to artists like us, and I have no idea how much that might be. Although I did hear that 6,000 streams of one song equates to £1.90.

We shot two cheap but effective videos and got on to *Later* with Jools. I only wish he had joined us for a number, and people tweeted to say the same thing. It was a big moment; we were back on the telly and we missed a trick. After the show we were invited around to Jools's castle for dinner with him and his charming wife Christabel. I remembered that when I first met Jools he would write, like everyone else, in my diary, and once he drew a Rolls-Royce outside a castle next to a princess, his dreams in a doodle. They all came true.

We shared stories around the table with Danny Baker and Jeff Pope, and then he took us to see his train set, which covered the whole of the top floor. It was magnificent. There was even an underground train network and scale models of the Thames down at Greenwich where we all grew up. His house was rebuilt with his loving passion for architecture; the detail is stunning. He has done well for himself and very much deserves it. I have always kept in touch with Jools, singing as a special guest on tour in his fabulous orchestra. Their arrangements of Squeeze songs go down well with his dedicated fans.

As a hobby while all of this was going on I had been working with Boo Hewerdine on some songs we had collected over a five-year period. I got to sing which was nice, it boosted my confidence in that neighbourhood. The album was the polar opposite of *Cradle*, but sadly it didn't come out as it clashed with Squeeze activities, which naturally take precedence. It was maybe over-ambitious to record twenty-three songs and try to strap them loosely around a thin storyline, but the songs really worked and will be released at some point. They are very much worth a listen. Doing other things in the background gives my life balance and I think I need that. It's good to prod around and write, it keeps the songwriting muscle in shape. Those songs will see the light of day, but first I have to find a window in which to release them. That may be tricky, but it will be worth it. There are some great songs floating around in my bottom drawer.

I'm growing more and more confident in my solo shows as well. I love the one-on-one contact I have with my audience, and these days I seem to know most of them. One of my favourite solo shows during a break from recording *Cradle* was when I was playing at the Arts Centre in a town called Oswaldtwistle, not far from the home of Peter Kay. I invited him along to introduce me. The small crowd of maybe 150 in total, were stunned to see young Peter come out on stage and walk up to the microphone. I stood in the wings. Twenty minutes later he finally introduced me as Glenn Tilbrook from Squeeze. When I walked on to the stage, he said 'Oh no, we've got the wrong one, the one who can't sing, ask for your money back!' I fell about laughing and indeed it was hard to sing a note without belly laughing all night long. 'Look, he doesn't know the chords either,' he went on to say – sadly he was not wrong. It was a memorable night for us all. The next day it was back to work, back to the studio for a check on reality.

The tour that followed the *Cradle* album felt very grown up; the production was key and many of the songs were supported by fantastic videos made by a friend of mine called Sam. We invested in a tailor to make sure the band looked good, and we made sure we took care of ourselves on the road. As touring goes I think I was as comfortable on and off stage as I had ever been before. It was a revelation not to be stressing about what other people might think. I started to put myself first, something I often find difficult. When men get to a certain age they start to wear their trousers up high just below their tits and not care. I think I was reaching this point in life. If I got things wrong, it was OK. I learnt from it and moved on. If I got things right I proudly owned my feelings and savoured the moments. What was not to like, the reviews told us that the new songs were just as good if not better than the old ones.

Touring in the past ten years has gradually grown; we have taken more care of our presentation and it looks and sounds great, and our audiences are growing in numbers. We of course travel differently and separately, Glenn in his bus which is his home from home, and me in the Audi sometimes with Gordon driving me, although I do prefer a comfy hotel. Suzanne has managed things well, a hard balancing act, the two of us with our very special needs. It can't be easy, and now with Rocket on board with their expertise I think we have a balance that protects us both. Julian Wright is expert at diplomacy and driving a good deal through the record companies' door. Eddie Grant has also been active in the delicate task of management. I feel safe in their hands, they are well respected and have good hearts.

America is still a very strong playing field for us and recently the long tours over there have certainly paid off. Old faces pop out of the woodwork and now too their children are at our shows, loving the old and the new songs. Our tours now include nannies for children, drivers for both Glenn and me and a complicated accounting system that nobody seems to understand, but we all get paid eventually – sometimes it takes as long as five months to get paid! It makes me feel like a jobbing plumber. For the first time in many years I can honestly say that I enjoy touring again; it's a great place to get to know oneself and learn how to cohabit with friends. The world is a smaller place these days so it's possible we could spread our wings, if I can get my head around the flying a little more.

At the beginning of 2016, after touring the UK, Squeeze were invited onto *The Andrew Marr Show* to play 'From the Cradle to the Grave'. One of the other studio guests that day was the Prime Minister, David Cameron, who before we went on told Marr that his government was planning to knock down council estates and build more houses in their place. This is a particular bugbear of Glenn's; he has always leant to the left politically, and feels really strongly about young working-class people being priced out of the areas they were brought up in. However, it was still a complete surprise to me when, as we were playing the song, he decided to change the words of the final verse. 'I grew up in council housing,' he sang to Cameron. 'Part of what made Britain great/There are some here who are hell bent/On the destruction of the welfare state.'

Predictably enough, the media went mad about the story – especially as Cameron, who obviously wasn't listening, sat there clapping politely at the end. Squeeze were back in the news again and suddenly I found I was a hero on Twitter, because people know I'm the lyricist in the band and assumed I was the one sticking it to the PM. I said to Glenn, 'I want to go on social media and remove myself from this because you should be the one taking the credit.' But he disagreed with me. So I was high-fiving people on the streets of London for days after the show as I was mistaken for the mastermind behind the lyrical changes. People always get the two of us mixed up; they stop me in the street thinking I'm Glenn, and I was once booked for a private show and introduced as him. I stood at the microphone and held my hand up. I got paid, sang, and went home happy. It was a stroke of genius when Glenn changed the lyrics that Sunday morning. David Cameron came over to us at the end of the show and said, 'You know I think that song is going to be a hit!' Wanker.

Later in the summer of 2016, we played at Glastonbury on the Pyramid Stage – a cathedral of happiness and a dream come true. It has housed all the greatest artists in its time and it was a complete honour to be there for the fifty minutes of our set. The band smiled and played so well, Simon so gracious, Lucy adding femininity to our songs, Stephen as dapper and professional as ever, and Melvin Duffy the sunshine in our sky. His smiles keep me warm and distract me from over-thinking. Louise and my daughter Cissy came to support me. She was covered in mud most of the time, as we all were; that's Glastonbury in the summer.

Glenn looked happy too, like I had never seen him before in his nice shirt and suit. He played so well; he is one of the great guitarists, and his singing is sublime and never ages. Our songs in his hands are incredibly safe.

Being on stage has changed very much over the years. I once felt intimidated and scared, shy even. I would clatter about in a haze following the shapes of the chords, trying desperately to get them right. The energy of the younger me and the younger crowds was so addictive, everyone bouncing about like wasps in a can. There was nothing better than chucking myself from one side of the stage to the other, high on the adrenaline of the moment. The younger me dished up the crowd with rough hands; stage talking was not polite and often aggressive. There was a swagger that we all adopted as we walked on stage, similar to how you see football players walking on to a pitch, shoulders up and down, head high, in for the kill. But I often looked scared and felt empty. Repetition of a song can often render it soulless, and remembering words has always been a mission for me, but somehow it slowly sinks in. I bluffed my way through the creeping success from the smaller pub stages to the larger arenas.

I have learnt to hold my own and not be looked down upon by others in the band. I feel like I have grown into the mature(ish) person I am today. The same rush and the same swagger applies, but there is no fear. I feel at home on any stage, in a small club or a large concert hall. In my solo skin I play house concerts, and that is very different, being in a living room with twelve people listening to me singing my songs. When I see myself on YouTube now, I see a very happy chappy, dashing about high on excitement, content with his lot, triggering off the other members of the band like a piston in a racing-car engine. And all this without the old Cipralex.

I do enjoy it, though. The pinnacle of 2016 was to play at the legendary Glastonbury festival on the Pyramid Stage, a peak experience that took me to another place, a place somewhat spiritual and free. It's not like walking on air, it's like being air itself.

As we leapt through our set, and the years, my eyes soaked up the growing crowds, who seemed to be miles away from the stage. Yet the connection to the front row and beyond was easy to embrace. It was our time to link arms with our songs and the people who have made them what they are on our journey. I saw many smiling faces and people singing, I saw flags and hats, I saw clouds and sunshine. Time raced by and it seemed as soon as we were on stage, it was all over and we were walking back into the wings. We hugged each other and hovered in our place, the place where we had triumphed. There were tears in eyes and lumps in throats, and with hugs all round we reluctantly shuffled back to the dressing room.

Like at every show, the audience is key: they are your reflection. They reflect your happiness and love, and sometimes all the mistakes you make too. When I sewed all of my dreams together as a teenager, they made a magic carpet for me to ride on. Being on stage at Glastonbury was like being on that magic carpet.

When I got home from the festival I watched us on the telly, and I was right: it was really great. I watched other bands too. Coldplay can grip a huge audience in the palm of their hands with such control; I find all that very moving. I loved the way they paid tribute to Viola Beach who had died in a car accident while on tour a few months earlier. Young lads on an exciting journey, but sewn together by their sudden and very sad destiny. The inspiration I had experienced at the festival made me want to look ahead and think about the next album, the next Glastonbury. I sat up at my desk and prayed. After all these years suddenly a spike of clarity mixed with fear had centred me in such a wonderful place. It's as though our songs and our journey had found their place back in people's hearts and minds, and I was feeling so excited about the future and what that might mean. They say a cat has nine lives, but I feel like I've had more.

ST PETER'S CHURCH

The very next day after I had driven home from Glastonbury with Louise, I received a text from David Enthoven: *Just saw you on BBC4. Big hug and looking sharp, Sir Christopher. David E.* It was uplifting to read his text, the very fact he took the time to contact me with his love really made my weekend complete. A few weeks passed by and we had turned the corner into August when I received a text from my old friend Chris Briggs, it came out of the blue. David was in hospital and was very ill. I was in shock. Lucy from his office called me to confirm the worst. I quickly sent him a text, and a day before he died he replied, sending me his love in return. I could not comprehend the magnitude of his passing; he was such a big figure in my recovery and in my life. Barny, who I had not seen for a few years, called me, and we met for lunch and shared David stories, of which there were many.

Barny and David were big on men's groups and discovering the male within, which meant poetry and tears in a cold open field. I once went on one of these weekends, New Age Warriors it was called. I was shitting myself – I had turned up to a disused airbase, where I was told to go to the man with the lantern in the opposite corner of the field. He then told me to cross back over the paddock the same way, ending eventually in a line outside a Nissen hut. We were told not to talk. One by one we filed into the darkness of the hut. When it was my turn, I looked around to see David. 'Go on, Diffy,' he said. At the door was Barny. I broke down and was led away. I drove home wondering what I had missed.

David ran a men's group of his own after that, and once I left The Priory I went there every week for a good kick up the backside. The group was facilitated by a very gentle but firm therapist called John McKeown from Liverpool. Ten men in a circle sharing deep feelings and being there for each other, risking and being supportive. As they were when my father had died, and when things at home at Old House Farm were less than perfect emotionally.

At David's funeral in the King's Road, the church was full to the rafters with friends and people from the music industry in which he had successfully spent his life. Behind myself and Louise was the quiet figure of Bryan Ferry, sat on his own off to one side. I went over to say hello and to ask if he was OK or needed anything; he passed me a casual nod. Brian Eno and Robert Fripp paid careful respects with quiet words, Phil Manzanera shook my hand and we exchanged stories about David and his passing. The church was also full of counsellors, most of whom I had seen over the years. Maureen was there, as was Gerrard from The Priory and Martin Freeman from Brighton, who I loved seeing. It's fair to say, I felt safe.

A eulogy was read by David's business partner, Tim Clark, who managed it without succumbing to tears as only a fellow Harrovian could have. David would have been so proud. He told the story of David's life in the music industry, from Marc Bolan through to Robbie, with Roxy Music along the way. He was bold and full of heartfelt anecdotes. Robbie Williams sweetly performed 'Moon River' with Guy Chambers playing beside him and Lucy Pullin, who worked with David, sang a beautiful rendition of 'Angels' that made us all swallow very deeply, letting the tears fall upon our cheeks. Such a wonderful send-off. When Craig Armstrong sat down to play one of my favourite pieces called 'Hymn 3' on the piano, I lost it. This piano piece is always with me when I fly, it's in my ears, it escorts me through the clouds into the air. His piano music is my meditation for my fear of flying. In my pew with Louise beside me my heart floated up inside my chest, I felt safe within as I said goodbye to my dearest friend, and as my eyes reached up to the sky through the stained-glass windows I cried.

I sat and looked out of the window above the altar as the sunshine poured in from above, and thought about my own mortality, my own life in its present form. I knew that in David I'd had a true friend who held up the lantern for me, showing me the way at each difficult twist and turn. Who would replace him now? Nobody could. But I would learn from his courage and from the way he gave so much and submerged himself in gratitude for the things he had in his life. I must do this too. I went to his homegroup NA meeting that week, and everyone in that tiny room wept and shared the love of David. A brick in the serenity wall had been taken from us, and all I could do was gain strength from his passing. I was heartbroken. His coffin was driven away with four Hells Angels outriders, they roared up the King's Road stopping the traffic as they went. The low rumble of the bikes made us all feel connected with David's wicked humour. He would have loved it.

A month later, Squeeze embarked on a sell-out tour of America. It was another five-week marathon, bookended by that enormous fear of flying I still suffer from, although it is getting slightly better. This was the last drop of *Cradle* promotion; after this we could focus on the future, a dangerous thing in itself. On stage each night I decided to take a piece of David with me in my soul. I imagined him being there with me. 'Smile, Diffy, be in the moment and enjoy yourself, tits and teeth, tits and teeth,' he would say. 'Have a fry-up, Diffy, if you feel low'; 'A Twix will sort you out'; or 'Call the missus and tell her you love her.' All sound advice. The tour was tough from one end to the other. But one thing that struck me was the friendship that grew between Glenn and myself; we gave each other space and we performed each night and enjoyed ourselves, mistakes and all. Mine not his. The band were playing so well together, like never before, and the future simply seemed ours to make. We fell into the last week of the tour exhausted, and there we were again, me and him in the dressing room embracing in a hug.

We had driven for three solid days and after forty-four complicated years together, I never expected a hug to mean so much. Just like on our first US tour, we travelled across the country, from the west coast with its warm and beautiful people to the east and the chill winds with even more beautiful people. We had come a long way from the Chevy van of 1979, the miles still seemed as gruelling even though there were many more comforts than there used to be.

Another year in the saddle drew to a close and all of my children gathered round the Christmas tree at home. I could feel the passing of time and the many Christmases before us all. This one felt really special. The girls, Cissy and Grace then flew to India which they seem to love, maybe one day I'll get there too. Louise keeps family well, and without her in my life I'm sure I would be driven back into that dark place. She has my back and is a real team player. In the past being a team player was alien to me, thankfully I'm still learning how important the commitment of relationships is. Not just with Louise but with everyone.

Christmas passed and in early 2017, Louise and I saw a house come up for sale in Firle. They are mostly owned by the Firle Estate and rarely come on the market. Not one in seven years in fact. We pored over the email and photographs and the next day went to see the house. And then a call from Peter Owen Jones: 'It's Peter, there's a house for sale and I think it could be your new home, come and see it.' Another biblical message from our vicar. We told him we were on our way. Peter is like all three of the main characters in *The Wizard of Oz*: he is made of straw, he is the tin man and the lion, but most of all he is the wizard himself.

Within two days we had the house under offer. At last a place to call home, a home that I will own with Louise. The first home I have owned for thirty-six years. It was time. Having always lived out of a suitcase, renting seemed like the best option for me in life until I met Louise, who very much believes in roots and ownership. I stood in the garden as we looked around the cottage. The house was next door to the church where I had been married, and in the village where I found my family and my feet again.

The bell struck from the Saxon spire of St Peter's church and suddenly I felt reconnected with my stumbling journey through life, from south London to the breathtaking Sussex Downs. When I heard the sound of the bell as it started striking the hour, time stood still for me while Louise and the vendors, two lovely ladies of the village, walked around the garden. I seemed to enter a zone of deep thought. I was off with the balloons. For that second I felt connected with the turning of another page, part of the long walk home. As I looked down the garden to see Louise so excited about the house and the plans being made there, I felt that perhaps this was the time to let go of my old values and embrace the home we are lucky enough to be able to afford at this time of my life. If only we could have gone to the pub to celebrate with some fruity wine, laid back in the afternoon and blissfully rolled over into a long nap. I could dream on. Eleven chimes passed and there I was, walking back to the car, the house was ours. Now all I have to do is work around the clock to pay off the mortgage – I've not had one of them in about twenty-nine years. We got home from the viewing and the phone rang: it was Glenn.

When I see Glenn's name pop up on my mobile phone I find myself in conversation with someone who I have now known all of my life. The only person I have known longer is my brother Lew which is a very deep thought in itself. I think we are closer now than we were all those years ago. How great is that? Relationships have come and gone, cars and guitars have come and gone, rehabs and tours have come and gone, yet Glenn still sits in the middle of my life like the musical maypole.

It was time to write the next album. I sat down at my desk looking out to the South Downs before me and started to write the lyrics. Another adventure was about to begin. Some predictable moments perhaps, followed by odd exchanges of unpredictability. That's the nature of our relationship. Writing takes me to my happy place. I feel at home dissolving myself in the many issues of the day, and in my imagination. January and February are always inspiring months to write. I love the darker nights and the cosiness of home, and when the house quietens down I can really sink into my word bath. I eventfully sent Glenn my new lyrics and waited for his response, which sometimes can take weeks. When he had read them, he said that they were the best I had written in a long time.

When the songs finally arrived back from Glenn in the form of his infamous demos, I pulled them down from my Dropbox – how I miss the C60 cassette – and listened hard, ears leaning towards the speakers in my car, the only place where I still love to listen to music. I was really happy to hear what he had written. It's often a magical feeling to hear his voice singing my words and to hear the songs glide in such an unusual way, from the serious chord jungle in one song and then suddenly back into the chic for another. The record at this stage seemed to be taking on a very different shape from the last, it seemed very exciting. The pressure of *Cradle* had lifted and I felt this time we could relax into a new, unscripted direction.

By March I was back up at Glenn's studio to gather round chord sheets with the band, just like on the album before and the many more before that, a daily drive of around three hours. There is a price to pay to live in the arms of nature, but I think it's worth it. We all sounded magnificent when we started to play, and why not? With the masterful Simon Hanson on drums, a better person would be hard to find for the job. A sweet man with a bright outlook on life, even when it sends him into a spin. Stephen Large on the keyboards, the ever-so-popular one who is on tour with so many other acts but finds time to put our band first, which speaks volumes. New on bass for this album was Yolanda Charles, who is smart and soulful and very adaptable with her playing. She knows a song and she feels where it needs to be, and couples up well with Simon. Laurie Latham set us up at the beginning of the session, but couldn't finish the album with us as he sadly had to record with Jools. Andy Jones, a friend of Glenn's, stepped in to focus things in the studio as Glenn had become swamped with ideas and inspiration. Andy was that gentle person who knew how to juggle the ever-changing studio emotions, and I really liked working with him. I was not helping very much, as my production skills are seldom useful, or always heard.

With twelve songs under our belts it felt like we were off to the races. Some of the new numbers sounded baffling in their arrangement but over time they sank into this thick skin of mine. I had the feeling that we were making another great record; a couple of the songs stood out as early favourites: 'Patchouli' and 'Innocence in Paradise'. Glenn worked really hard producing the album, putting in maximum hours to place the songs in production. Fourteen albums down the road and his strive for perfection I still find inspiring. I may not have always recognised this, but playing back the new album I can feel the love we still have as songwriters, and for each other. We stand out from the crowd as gifted songwriters. Nobody sounds like us. It's been some journey and I hope it goes on for many years to come. He reminds me of a brother, someone who will look out for you and give you their shoulder to lean on, and at the same time manage to bring out the complicated emotions that only time can dissolve.

During the recording we took time out to head back to Glastonbury, this time for a duo show on the acoustic stage. Only a year and a chapter since the last visit to Somerset when we held our own on the Pyramid Stage. We went down on site a few days early this time so that we could write and record in Glenn's RV. Sadly the heat got to us both and that never happened. This year was incredible, I managed to play three times in the space of one day, with Jools on the Pyramid Stage, with the inspirational Gilson on drums, and with Glenn on the acoustic stage, plus a BBC TV slot singing *Up The Junction* backed by Masters of the Kazooniverse. It seemed strange with so many other past members of Squeeze being around on the weekend. Paul Carrack played a fine set and sung three of my songs in a row on the Friday. I was welling up with pride as he sailed through his version of *Tempted* and *Bet Your Life*. Having Glenn on stage with Jools on the Saturday would have been a special TV moment but it was not to be. Jools thought it was a great idea but best saved for the future. Our acoustic set went down well, and we raced through our hits like men with trains to catch. I think we were both looking forward to some new songs joining the canon of our acoustic repertoire. Grace and Cissy joined me and Louise and it made for a calm and very special family weekend. They got to party and I got to blag meal tickets backstage and wristbands.

I got to hang out with Johnny Depp, a name I find embarrassing to drop. We had met before at a previous show in LA but this time we spoke for over an hour. He was softly spoken and leant into my every word, which felt surreal. He dressed in the way that he does, like a pirate. We tried to get on the side of the stage to see Radiohead but it was full on the gantry where guests stand to watch. Beside us on the stairs also stood David Beckham. There I was between two massive celebrities, neither of whom could get the right wristbands. I tried to help by talking to a passing tour manager. Johnny then said to me, it's OK I think I'll give this one a miss. When the Foo Fighters played we were there again trying to get side of stage. The same thing; no special wristbands. Along comes Liam Gallagher with his 30-strong entourage and they walk right by us up the stairs on to the gantry. It was like a pub arriving, them all drinking and smoking like the lads they are. His brother Noel we met earlier the day before, a true gentleman, who when I introduced him to Louise said I was punching above my weight. He may be right about that. Soon after that comment Mrs Difford was having her picture taken with Brad Pitt, and she looked very happy with herself. He said he was a huge Squeeze fan and shook my hand. And me just a simple bloke from King George Street with no such celebrity to match his. The real celebrities are the backroom staff at festivals, the dressing room managers, the drivers in their Land Rovers, and the kind people who give out the wristbands. I ended up with an armful. I have never been completely comfortable with the celeb palaver, much preferring to ride shotgun with the crew, or keeping it simple with my close friends along the way.

Before we left the magical staircase that leads up to the Pyramid Stage, Lou and I watched Barry Gibb. He sang Staying Alive and the whole festival burst into song and dance. For me nothing could top this, but it did. The next band up were Chic. They had me crying with deep emotion. If only Squeeze could get a crowd reaction like that. Maybe we do, I sometimes just don't recognise it. I'm not sure what it is when I see bigger bands take to the stage. I get very churned up, not envious but full of joy. It's what I was seeking all those years ago when I first saw The Who on stage down at the Charlton Football ground and when I began to write songs with Glenn. I guess I get all the emotional stuff from my mother, who would cry watching the weather forecast.

When I look back at my relationship with Glenn I feel blessed that we have survived so long. I think we still have the same differences we always had, but today they seem more transparent. Keeping a good relationship tidy is bloody hard work sometimes, but it's worth it if you work at it. It's taken a fair amount of beer, wine, therapy and song to get there, though. It's also been very complicated. I don't think it could ever have been simple.

'Give Me the Simple Life' is one of my favourite songs. It has become my daily mantra over the years, yet that simplicity eludes me. It seems that Squeeze are as popular as ever, Glenn and I are writing great songs again, my solo career is settling in, however chaotic it seems, and I'm loving the commitment to the future with Louise. All of this keeps me busy and the simple life is far away in the distance, which is just as well. I can't imagine myself shuffling about in the garden, or sitting and watching daytime TV like my dad ended up doing. Those twilight years need to be filled with ambition.

I've always wanted more in life, always looking over other people's shoulders to see if there is a greener field for me. The addict loves more, more of everything. My recovery meter often goes over into the red when I'm not on my game, when I'm seeking happiness in the out of reach. I will never be anybody other than myself and although I can dream of being more successful or more talented, I just have to accept that it's OK, there is no need to be wanting. I feel rewarded with love and happiness by just trying to stay in the moment.

When I was a young boy all I ever wanted was that red tractor in the toy-shop window, that ice cream with the 99 Flake. I wanted more pie, I wanted the best BMX bike, I wanted the latest Airfix model aeroplane. I just wanted. I have been trying to fill the hole in the doughnut for far too long, and that takes a lot of effort. I still want to have it all, but then who doesn't? I have everything I need really: a good wife and family, a great band and some wonderful friends. Songs and words for days, and a diary so full I can't even find the time to sit in the garden and listen to the birds sing.

There simply is nothing to complain about, but the fear that it all might go horribly wrong still follows me around like the old black dog.

Even now when I'm twenty-five years sober I have to stay alert, but also know when to celebrate with the still and sparkling. Celebrating my 25th sobriety birthday this 4th July, I looked out of the window at the panoramic view across Greenwich, a mile downstream. I was in a hotel, table for one, down by the O2 Arena built on the site of the old gasworks. Here many years ago I played in the mud while by father tended to the allotment and nodded to his mates as they passed on their way to work. Off in the distance I could see Greenwich Park and the Observatory on the hill, where I used to sit while hopping off school. I could see the church steeple of St Alfege where I had been married in 1979. I could see the ever-changing skyline of London shimmering in the sunset which has risen up over the Isle of Dogs like masses of steel and glass Jenga pieces to obscure the evening sky. Over the horizon heading east of London I could see where my daughters Grace and Cissy now live, and by turning my head in the other direction I could see towards Charlton, where both my parents

are buried. I was staying at the hotel to break the relentless journeys up to the studio each week. I was becoming my car and my
car became me. Twenty-five years clean in the saddle was posing
me some long questions, none of which I could answer. There I
was, with this poetic view of my past life just beyond the glass
window of the restaurant. I was thinking about friends and how
many you can have in your life. How many real friends that would
take that silver bullet for you are, of course, hard to number, but
one thing was for sure that Louise would always stand by me if
times got tough. My children also would do the same. They are all
so wonderful and kind, sending me balloons, two golden balloons
saying 25. I had so many calls and messages on the social media
congratulating me I felt overwhelmed. It was a day of beauty and
friendship. And a table for one. Home was not far away now, with
the new house and the future being just one day at a time away.
What else could I need in life? In some ways music has become
the oil that keeps the wheels from squeaking, but it's never that
simple. The squeaking wheel keeps on turning, and for the time
being it's only me that confuses and complicates how that wheel
turns.

When I was a child, to be told to speak when spoken to by my
mother gave me the backstage pass to my imagination, and there
I found the many songs and stories I have written and have yet to
write. I still love being in a band, not the gang it might have been,
but to hop around on stage is still a thrill for me. I still want to
be that guy who sings 'Cool for Cats', and I still want to be a little
bit famous. All the big cash is sadly gone but I have socks in my
shoes, I have food on the table and a smiling face to wake up to.
My dad always said if you join a band you will become an addict, a

drunk and skint. Seems like his tender advice was right. However, I have amazing children who make me proud, and the escalators up to the next floor of adulthood seem to be running just fine. Over the years I have certainly idled and stood still where I could have taken in more of what went on around me, but that's what makes me who I am. I think I'm happy with that. I've never known from one day to the next what was going to happen, but something always did.

When the Beatles' van broke down in 1965 it was on the side of the road, having veered off it in some snow. Ringo said, 'What are we going to do now?' And John said, 'Something will happen,' and I'm very much like that, because something will happen – it always does.

Forty-five years ago in my little bedroom at Combe Avenue, on my single bed with my Bic pen and notepad by my side, I dreamt of being on *Top of the Pops* – tick. I dreamt of touring in America, which I used to visualise with my mother on the rocks at the Giant's Causeway – tick. I dreamt of having a family – tick. I was surrounded by posters of my favourite bands, vinyl records stacked up on the floor, my nylon-string guitar leant against the wardrobe. I was filled with dreams but lived mostly in fantasy, I was safe there. I think I was floating in a dream when I took a 50p piece from my mother's purse and placed an ad in a sweet-shop window for a guitarist to join a band. There was no band, there was also no record deal, there was nothing but me and my unmanageable grip on reality. I feel so blessed, and still I find it amazing that with that 50p, I found the rest of my life.

And now if you can excuse me, I'm going to have a little cry.

The Serenity Prayer

God grant me the serenity
to accept the things I cannot change;
courage to change the things I can;
and wisdom to know the difference.

Living one day at a time;
enjoying one moment at a time;
accepting hardships as the pathway to peace;
taking, as He did, this sinful world
as it is, not as I would have it;
trusting that He will make all things right
if I surrender to His Will;
that I may be reasonably happy in this life
and supremely happy with Him
forever in the next.

Reinhold Niebuhr

RAINBOW'S END

It was September 2017 and my book had just been published. I was excited, but for the time being I had to put those feelings to one side. I was back in the rehearsal room with the band, running though the set for the Join the Dots tour. My book had been getting fantastic reviews, both in the press and with fans who emailed me via my website. The arc of my story seemed to have touched many people.

Squeeze had a new album up the flag pole called *The Knowledge* which also attracted great reviews, as Squeeze always seem to do. So it was time to put the tour on the front foot and the book on the back. With my confused feelings I ploughed on through the many sheets of chords that I always need at the start of any long tour. I'm a slow learner but my enthusiasm hopefully outweighs my dyslexic overview of life.

Touring the UK followed the usual pattern: wake up and drive for hours, mostly through slow traffic, get to the show and be greeted by one of our team, either Carly our tour PA or our tour manager Gary Weston. Gary is one of those wonderful human beings who calmly gives you all you need and makes sure you are on time in the right room with total peace of mind. I had my own dressing room on this tour, like a dog with a kennel all to himself, I padded around trying to settle. Carly is the kind of person who softly enters the room with just the right amount of concern at the right time, she is such a good soul. They are two great people to have at the entrance to the travelling Squeeze circus. Catering is often delightful, and at 5 p.m. there's a three-course meal followed by a nap after sound check in a dark dressing room. Sound check is normally a time to check the sound, as you would imagine, but everything these days is digital and logged onto a memory stick. It's always fantastic and thanks in many ways to our monitor man Peter, who otherwise tours with Steely Dan in America, another band with a duo of powerful grace. Sadly, Walter Becker died in 2017 and it made me think about my relationship with Glenn on a very deep level. One day one of us will pass on, and the other will be left to think about the importance of the time we spent together over and above all of our differences. Deep thoughts for a deep tour.

Before the show starts, we all gather to put on our in-ear monitors. We make our way to the side of stage and stand there as the opening video rolls by on the screens behind us. At this point we disappear into our own safe worlds where only the songs and the immediate future mean anything at all. We then stroll on and face the music. On the UK tour we played to sold-out venues up and down the country and the people we played to seemed to like the set of new and old songs. We delivered. The UK tour was a triumph, so why was I was starting to feel so flat? Maybe because I was. Five thousand miles in the car and that self-imposed isolation didn't help my mood, but there were few alternative options. I bathed myself in Craig Armstrong, Radio

Three and some recent demos I had been working on.

The highlight for me on the UK tour was performing at the Royal Albert Hall, where we had the NHS choir with us on stage as well as Cara Mchardy. Nine Below Zero became part of our show too, lending brass to our songs and the magnificent harmonica-playing of Mark Feltham, not to mention the gentleman who is Dennis Greaves on guitar. It was a memorable night. After the show I took time to linger in the green room with Louise, but I noticed the absence of many people I knew; the band were already beginning to fade into the long corridors. It was like being in school when most of your close mates have already left for the summer holidays and you are left by yourself at the gates while your mum comes to collect you.

The American tour began a few days after the UK tour ended, starting in Disneyland Florida. There was nothing overly animated about our show that I can remember; we waded through our set slightly jet-lagged. We performed just before the fireworks on the lake behind the stage. Supporting the fireworks needed a light touch, so we only played two short sets each night, a chicken in the basket kind of show. I had not done a tour on a bus for a while but I enjoyed the ride. The band had some gentle late nights and I slept at the back with earplugs in. The shows went well, we travelled for four weeks and played mostly sold-out shows. Days off in hotels dragged, I often felt a little depressed as I surveyed the situation around me. I slept all I could and learnt to tell the time from shards of light that entered my room through the ill-fitting curtains. There was a disengagement within and I could not put my finger on it – the band played out of our skins yet for me there was something missing. I felt myself slipping from the stage, retreating slowly and regretting disjointed moods. It was brilliant playing the songs, old and new, they seemed to make good bedfellows and there was nothing really to complain about. We were on the very top of our game, so why was I finding it all so complicated?

The highlight of the US tour was playing back in New York, at the Beacon Theatre. The room was heaving with love, it was a great night full of magical moments. But in the green room I felt the very thing I had felt back at the Albert Hall: lonely in my own company. The black suit, the black guitar and the black dog, we all went walkies together in front of a very lively New York crowd. The memory I will always take from that show was being visited by my four children Natalie, Riley, Grace and Cissy, who had flown in for the week just to hang in the city with me. Their support quickly raised my mood for the last few shows.

My flight home at the end of the tour was tough. The turbulence tossed me around in my seat and as I reviewed the weeks that had just passed by in my tired head, I felt wasted. Home was not far away and as the tour came to a close, like on all tours, you say goodbye to everyone knowing you won't see anyone for months. As I have said before, being in a band is often like that: merchant seamen who get back on shore and head off in all different directions. Both tours were the most professional I had ever been involved in; the production was first class and the playing was possibly the tightest we have ever sounded. That glue that sticks a good band together was sometimes unavailable to me, I think that over time the adhesiveness of friendship and music had come apart, leaving a void. I take full responsibility for my part in the fog that was created over that period of touring, but for me it has now lifted. I feel optimistic that I can find a feeling of togetherness in the future, I will just have to work harder and put myself back on the stage, in the centre where I belong.

The last show of 2017 was in December at St Mary's Church in Rye, a very special place, where I had got sober twenty-six years ago. It was a duo show, just me and Glenn – we had committed ourselves I think for a little Christmas pocket money. The feeling of being back in that building with all those prayers stood me in a very good place, and I felt very spiritually aware of my strengths and my weaknesses. We played together with such power and it was hard not to recognise the emotions that were flowing through me like water over a rock from a mountain stream. Some of the lyrics hit me like salmon leaping in the air, the evening was a mixture of psychodrama and song. It could have been the release of tension from the very long tour where we had been in each other's company for such a long time, and it could have been deeper than that. Walking back to my car after the show I stood and watched the nicotine-amber light from the street coldly outline the spire of the church. I drove home quietly without the radio, without the world. It was as if the future and the past had suddenly collided in my heart, and in that moment something changed. As if a penny had dropped.

During the months before all the touring with Squeeze I had put the brakes on promoting my book to favour the new record. *The Knowledge* did really well, but did not sell as many copies as the previous *Cradle* album. I was proud of my work, and I think I reached a new level of lyrical openness with the way that I wrote songs with Glenn. Before the recording I was offered forty shows with Jools, which I loved. I came and went from the studio but never missed a session and gave 100 per cent of the time I had. I kept the tiny wolf from the door by also taking on more and more solo shows. These days I have to work three times as hard as I once did back in the golden days of the Eighties. Royalties have fallen off the map so it's impossible to stand. I played ninety-eight shows in 2017, and I found out at the Rocket Christmas party so did Elton. Mine with a slightly different outcome.

As 2018 fell into my lap I sharpened my pencil and wrote some lyrics for both Jools and Paul Carrack, which bore great fruit. Four new songs with Paul got me excited about writing again, I was so moved by the sound of his voice on my words. With Jools I felt at home, we had fun and I hope I gave him some words to orchestrate. I really appreciated him giving me the space to co-write with him once again. I started the new year full of renewed inspiration. The builders were on site and the new house in Firle was uppermost on mine and Lou's minds. My first home in thirty years. There was also some clear time to promote my book which I felt was long overdue. The book was even up for an award!

The book tour raced towards me, so I sat one afternoon with Boo Hewerdine for a few hours working out a set – that's all it took. Boo is a funny person to tour with, dry and full of conversation, an excellent wingman. We laughed and shared so many stories on the tour, all of which helped to pass the long hours in the car. Four weeks of touring and a further 8,000 miles reduced me to the bones of a very tired man, however it was worth it and it was liberating. At first the shows were slow and not so well-attended, but by the end of the run we were selling out everywhere we went. A lovely feeling. My stand-up abilities improved as we made our way up and down the country, and my playing and singing felt more relaxed than ever before. I tried to perfect my timing and took advice from actors and comedians, I was beginning to tell my story, make it funny and sing vaguely in tune.

There was no dressing room to pad around in on my own, no people to meet me at the stage door, no crew and no large pay packet, it was but another side of the very same coin, this one slightly less pressurised. I was back in touch with that young man who sat in his bedroom in the early Seventies on a council estate dreaming of being in a band. The band I dreamt of being in was touring in Australia while I was on the last few motorways of my book tour. I saw the pictures on the internet of a very happy team performing upside down. I did have the choice to go on the tour, but turned it down due to the flying phobia that at present dogs my days. I had mixed feelings about what I saw and read but I had to follow my instinct – being in the air every day of the week was not for me, it would have finished me off although naturally I regretted not being there. The band looked happy and I was pleased for them. After my shows I stood and signed souvenirs (which is what CDs and books seem to be). As I mingled with the crowd who never once asked me why I was not in Australia, I felt like I had made the right choice, for now at least. I became friends with a pilot called Andy, a Squeeze fan, and he invited me to spend some time with him in a flight simulator at Heathrow – he was sure he could help me with my phobia. I sat in the hot seat while he programmed in some heavy weather, engine failure, and cross winds on landing. It was so real, I was nervous, but after many hours I came to understand that the plane was built to take all of this and more, and that the computers on board were really in control. The hours in the simulator helped me without a doubt, so maybe another tour in future might not fill me with as much dread. All fingers and flaps crossed.

The book seems to have held up a mirror of my world not only for me but for others too, and by being so honest and present I have risked some friendships in the paragraphs of my journey. I have loved being within the spine of my book, it has provided me with a self-analysis of what I do and where I am. Being in a band with its complicated dynamics will always be my first love, but writing and telling stories seem like home to me now. I find that people are generally disengaged with music, it's almost like the old passion of listening to records has changed. No longer can you rely on selling CDs at gigs, no longer can you risk being with a major record label, no longer is it good enough just to be onstage and expect to be loved from the back row forward. A new way of engaging is what's needed, a way of embracing your fans and respecting their needs. I think our fans like a nice seat, a good story and a light dance somewhere towards to end of the show. That's not a bad night out. I remembered the days when I would get a 53 bus up to London to buy a new album, take the same bus home and then play it on my record player. Today I hold my phone to the speaker and within seconds I have the song there on my phone.

These days it's all about playing live, it's all about the present moment and the experience of being in a time and place with other people of like minds. The gathering of souls is something very special. Without writing my book and going on tour I'm not sure I would have reached this understanding. I may have possibly managed to open up a can of worms in my head, but silkworms I hope.

Looking back the most moving part of the book for me was when I had to read it for the audio addition and suddenly my words were connected with the person who wrote them. Me. I sat in a booth for four days being swept out on a sea of deep emotions, I was adrift with myself and needed to find dry land. I had not prepared myself for this and felt the weight of my words pulling me in all directions. Johnny Mercer's lyrics to 'Moon River' pop into my head as I try to resolve so many feelings about what has happened since the publication of my book. The song is really about friendship. It tells of the importance and joy of having friends who are not just there when you are down and sad, but throughout your life. We are dream makers and heartbreakers, we are drifters. Some friendships are wider than a mile and it's the effort needed to cross that divide that will keep me with the ones I love. 'Moon River' depicts a very classic drama, that of young people who leave home, which is sometimes a simple place, to search for fame, fortune and happiness, and are never able to return or feel at home anywhere but in that very sacred place. I have been on this journey myself for many years. Writing my autobiography has put me in touch with every twist and turn. I feel very proud of what I have written be it factual or fiction, I feel totally lifted by the praise I have received from far and wide. The penny that dropped at Christmas 2017 in Rye could have been the realisation that that not everyone needs to be on the same page as you. I feel ready for the future and the next chapter of my life. I will remain in search of my rainbow's end with my huckleberry friends, real or imaginary, and prepare myself for the changes that inevitably will face me down the years. I put an ad in a sweet shop window and the rest of my life just arrived.

I did an interview for the book down an ISDN line to a journalist in Madison, Wisconsin. He asked me if I had reached that fantastic place I talk about in my book. It was a very good question, and my answer was very definitely yes.

ACKNOWLEDGEMENTS

I would like to thank all the members of Squeeze who have given so much to the songs I have co-written, in performance and during various recordings. I would also like to remember Kevin Wilkinson and Matt Irving who have passed away gently along the way.

I take my hat off to all the crew who have pushed my amps around the many stages of the world and tuned my guitars, from Deptford to Detroit and back again.

Love and gratitude to managers David Enthoven, Matt Thomas, Julian Wright, Shep Gordon and John Lay, and to Suzanne Hunt.

The photography within these pages has kindly been provided by Jill Furmanovsky, Ron Reid, Lawrence Impey and Danny Clifford, among others. Thank you.

I would hold my umbrella open for the very generous Elvis Costello and Elton John, Christopher Guest, Cavan's own whippersnappers The Strypes, Niall Walsh, Marti Pellow and Bryan Ferry, and all of the inspirational people who have been the cornerstones of my musical career.

My ever-patient publisher Alan Samson, editors Rufus Purdy, Celia Hayley and Holly Harley, the Orion team Hannah Cox, Helen Ewing and Carey Brett, and my literary agent Clare Conville.